Why Don't You Just Leave Him?
A True Story of Living Through Domestic Violence

Stacey Jameson

First Printing, 2019

Second Edition, Published 2023

ISBN: 978-1-3999-6289-6

Contents

About the Author..1

Introduction 2

Prologue 3

The early years 6

Love's Young Dream 13

The Bully Boy 19

Reunited..28

Pregnant and Scared 31

The Wedding 38

Trouble and Strife in Married Life..44

A Little Baby 54

Taking Baby Home 64

Calling the Police 78

Baby Number Two...84

A Little Independence 90

Something Amiss...98

The Other Woman...108

New Home, New Start 120

Troublemaker 127

Nights Out 131

Leon's Fantasy 135

Suffer Little Children..142

Falling to Pieces 146

Lady of the Night 154

Marriage Guidance..160

Christmas Time...163

The Never-Ending Cycle 169

The Winds of Change 176

Refuge Life 184

The Epiphany 195

Losses and Gains..210

A Letter to Myself..214

Home Sweet Home..219

A Chance to Love Again 227

The Aftermath...253

If It's Going to Be, It Starts with Me 257

Fifteen Years Later – Life Goes On 261

Love at Last 268

Elsa 272

Date Night 277

New Year, New Life 281

The abused wife. A Poem by the Author 289

A letter from Stacey 291

Acknowledgments 292

About the Book

This is a story about a young woman who was trapped in a relationship that was violent and abusive. Coercive control drove her to the depths of despair.

For all those out there who think there is no light at the end of the tunnel when you are in an abusive relationship, the time will come when you have the strength to find a way to get out, and you will say: *You have no power over me.*

About the Author

I was born and bred in the Black Country, where people are salt of the earth. I was lucky enough to have been a teenager in the eighties, and now I look back on it as an amazing era. Sadly, I was so caught up in the distress of my parents' divorce as a child that I never really got to enjoy that amazing time.

I love to start the day with a quick yoga routine – not that I am good at it but I am hoping it will help me age a little more gracefully. It also sets me up nicely for my day at work. I also love meditating, which has helped me develop a lot of much-needed self-awareness, as you will realise when you read my story.

I work in administration, but my passion in life is to get a message out to young people to take care of themselves and be their own best friend, to see how important the choices they make in life are. I now live in a rural village and relish the peace and tranquillity that that brings. A vast difference to how my story began.

As a teenager longing for love and acceptance, I was only thirteen when I met Leon. It was such a crucial time in my development and I thought I had found the love of my life who would rescue me from my oppressive home existence. I couldn't have been more wrong. If only I had known that living with him was going to be so much worse.

When he became my husband, he used to say to me, 'Don't ever try and hit me back because if you put me down and I get back up, I will kill you.'

It's an assumption that some people stay in a violent relationship because they choose to stay. It is often because they are too weak from all the abuse, frightened because they fear the repercussions of leaving, or conditioned because they don't know any better, that they stay. But there is also so much more to staying than these reasons alone.

An abusive relationship doesn't have to lead to murder to be bad – the day-to-day of living with an abusive partner can be the slow death of a person's spirit emotionally and physically. As a mother, wife and daughter, I was weak, frightened and conditioned – and so much more.

This book is a work of non-fiction based on my life, experiences and recollections. The names of people, places, dates, sequences, and the details of events may have been changed to protect the privacy of others.

Introduction

People speak from where they are at that time in their lives. Emotional and social experiences change with age. I can only say this in my defence, looking back at what I was implicated in. From my not-so-wise teen years, when I was embarking on the journey of life and love, it was as if I had been living under the depths of a murky sea, unaware of the light and land above. The only thing I knew was my environment, not what was beyond.

When I started to recover from the trauma of my violent marriage it was like coming up for air and seeing above the seabed. I saw a beautiful, picturesque stretch of white sand in front of me. Now I am on dry land, feet firmly on the warm sand, living freely, with the sun beating down and warming my back. I can now look into the sea and remember my struggle in there. That had been my environment and all I knew – but now I know better.

Prologue

It was a cold November teatime in 1994 and the wind was bitter, turning the rain that was falling ferociously from the grey sky into glass sheets on the roads and pavements. The paths underfoot were as slippery as an ice rink.

Walking along the streets of the Black Country with my arms folded, trying to defend myself from the wind as it nipped into my skin, my only protection from the elements was a thin T-shirt. I hadn't had the time to put on a cardigan, let alone a coat.

The rush-hour traffic slowed down as it reached gridlock at a traffic island that was renowned for queues at this time of the evening. As the traffic was at a standstill, I took the opportunity to cross the road while the drivers in their cars were waiting for their next chance to move forward. My face was screwed up in a wasted effort to take cover from the harsh wind as it blew bitterly into my face, which was cold and wet. A combination of tears and rain mingled with despair. If the drivers had looked more closely at me rather than being engrossed in their own thoughts, they would have noticed my bare feet. What a sight I must have looked. I was about twenty-five, with shoulder-length, blonde hair and blue eyes, walking the streets in this awful weather in nothing but a T-shirt, denim jeans and no shoes or socks. My clothes had been clean and my hair tidy – until the wind and rain had bedraggled them.

Into sight came a red phone box just yards from the traffic island. Jogging to get to it, breathing hard from the cold and a heavy heart, I hurried into the cubicle, made a reverse charge call to my husband at home and asked him, reluctantly, to come and fetch me. He questioned me in his usual accusing style, implying that I had been gone for so long I must have been seeing another man. He was unable to believe I had been walking around outside all this time in this awful godforsaken weather.

There was no doubt that there was trouble in store for me once he came to collect me, but where else could I go? I needed to go home. Home was where my children were, and I didn't want to leave them with him any longer in case he was spoiling the atmosphere for them with his bad mood.

The ironic thing about it was that the reason I was out walking the streets in the first place, feeling ashamed as people were driving past, was because I had run out of my own home to get to safety.

What had started off as a normal day had, as usual, taken a turn for the worse. We lived in a beautiful detached house and shoes were not allowed to be worn indoors; that was one of my husband's rules. The rule was a great hindrance to me when I needed to get out of the house quickly! On this particular occasion, I had once again said or done the wrong thing and heard my husband shouting angrily as he desperately tried to get to me to give me a thump. Fortunately, I was graced with the foresight (as the 'wrong-doing' had literally just been done) to run. Having made it halfway down the stairs already, I heard him at the top about to follow quickly behind, so instinctively, I made a rash decision to risk jumping down the other half of the flight of stairs to save valuable seconds in my escape.

The front door was just yards away from the bottom of the stairs. Could I make it out of the door before I felt myself being dragged backwards by my angry husband's strong, adrenalin-fuelled arms? My feet crashed to the bottom of the stairs – I felt like a ninja, and I had made it to the bottom without breaking my ankles in the force of the fall. No time to be smug, a few more steps and I would be out of the door with my feet carrying me as quickly as they possibly could to freedom. I focused on the brass catch of the door – it only needed to be yanked down and I could pull the door open and be out into the street and the safety of prying eyes.

Miraculously, because my nerves were making me tremble uncontrollably, I managed to push down the door catch with my right hand. I was shaking so much it was making the task a lot more complex than it should have been. Flinging the door open, I jumped over the front doorstep, feeling the concrete ground that a moment ago had been soft clean carpet beneath my feet. It was hard and cold underfoot as I ran up the path leading to the street.

He still hasn't caught me, I thought. I didn't need to look back; I was too fearful to check. I was just reassured by the fact I had made it into the street. A place of solace, the outdoors – in the public eye. I knew he wouldn't follow me outside; he liked to keep up appearances in front of the neighbours, so he wouldn't make a scene out here.

Now what to do? I couldn't go back in the house because he would be even more enraged that I had had the nerve to defy him, and I had run quicker than him in the process. So, I just kept on running, feeling adrenalin coursing through my body. Finally, I got a stitch and eased into a slower pace. It was starting to rain and the traffic was getting heavy. I heaved a long deep breath of relief. I had managed to escape him.

This is not how I'd imagined my marriage would be as a child. How did my life come to this?

The early years

Dad and Mum were about seventeen when they first met at the local dance hall. They were both the youngest siblings in families of seven. Like Yin and Yang, Dad had jet-black hair, olive skin, and eyes set like blue jewels sparkling in his very handsome face; my mother had long strawberry blonde hair, fair skin and beautiful green eyes. My father was really into his Royal Enfield motorbike and was very popular with the young girls. This was the sixties, the era of Teddy Boys and the Beatles; my parents were teenagers in the bosom of rock-and-roll. They met, fell in love, and out of that love came me, and then reality set in – too young and too soon, responsibilities fell on them. To add to their pressure, fourteen months later, my sister Hannah was born.

Strangely, throughout my childhood, I couldn't wait for the day when I would be an adult and finally get my freedom. In my dreams, I would marry my prince charming and have the perfect family – a boy first, followed by a girl. We would all live happily ever after, not like my mum and dad. It was a case of having to get through my years as a child before my beautiful dream would come true – or so I thought.

We lived in a respectable little cul-de-sac in a highly sought-after area. Dad always worked away from home; he was an engineer and very fortunate that he had found his vocation in life at such an early age. He would often spend time on the oil rigs out in the North Sea. He was a workaholic, an ambitious young man with high hopes. He thrived on travelling all over the world to do the job he excelled in.

It was because Dad earned such good money that my parents were able to buy their first house. It was a lovely three-bedroom, semi-detached property set in a quiet, typically British, suburb. He and Mum even had their own cars. For most people, it was hard enough in those days to have a car at all. But their affluent lifestyle wasn't enough to buy them happiness. Mum was bogged down with two demanding babies, missing out on her youth, and Dad was too focused on work and making it big in life to appreciate how she was feeling. Mum would spend many a night at bingo to break the routine of housework and children.

It was then my kindly old grandmother would take care of us. When Dad was at home he was strict, but fun too. He forced us to eat our greens, saying it would put hair on our chests. My little sister Hannah and I would always heave, but he wouldn't let us leave the table until every bit was gone. Mum would always stick up for us and say, 'Oh, come on, Michael, they've had enough now.' It didn't matter, he still made us eat it all up.

The nights when Dad was at home, I remember lying in bed in the dark, hearing the sound of raised angry voices downstairs. It was horrible; they always seemed to be arguing. Banging, thumping, thudding, yelling, and the constant sound of my parents at each other's throats would echo up the stairs.

Sometimes, I'd see Mum sporting a black eye, but she would always say she'd bumped into the door. One morning, I noticed holes in the wall of the downstairs hallway and realised that they must have been from a knife because Dad had been stabbed in his buttock and had to go to hospital.

It's not surprising I was a fearful child. Every single night, I lay with rosary beads round my neck and Jesus statues round my bed. Dad's side of the family were devout Catholics and that's how I'd acquired the holy artefacts. Grasping the rosary beads in my hand, I would pray that the demons in the night wouldn't come to get me. I was petrified of the dark. I used to have recurring nightmares, but I was too scared to call out to Mum in case the man who I dreamt about, who stood in the corner of my bedroom with an axe, got me. So I lay there silently terrified until morning light when, very often, my nanny would come and wake me up, and help Mum get us ready for school.

When I was about ten, my mother gave birth to a baby boy, Luke. Having another child was my parent's last-ditch attempt to patch up their marriage. My father had always wanted a son and my mother had given him what he wanted. Unfortunately, it was around this time that Mum hired a private detective to follow my father and discovered that he had been seeing another woman. So, she started divorce proceedings.

Dad left home and our lives were turned upside down. There was often trouble with him turning up at the house. To try to make ends meet, Mum got a little job cleaning the coaches at the local coach firm and started seeing a man, Tony, who worked there. He was nice to us; he made us laugh. When he came to see Mum, sometimes he would bring pork sandwiches for us. He looked like the comedian Russ Abbot; he had a comical appearance, with brown eyes like laughing slits in his face. Although he was a heavy drinker, Mum seemed happy when he was around, and we loved the good atmosphere.

One morning, my sister, my baby brother Luke, Mum and I were all still in bed fast asleep when we heard a horn blasting loudly outside the house. 'What's that?' we all yelled, leaping out of bed and darting to the window in my mum's bedroom to see what all the noise was about. There, at the neck of our narrow cul-de-sac was a great big coach, full of people off on a day trip, bemused faces all staring back up at us through our bedroom window. Sitting at the wheel of the coach was Tony, tooting the horn without a care for the neighbours, or the impatient passengers.

Mum opened the window and gestured to him to go away; she was giggling like a schoolgirl. He leaned out of the coach and shouted, 'Come on, we're going to Blackpool!'

We nearly didn't go because Mum was concerned she hadn't got time to put her make-up on. Under great pressure from three pleading children, and a coach full of fed-up people, she surrendered. Quickly, we all got dressed and were on the coach in five minutes flat. That was one of our many trips to Blackpool. Mum and Tony split up eventually; I think it was because of his drink problem and, as time began to show, she was still working through her feeling for my father and the breakdown of the marriage.

As a result of the divorce, we moved from our lovely fine house to a nearby, not-so-fine, house on a rough council estate. Mum saw it as a new start and would get herself dolled up to go out most weekends. When Dad wasn't working away, we would stay over at his on a Friday night and he would always pop to the pub for a pint and bring us a takeaway back of roe and chips. It was a real treat. On Saturdays, we would clean his house and go to the launderette and do his washing, in return for five pounds' pocket money, which was a lot of money to us kids. Dad was really strict, but we knew he loved us, he was just old school and very preoccupied with work and the backlash of the divorce. We were grateful for the pocket money anyway, as Mum couldn't afford to do that for us.

I can remember the rare occasions in the eighties when we were treated to a fashion item. I was once given what was called at the time a Y cardigan and that lasted me for years until it was well out of fashion, and some jeans with a red stripe down the leg. Hannah and I always felt inferior to all the other girls who went to school because of the way we looked. Don't get me wrong, we were clean, but we were definitely not fashionable. The majority of our clothing came from a box of second-hand clothes my mum's brother let us rifle through now and again.

Mum always seemed to be taking Dad to court for maintenance or something or another. We were her little pawns, stuck in the middle of the cruel divorce game. I loved Dad so much, but I couldn't ever let my mum know that because she hated him, and was of the mind that, out of unspoken loyalty, we should dislike him too.

Once I told a friend of mine that I hated Dad. I don't know why I said it but it seemed the right attitude to have. When I left her later that day, I cried my eyes out with guilt for saying I hated him, because I didn't and I knew how hurt he would be if he had heard me say such a terrible thing. It was beyond the depth of my understanding at that time, but Mum was influencing my feelings towards Dad. She was always telling us terrible things about him, and it seemed respectful to try to merge into her way of thinking. It made life easier for us and she expected our loyalty. We didn't want to get on the wrong side of her, and of course she was our mum and we trusted everything she said. She was always drumming it into us: 'Never bite the hand that feeds you', which was her way of saying that we should have total respect for her.

When Dad got a serious girlfriend called Helen, she told us that Helen wanted Dad all to herself, she would do anything to achieve that. Of course, because we were children and we trusted our mother, this created a barrier between us and Helen.

We were childishly innocent and couldn't see that Mum was just using us as tools to create problems in Dad and Helen's relationship. On many occasions, she banned us from seeing Dad, blaming maintenance payments, but it was just another way of hurting him. She was using her control of us as children to stick the knife in. The trouble was, however, that it was hurting us greatly too.

It broke our hearts when Dad would phone to speak to us and I would hear Mum telling him that she wouldn't allow it. We would be sitting in the background, worried that Dad would think it was us who didn't want anything to do with him. We had no power to do anything about it and we so wanted to let Dad know that we wanted to see him too, but how could we?

The situation got so bad that my father started pulling up outside the school. A large grass verge surrounded our primary school playground, and now and again I would see Dad's car parked in the street. My sister and I would yell with excitement, running down the grass bank shouting, 'It's Dad, it's Dad,' and waving frantically until we reached the wire mesh fence that separated us. We would spend a few moments talking to him through the fence, but then the dinner ladies would call us back. My sister and I would wipe the tears from our eyes, walking back up the grass bank as Dad's car disappeared around the corner.

Over the years, as Mum tried to control how much time we spent with Dad, we began to see him in secret. By the time I started secondary school, he would pick me up some afternoons for an hour or so, and I would lie to Mum and say I had to stay late for games or something. The guilt at lying to Mum would eat away at me, but by the same token I wanted to spend time with my dad; he had done nothing wrong to us after all, and I missed him terribly. He was more level-headed than Mum; he never spoke with bitterness and anger. He was more interested in how I was getting on at school and making sure I was staying on the right path in life.

One day, I got back from school and my cousins were at our house fussing round my mother, who was sitting on the chair crying. Immediately, I worried something terrible had happened. Had someone died? Tentatively, I entered the room, not knowing what to expect. Mum exploded, 'Have you been seeing your father?' My heart sank because I had been caught out.

Sensing the brewing storm, my cousins made their excuses to leave. I didn't want to be on my own with her. I knew I was in a lot of trouble. I admitted I had been seeing him and she was so angry, 'How could you? You devious, deceitful liar, you...' She must have called me 'devious' a hundred times or more. Then she just went on and on about how I was sly and deceitful.

What could I say? I had been devious and deceitful, and she had found out. I can't remember if she hit me, but the insults were more damning. She constantly labelled me as devious after that. When you're told you're a certain way by a parent at such a young age, it latches onto your persona and knocks your confidence in life. Hence, I always felt as if I was a bad person, not worthy of anyone's trust. I felt I had to grovel to people all the time just to be on an equal footing and for them to trust me enough to see that I wasn't devious. That's why I always felt beneath people in general.

Mum was becoming increasingly bitter, and it was no surprise that her favourite drama on the television at that time was *The Life and Loves of a She-Devil* by Fay Weldon. The story of a calculating lady who, after divorcing her husband, made it her mission to destroy his life, it seemed to reflect my mother's mindset.

Mum suffered with depression and a bad back. She had awful bouts of sciatica, which left her lying on the settee, moaning and agitated. Oddly, the sciatica was never about on Friday and Saturday nights when it was time for her regular nights out at the local clubs.

At the top of the road where we lived there was a big block of council flats and each afternoon, after finishing school, I would walk past them and down a grass verge. At the bottom of the grass verge, our council house would come into view. I never wanted to go home, so I would stand for a few minutes wondering which personality would be present when I walked through the door. Nine times out of ten, unless we had visitors, Mum would be in a horrible mood, and for that, we all had to suffer. She would very often be asleep on the settee with her bad back, and when she woke she would always ask, 'Have I been asleep?' Before we had chance to put our school bags down, she would send us to the shop for her cigarettes – twenty Benson and Hedges. Many nights, I would lie in bed wishing so much she would get a serious boyfriend who would look after her. Then we wouldn't have to bear the brunt of everything that was wrong with her life. I figured that all my friends who had mums and dads who were still together were so lucky, because their parents were busy taking their moods out on each other rather than on their children.

My mother had nobody to take her anger out on other than us – and she had a hell of a lot of anger. If there was a man about, Mum would usually have her nice side on display. The added bonus here was that if she was in a bad mood and couldn't contain it, she would take it out on him and not us. It was a relief to me when she had someone else to focus on. Living with her made me realise that this was not what I wanted for my future children. I didn't want to instil fear into my children like the fear I felt of her, or for them to feel the pressure inherent in having a lonely mother. So I concluded that when I got married, come what may, my marriage would be for keeps. My children would grow up with parents who were together – they would never know the feeling of having parents who were apart. It was all going to be so perfect, or so I believed.

The pressure of bringing children up on her own was immense for my mother; very often she would scream at us that she wished she was 'six foot under'. I never knew what that meant when I was little, but I knew it was something horrible because she was so distraught when she used to yell it at us. We had to stand there and take it. There was nowhere to go, but then we didn't know any different. Life with her was like a test of stamina – see how much you could take of being constantly made to feel like a burden, and take it on the chin.

There were many outbursts of anger from my mother throughout my childhood. To me, it seemed so unfair – in my innocent child's mind, untarnished and unspoilt – that she had to live with all the hurt and pain caused by my father and the terrible things he had bestowed on her. She had been left with the nuisance of us and we were lucky to have none of the worry. We had no problems, and she was bogged down with them. Therefore, in order to ease the guilt I misguidedly felt, and to help my mother alleviate her pain, it seemed only fair to me that I should bear the brunt of her anger without question. It wasn't for me to rebel or have an opinion. It was my duty to be her anger sponge, to absorb her pain. That was my way of dealing with the guilt I felt for being a carefree child, that was my way of taking the burden off my mother. I conditioned myself to believe that being upset was irrelevant. I didn't have the responsibilities Mum had. It was up to me to take my mum's frustrations and soak them up, and to be the same with anyone else. It was a skill I developed to survive, and I carried it through my life, not realising that what I had assumed as a child was a good way of getting through situations with angry people was actually setting me up to fail throughout my life in a massive way. It led me to be passive, easy prey for the aggressive people who continued to come into my life.

Love's Young Dream

All the girls at secondary school were getting attention from boys but I didn't get that much. Most of the girls who had the doting parents, also had the most fashionable clothes and always looked pretty and fabulous. The boys would flock round them, whereas I was unnoticed. I always felt inferior to the popular clique in my dowdy clothes. I really longed for a loving boyfriend, to have someone who was there for me, to make me feel loved and cared for.

My nickname at school was Nervous Stacey. The naughty boys in my class often amused themselves by craftily getting their penises out in class and then calling my name. The first time, unaware of their antics, I looked round to see what they wanted and they were sitting there with their penises proudly on display. Blushing like a tomato, I looked away quickly and heard them all erupt with laughter. I must admit I found it quite embarrassing, yet funny, that they enjoyed teasing me in such a vulgar way.

In my leisure time, I used to hang around the youth club behind my house. It was a dirty little portacabin full of old settees and chairs that had long seen their best days. A big snooker table was the centrepiece of the room. There was also an old-fashioned music centre in teak casing that always had the radio blasting out the latest hits from 1983. Overloaded ashtrays cluttered the room, exuding the stench of stale cigarettes. Most of the kids and the unemployed adults would hang out in there, smoking and playing pool. Everyone knew everyone's business as it was the gossip haven of our scruffy council estate. That said, though, we spent some happy days in that dingy old building.

It was there that I first saw Leon McCabe close up, leaning over the snooker table, eyes focusing down the long wooden snooker cue in an expression of serious concentration. He was thirteen years young, the same age as me. I'd seen him walking to school on many occasions with his older sister, Mandy. They always walked hand in hand. It was a sweet sight to see, the protective older sister holding her little brother's hand, and it didn't seem to bother them what people thought. They were obviously very close. Their lovely relationship intrigued me, and Leon in particular intrigued me very,

very much. It was literally as if Cupid was hovering over me and shot an arrow through my heart.

Leon was smaller than most of the boys his age. His face was so pretty he almost looked like a girl. He had lovely olive skin, brown hair and hazel eyes, and a slightly disproportionate nose, showing the signs of the onset of puberty. He was always dressed very neatly in fashionable clothing – unlike me. So, I started to hang around him as discreetly as I could, hoping he would notice me.

Over the weeks following my first sighting of Leon at the youth club, my friends and I made friends with Leon's pals. We started socialising more in the youth club, and after it finished, we would walk around our housing estate talking and having a laugh.

One night we went back to our mutual friend Davina's house; her mum was out so we all took full advantage and piled in there, playing music and flirting. My friend Pauline was now going out with Leon, and it transpired that his best friend David wanted to go out with me. The term 'going out' in those days meant you were girlfriend and boyfriend, but it was all completely innocent; it was no more than a label and the only time you saw each other was when you were out with your friends.

Pauline told me that David wanted to go out with me, and I was quite straight with her, telling her that I actually preferred Leon. 'Well, that's it then, I'll ask Leon if he will go out with you, and I'll go out with David instead' was her surprising response.

'Are you sure you don't mind?' I asked, delighted with her perfect solution.

'Nah, I'm not bothered about Leon, and I know you like him.' It was as simple as that. She went into the kitchen to talk to Leon about our plan and came out two seconds later saying, 'Leon said he will go out with you.' That night, Leon held my hand. It was dark and all the stars were out, and I felt safe as he walked me home. We arranged to meet at the bus stop on the estate in the morning and get the bus into town together to make our way to school. It felt so good to have someone so handsome interested in me. That night I could barely sleep I was so excited for the morning when I would be meeting my boyfriend to travel to school. From then on, we were pretty much inseparable.

I was absolutely infatuated with him. School dragged as I sat watching the clock, waiting for home time when I would rush back, get ready and be straight out of the door to meet Leon. A few nights went by of walking round the streets, holding hands and getting to know each other before we decided to take things a step further.

We both knew what was going to happen as we went up the dark gravel road that led to the field behind my house where the youth club was. We walked around the back of the building and that's where we had our first kiss. It was wonderful and I felt as if I was floating on air. Leon was smaller than me and had to stand on a box for the kiss, but I loved every second of it.

When I got home, I told Mum I had a boyfriend, but when I told her who it was, she went mad. She knew his mother and said they were a horrible family, and I should stay away, but nothing would keep me from Leon. I was smitten.

We walked to school together, spent all our spare time together. A lot of the time I had to take Luke everywhere with us, which was a bit of a nuisance as he was only three years old and quite a handful.

I loved Luke with what I imagined then was a mother's love; he was like my baby, and I think I was more like his mother than his sister in a lot of ways. He loved girlie things and girls' toys, and I used to dress him up as a little girl. Luke was rarely at home and if I wasn't looking after him, he would often stay at one of my mum's older brothers or sisters' homes, which was a good thing given how Mum suffered with her mood swings.

At night, Leon and I finally had time alone. We would walk the cold streets together hand in hand, chatting and bonding. He would confide in me about his problems at home with his parents arguing and fighting – his dad was either cheating on his mother or hitting her. This time spent with Leon was incredibly comforting to me and we both had a common denominator –problem parents.

As soon as I got in from school, I would get changed to go straight out to be with Leon. He made me melt looking so good in his adidas tracksuits. Mum used to go mad that I was spending too much time with him, but when I was with him, the time went so fast. The fact that he found me interesting and attractive was wonderful for me. No one had ever made me feel so special and important. We would spend hours talking and laughing.

We talked about our lives. His life was different from mine because his parents were together, he was from a solid unit. Whereas I came from a single parent household, and it was good to exchange stories on how this affected our lives. It made me wish my parents were together and then maybe I could have an adidas tracksuit.

My life now seemed fun, and I always had something to look forward to. Meeting him had changed my world. My heart was his. I only had to look at him, be in his presence, and I felt so comfortable and happy. We were in love.

One night, Mum sent me to the curry shop to fetch her usual supper of beef curry and fried rice. While walking back, Leon and I were larking about and, to my horror, I accidentally dropped the food. The curry splattered all over the pavement and there was no way of recovering it. I was petrified about going home and telling her.

Mum went berserk when I got back and reluctantly broke the news about the curry. It was so humiliating that she got angry with me in front of my boyfriend. She started hitting me, hard. I was by the wall with my arms flailing, trying to protect myself. Leon stood there watching the whole thing. I thought he would be horrified but he was amused. He just stood there, laughing, which was even more embarrassing.

I put it down to him being nervous. Seeing his amusement just fuelled my mum's fire and she yelled at him to get out of the house. Leon's parents would never have done anything like that to him, I thought. I admired them, they were proper parents, so wrapped up in themselves they didn't have time to put the guilt on their kids for having a life.

I loved going round to Leon's house. It was immaculate, like a show home. You always had to take your shoes off to go in there. His mother, Diane, was very beautiful, with a rough husky voice, thick black hair and strong, arched eyebrows. Les, her husband, told me that when they first met he thought she looked like a film star, she was so glamorous. She was of French descent, and I really liked her.

She seemed very pleasant and over time I became her confidante. She made me feel so grown up; she talked to me in a way my mother would never do – almost like an adult equal – and she valued my opinion. She made me feel as if she respected me. She told me all about her problems with her husband, who had a terrible temper and had been caught out a few times having affairs. Maybe there was violence and aggression in that household at times, but never when I was there. I knew they had their moments, but the majority of the time they seemed fine.

On the whole, the vibe in their house was better than the lonely, bitter one that my mother gave out, so I loved spending time with them. Leon regularly had new fashionable clothes, and pocket money to do things like get a snack or cigarettes. His mum and dad being together provided a unity, a stability that I lacked in my own life. Leon and I were allowed to sit in his bedroom and his mother would bring us cobs and crisps on a tray, and a regular supply of coffee. There was no way my mum would have been like that with me. I was rarely allowed to have Leon in the house. She let him in and did him a bacon and egg sandwich once or twice, but most of our time was spent at Leon's.

His parents took us on day trips to places such as Weston Park. I loved sitting in the back of the car being part of their family. Compared with my way of life, this was luxury. They seemed so normal and well adjusted. So desperate for some sense of belonging, I was completely seduced by them.

One day, his parents kindly took Leon and me out for a meal at the motorway services. They seemed very nice and the whole day was such an adventure. It was great being out with his mum and dad, their united little family. I envied Leon having this family round him. Les and Diane had each other to lean on so they didn't have to lean on Leon. It was all very light and happy. That day, we all got into Leon's father's car and drove out to the services. We were queuing for our meals when the next thing I knew, I looked round and Leon and his parents were sat down at the table looking at me and laughing. Confused, I wondered at how quickly they had got served and paid for their meals, as I was still wondering what to choose.

They kept waving at me in a gesture for me to go over to them and sit down, but I couldn't, I hadn't paid for my food. Then Leon came over and told me to come and sit down with my food, and slipping a supportive hand under my elbow he firmly guided me to the table. Nervously, I went along with him, realising that they weren't actually going to pay for the meals; they were stealing! They were also condoning us stealing. It didn't feel quite right, but they all found it so amusing. This was exciting; I had never known adults who behaved like this before. So, I sat myself down at the table and they all laughed. Then they bragged about how easy it was to get away with stealing the food at the services. My parents would have gone mad if they had witnessed what was going on, and obviously I had no intention of telling them because they would have stopped me seeing Leon and his family in an instant.

The Bully Boy

The relationship between me and Leon began to change by the time we had been together almost a year, as he became increasingly jealous and insecure. It was a subtle change, one that developed over time and it didn't really trigger any red flags for me, as I was already used to living in a household with someone who was irrational at times. Leon started to question me about speaking to other boys at school, and made it clear he did not like it. Admittedly, I was just as jealous as him, but I did not make any rules about who he could and could not speak to.

We spent a lot of our spare time at his parents. It was a joy to be treated as part of Leon's family. I felt privileged, and had a sense of belonging to a wider social circle, with people who clearly thought a lot of me. Without Leon, I wouldn't have my lovely new family. Leon's mum was like a mother to me; she talked to me and made me feel good about myself. I knew if I lost him, I would lose the family I had become part of.

As time went on, Leon became bit of a bully. It was so gradual, I didn't even seem to notice it happening. He always seemed to be picking on weaker kids, and harder kids were always picking on him. Our housing estate had that dog-eat-dog culture. One day, he chased one boy who was being really mouthy to him until he caught hold of him.

In my eyes, the kid was just being a cheeky little blighter and taking his chances, like kids do. The boy's name was Stanley, but his nickname was Sausage, probably because he was lithe, tall and seemed a little slow. Unfortunately for him, when Leon caught up with him he threw him into the bush and all I could see were Stanleys stick-like legs frantically waving out of the privet. The kid was petrified and Leon laid into him really badly. He just kept punching him really hard, over and over again; the sight of it made me feel sick. I was sobbing and trying to pull Leon off him as I begged him to stop, but this just seemed to inflame his cruelty and he continued until he ran out of breath. Sausage seized his chance and ran off as fast as his feet would carry him, twisting his head and looking back yelling 'nob-end'. Leon, realising I was upset, then justified his actions by saying the kid had been insulting him and his family for months and had it coming.

It wasn't long before Leon's nasty streak started to surface with me. He was very possessive, always questioning me about where I'd been and who I'd been talking to. Over time, this escalated into aggression and control.

One day, we had been arguing about something really trivial, so trivial I cannot recall exactly what it was but I know I had made him unhappy. It may have been me talking to another boy or something like that. We were walking up the grass hill around the back of the maisonettes at the top of my road when he struck me for the first time.

He was getting more aeriated and pushed me against the nine-foot brick wall that housed the washing lines for the tenants of the flats to dry their washing. It was a secluded area other than the windows of the flats surrounding us. Maybe Leon assumed no one could see us because it was there that he first struck me with a sharp slap to the face.

I felt shocked. I think he was equally as shocked because he could not apologise enough. He immediately hugged me, rubbing my shoulders, 'Sorry, I'm so sorry,' he said, looking bewildered by his own behaviour. That should have been the point of no return, where I walked away. But I felt sorry for him because he was clearly regretful of what he had done.

Later, this behaviour would rear its ugly head again – with a little more viciousness each time. A slap, and then a pull of the hair, always quickly followed by a heartfelt 'sorry'. Bit by bit it started to happen more often, until I was in love with and petrified of him at the same time.

He was always very sorry afterwards and would come knocking on my door, upset, begging me for one more chance. I always felt deep pity for him when he was upset. He wanted, loved and he needed me. It became clear that he was mixed up in his head due to what he often described as living in an unbearable atmosphere at home, with his parents arguing. His home life caused him a lot of stress. We always found excuses for his behaviour. However bad he had been to me, it was automatically dismissed in my mind. I suppose I was a prime candidate for Leon as I always saw the good in everyone.

The erratic behaviour continued, and I naively used to think he must love me so much to get so jealous over me. Only, it wasn't love. It was control, although I didn't see it like that at the time. For me, guilt and pity for others came as a priority above any respect I had for myself. Leon made me feel so loved and so complete. Of course, I always gave him one more chance, until one more chance turned into chance after chance, and the threat of 'one last chance' had no meaning any more. He and his family were my world, and when we got on well I felt so completely happy.

I was all he had, and I thought that we had a special understanding. We were kindred spirits, united by tainted parenting.

]It was 1985 and with the release of the film *Rocky*, all the kids were in awe of the Italian stallion, especially me. As a typical teenager, I had a few posters on my bedroom wall of Sylvester Stallone. I thought he was gorgeous. One day, I was in my bedroom and I noticed that my favourite poster had been crayoned on deliberately. Confused and angry, I couldn't work out who had done it. Leon hadn't been in my bedroom; he wasn't allowed in the house much at all. I knew it wasn't Hannah or Mum because it wasn't the sort of thing they'd do. That left one answer: little Luke.

So being an upset teenager about my Rocky poster being vandalised, I screamed down the stairs to Luke to come up at once. I began shouting at him saying, 'Why have you drawn on my poster?' and before he had a chance to answer, Mum ran up the stairs at ninety miles an hour, her feet thudding on each step in temper. 'What the bloody hell's going on?' she shouted. I showed her my poster and began saying that I thought Luke had damaged it.

'Have you done this?' she shouted at Luke.

Luke shook his head, frightened, and said he hadn't.

It dawned on me then that he was telling the truth; we were all scared of Mum and knew better than to tell lies. In an effort to save Luke from a beating the poor little boy did not warrant, I desperately tried to backtrack. I'd realised that somehow it must have been Leon, but now it was too late! Mum started smacking a crying Luke really hard.

Luke was begging, 'I haven't done it, I haven't done it.' You could see the poor kid hadn't done it. I was trying to get Mum to stop, saying, 'Leave it now, it doesn't matter.' It was no good; she wouldn't stop hitting him and shouting and swearing. I felt so ashamed of myself for being such a coward. I should have said that it must have been Leon, but I couldn't. I knew if I did she would hit me for starting all this trouble, and want to know how Leon had got into my bedroom – I was absolutely petrified. I felt sick. My poor little brother was only about four. It was clear from the way he was pleading with her that he was innocent. How could she not see that? As his own mother!

Finally, Mum stomped off downstairs leaving my little brother sobbing. Luke looked at me and said, 'I didn't do it, Stacey, honest.'

I wrapped my arms around him and we were both crying, 'I know,' I said. 'I know.'

It was sickening; my poor baby brother. Immediately afterwards, I was so anxious to see Leon to ask him if it was him, and when I saw him, I told him all about the trouble he had caused. He didn't need to admit it to me verbally as the amused expression on his face told me he'd done it. I was so angry with him, but as usual he talked me round, and I forgave him in the end.

As time went on, Leon's attacks got more and more frequent. One day, we were walking to school together and he wanted to search my bag – that was what Leon was like, he needed to keep a check on me. In my bag was a vinyl record of a song called 'Take On Me'. I had borrowed it from a geeky lad called Gary at school. Leon demanded to know who I had borrowed the record from and then proceeded to stamp on it. I was really upset because it wasn't mine, and I didn't have the money to replace it. I was already worrying in my head how I was going to explain to Gary that I hadn't got his record and that he would have to wait until I'd got the money to replace it.

We were standing by pointy iron railings near some waste ground when Leon grabbed my green canvas school bag and kept smashing it through the spikes on the top of the railings, tearing big holes into it. As I began shouting at Leon to stop, he got more livid, grabbed me round the throat and threw me up against the railings. He kept pulling my hair and slapping my face. Then he started pulling me towards the church and when we got around the back of the church, he kicked me a few times in my shins, then he grabbed my school bag and swung it round and round and flung it high in the air until it landed on top of the church extension. He stepped back towards me, breathing heavily, and grabbed me, pulling me to him, his eyes now narrow with confusion.

Bedraggled, I pushed him away and made a run for it, Leon chasing, shouting after me. He was out of breath, and I could hear his cries. 'I am so sorry, Stacey. I can't help it. I love you so much I couldn't help getting jealous.' He was sobbing, his shoulders heaving up and down. 'What have I done, Stacey? What have I done?'

Not knowing what to do, I kept running, not daring to look back. I made my way up to the bus station and clambered thankfully on to the school bus that had just pulled in at the stop. All I can remember after that was getting to school looking as if I'd been dragged through a hedge backwards and arriving late for my geography lesson. Pushing the classroom door open, I apologised for being late, and, with my head down, I made my way to my seat.

The teacher made me stay behind at the end of the lesson. She was being very nice, and she managed to cajole me into explaining the state of my red tear-stained face to her. She gave me a jolly good talking to about how what had happened to me was very bad, and that that sort of behaviour only gets worse over time, and that I should talk to my parents and keep away from Leon.

When she mentioned talking to my parents I instantaneously dismissed this. I did not feel I could talk to either of them. She had everything together in her life and the only security I felt I had was Leon, regardless of how badly he was treating me. She would have been a brilliant mentor had she had more regular time for me, but as a young person I just slipped through the net. A mere conversation was not enough, given the emotions I was up against and my lack of wisdom.

Eventually it was home time, and I caught the bus back to town, my heart feeling heavy. All the drama had gone and it was back to just me. The bus bumped along with kids from my school, and mothers with crying babies. Everyone was either absorbed in their own world, or chatting to the person near them. I felt so alone. There was going to be nobody waiting to walk home with me, and the prospect of going home to my room was dreary.

Stepping off the bus, I heard Leon call me and I turned around in disbelief to see him sitting in his school clothes on the damp wall, his mop of brown hair almost falling over his gentle brown eyes. He must have been waiting for me and it made me feel sad for him, it made me want to hold him. He stepped up to me, and I stepped back; he held his arms out to me, regardless of everyone in the bus station staring. The hurt in his eyes mirroring the hurt in my heart, he stepped forward again and put both his arms around me really tightly. Relief flooded through me, and although I knew in my head I should have pushed him away, my heart said different. Our heads touched, my forehead against his, and he kissed me on the mouth. My heart was beating so fast. 'Stacey, I love you so much,' he sighed, and I knew he did; all my anxiety dissolved.

There was no way I was going to tell my parents and let them stop me seeing Leon. He couldn't help himself; he needed my help, not for me to turn my back on him. When he was in a good mood, he made me feel so happy and loved. No one else could make me feel so complete.

Inevitably, over time, we had to start seeing each other in secret because my parents knew the relationship was unhealthy. I got caught seeing him in secret one time by my mother; she followed me without me being aware, and when she caught us she took me home and gave me a good hiding – but it just made me want to be with Leon even more.

I carried on seeing him in secret, but it all went sour again one night when Leon saw me home after we had met up. When we were saying goodnight, hidden behind a bush, I said something and he lost his temper with me. I can't remember what triggered him, but he slapped me really hard round the face and pulled my hair. Mum must have heard the commotion as I made a dash for my front door. She swung it open and I ran into the house crying, Leon standing outside defiantly in full view.

All I could hear was that Mum hit the roof. 'What the bloody hell have you done to her?' she shouted.

Leon shouted back, 'Fuck off, you whore.'

Then he bolted, and Mum ran after him yelling, 'Who are you talking to? Get back here!' She didn't catch him though.

I listened in disbelief. How could he have spoken to my mother like that? He'd done it now, for both of us. I wasn't concerned that he had just beaten me – I was hurt he had disrespected my mother so awfully. What hurt the most, strangely, was knowing there would be no going back for us.

Mum got straight on the phone to Leon's parents. She told them to keep their son away from her daughter, and told them I looked as if I'd been dragged through a hedge backwards. Mum belted out her orders, 'Stacey, you had better keep well away from him this time or woe betide you.'

What else could I expect? I lay in bed and couldn't sleep for most of the night, going over things in my head. I had to be strong. I was trying to focus on him calling my mum a whore, and all the terrible things he had done to me over the last two years, knowing how wrong they were. Still, ridiculously, I was convinced that he really loved me. So, I sobbed myself to sleep because I knew now that his parents and mine were involved and, especially after what he had done, that we had to be over. Although I should have been relieved, I wasn't. I was heartbroken, I hadn't just lost him, I'd lost his family.

The next morning, I got up for school and I was so hoping he would be at the top of the road waiting for me, but he wasn't. *Maybe he will be at the bus stop*, I prayed, but he wasn't. My heart was sinking with each corner I turned. The school day dragged and when I finished, I expected him to be waiting outside the school, heartbroken like me, but he wasn't. Each time he wasn't where I expected him to be waiting for me, I felt a wave of anxiety and desperation – the feeling was hideous. He never usually gave up!

Instead of feeling relieved that he and I were over, I became more and more infatuated with him. Just after we split up, I'd purposely walk particular ways to school in the hope of bumping into him and I would make friends with people who were friends of his friends. The first time I saw him again, I was purposely waiting in the shopping arcade on a school morning because it was raining. I knew the chances were he would take that route. I saw him walking down with two older girls and I felt my heart pumping so hard with excitement I thought it was going to come out of my chest. I was blushing so red I hoped my face would calm down by the time he neared me and not give my embarrassment away. Trying to act casually, as if I was expecting someone else, I waited for him to walk past me hoping for eye contact. I needed to see his reaction, to see if he had been missing me the way I had been him. Finally, he came within eye distance and glanced at me, then, as if I was just another random stranger he didn't know, he continued his conversation with the girls he was talking to and walked on.

As he walked past me and disappeared, tears sprang to my eyes; I was disbelieving that the boy who had loved me didn't love me any more. He obviously hadn't given me a second thought. I tried to be angry and tell myself that it should have been me blanking him, but him pleading with me to come back. I knew we were no good for each other, but I couldn't fight these overwhelming feeling of loss that kept playing in my mind.

Memories plagued me of when we first met and how gentle and affectionate he had been. How could our relationship have turned so bad? Thinking back, I remembered how it started. We were only thirteen. In our first week together, waiting at the bus stop to travel to school, he had held my hand and I felt safe and my heart soared. We boarded the bus together, we sat down and snuggled up. He said, 'I have something for you,' and took out of his bag a grey velvet jewellery box. Taking it from him, I felt so coy, no one had ever made me feel so special. Opening the box gently, I saw enclosed in the crushed red velvet lining a silver digital watch.

'Wow,' I said, feeling touched, 'why have you got this for me?'

My heart stirred when I remembered his answer, 'Because you are my girl.' With that feeling of belonging to someone so intently that it didn't matter what went on with the rest of the world because I was no longer alone, I was part of someone else, I felt stronger and happier.

The desire to be happy like that again came from relating to the lovely moments we had shared. Our connection with each other was so intense I felt as if no one could ever make me feel that way again. My obsession grew worse and I could not stop thinking about him, daydreaming about him, fantasising about bumping into him and him begging me to come back. All I talked about was him, I must have really got on my friends' nerves. It was so painful to feel like this constantly. I wondered what he was doing, who he was seeing. I frequently heard he was going out with different girls. My heart was with him though, so the thought of going out with other boys just made me feel physically sick. It may have been naive to think that we could have those happy times back, but I was only a teenager, and through all the pain I could not see any sense.

To make things worse, Mum was still suffering from depression so being at home was miserable. There was no love in our house, just the pressure cooker of irritability. Each night, I would cry in bed and pray, 'Please, God, end my pain. Please make Leon want me back, and I'll do anything. I don't care if he hits me or goes off with other women, as long as he is mine. Please, God, make him marry me so that we can be together forever because I can't go on pining for him like this forever.'

My mind was in a dark tunnel, with no concept of the wonderful position I was in, being so young and having my whole life ahead of me to start afresh. It was just not getting any easier. There were a few times I sat at the kitchen table, in the dark, crying. Mum would be out and I'd be in so much pain emotionally I would think about killing myself, but I then I'd think about how much it would hurt my family if I did and I knew I couldn't do it to them, so I had to continue bearing this awful feeling of unrequited love.

Then I heard that Leon had joined the navy, so I tried hopelessly to get over him. There was an advertising campaign at the time promoting the dangers of heroin. Everything the advert said about addiction was how I felt for Leon – he had become my addiction. No matter how bad he had treated me, rightly or wrongly I still craved him every second of every day. Even when I went to sleep, I would dream we were back together and happy again. It used to hit me like a ton of bricks when I woke up, realising it was only a dream. I used to lie there crying into my pillow, feeling sick. It was my first overwhelming experience of a broken heart.

Reunited

It was 1986, I was sixteen going on seventeen. Although I had finished my CSE exams and was quite pleased with my grades, I was still at school for another year. Mum insisted I went back to school to redo them, which was a complete waste of time because I'd already done them to the best of my ability. It wasn't because she was concerned about my education, she just wanted me to stay on so that she could continue getting her full social security benefit. So, the school put me into a class with pupils of the year below me that I'd previously been in. All my year left school and got jobs or went to college.

Around this time, Dad was encouraging me to try and join the Royal Air Force. I wanted to make him proud, so I went along with his dream. We drove over to the local RAF careers office and pulled up outside. Dad said that I should go in there now and tell them I was interested in joining. I bounded into the office and the officer sitting behind the desk looked a tad amused at me in my jeans and pink leg warmers. Feeling intimidated, I blurted out literally what Dad had told me to ask, thinking it was the right thing to say, 'What can you do for me?'

The officer tapped his pencil on his pad trying to hide his smirk and then he passed me some leaflets about joining the forces. The following week, in that same office, I sat an aptitude test – and, as I had expected, I failed. Dad was unhappy as he had great visions for my future. I, on the other hand was relieved, I knew I would be way out of my comfort zone among all these professional, capable fighters.

Hearing through the grapevine that Leon would be in a club in my area that evening, I intended to get myself in there as well. I dressed up and tried to make myself look older by stuffing my bra with socks. Looking in the mirror, I was very pleased with how good I looked with my thick make-up and long blonde hair. When I arrived at the club, I felt like the belle of the ball and I was getting quite a few admiring glances. Of course, there was only one person I was interested in seeing and that was Leon.

Seeing all the attention I was getting, he made his way over to me and, to my delight, he seemed to be taking a genuine interest in me. I tried to act blasé about it, but inside I was so happy; I had been waiting for this moment for so long. We began to chat and catch up on things and he offered to walk me home. The navy had seemed to make him mature, and I was relishing the fact that so much time had gone by that the things he had done to me and the name he had called my mum was now hopefully going to be a distant memory. I felt selfish for going against my mother, but there was no way I could continue living without him. It was just as in the advertisements I had seen, he was like my heroin, that's the only way I can describe it. It was a wonderful evening for me as he walked me home. Our relationship began again from that night and I was so happy. Because Leon was in the navy and I only saw him when he was on leave, we hardly saw anything of each other, but when we did see each other there was never time for the violent side of Leon to rear its ugly head; it had died a death, thank goodness. I lived for the weekends when we could see each other.

Mary, a lovely middle-aged lady I used to babysit for, kindly let him stay over with me when I looked after her kids when she went clubbing. It was great for her because she always had a babysitter on tap, and it was good for me because it gave Leon and me somewhere to spend the night together. We were very immature and didn't think of the consequences. We didn't always use condoms, as I was too embarrassed to buy them, so I relied on Leon getting them. When we didn't have one, I begged him to be careful, naively believing that we would be safe. However, one night when we had unprotected sex I could tell he had gone the whole way, without pulling out. 'You haven't come in me, have you, Leon?' I asked him, petrified of the answer. He said that he had, and started laughing as if it was some big joke. 'Oh no, no you can't have? Tell me you haven't? Tell me you're joking,' I pleaded.

Petrified, I kept pleading with him to tell me the truth hoping that he'd say he was only tormenting me, but he was telling me the truth and he seemed to find it amusing that I was getting in such a state about the thought of being pregnant.

'Don't be daft, you won't be pregnant,' he laughed, pulling up his trousers and getting ready to go. How could he laugh about something that could be so serious? Maybe it was because he wouldn't have to suffer the consequences with his parents, or his entire life, as I would have to. Maybe it was because he'd seen his seventeen-year-old sister, Mandy, get a council house and the support of the state by having a baby, and that's what he wanted for us too?

Naively, I believed what he said, and tried not to worry about it, but after some time I realised my period hadn't come. I scraped some money together then went to a chemist and bought a pregnancy test. That night, I stayed at Mary's and decided to do the test there. I couldn't risk leaving a pregnancy test lying about at home. It was a school morning. I followed the instructions, urinated on the sample paper, and I sat on the bed waiting for the result. Five minutes went by and I looked at the results it was POSITIVE.

My mind went crazy as I screamed inside, 'Oh my God, no it can't be, it just can't be.'

But   it   was.

Pregnant and Scared

I had never been so scared in all my life. The double strips facing me on the test kit telling me it was positive were undeniable. I just couldn't believe it.

The room was spinning. Panicked thoughts raced round my head – the main one being mother. She would kill me. Sobbing my eyes out, I collapsed on the bed. There was nothing I could physically do to change this. It wasn't possible to expel it from my body; it was inside me. It would grow inside me, and in time it would have to come out. If only there was a way I could deal with this without my parents having to know.

Eventually, I got myself together and ran down to the house of a friend with whom I sometimes had a lift to school. Her house was always so busy in the mornings. Her mother was up rushing Laura along to get ready. The smell of toast and coffee was so comforting, it was always warm and snug in contrast to my home. When she saw I'd been crying, Laura got excited, avidly waiting for the gossip. Begging her not to tell anyone, I confessed I was pregnant. She was smirking, trying to look concerned. Why couldn't anyone understand how bad this was? This devastating news was certainly not amusing to me. This was my life and there seemed to be nobody I could turn to. Laura's mum dropped us off at school and the news spread.

As time went on, I became conscious of the fact that there was a life growing inside me. At school, I spent most of the time running out of lessons to be sick – I felt awful. Every night, I lay in bed crying and wondering what to do. The life inside me was no longer 'it', but had started to feel like my baby. Rubbing my tummy at night, I would gently tell my baby not to worry, that somehow everything would be all right. I was getting attached to the innocent little life forming and started to think that maybe having this baby would not be such a bad idea after all.

Fantasies of me in my own little council house, living blissfully with Leon, our own perfect little family, his parents visiting. It would be wonderful. Living with my mother was horrible, and I suppose the pregnancy started to feel like a solution to get away from her.

My bedroom was always freezing, the ice on the windows thick outside and inside; you could see your breath if you breathed out into the air. Although we had central heating, it was never used, or very, very occasionally, but it made such a difference to the house when it was switched on. The house turned into a pink paradise, as all our bedrooms were painted pink. I would sit with my back up against the radiator, enjoying the feeling of warmth; it was nice just to be able to sit in my bedroom when it was rarely like that. Usually, we all sat downstairs in front of the living room gas fire. The hot water was rarely on either – only when Mum had her bath and we used her water afterwards.

The day Leon phoned me from work and I told him I was pregnant, he laughed and said he didn't believe me, so I was left to deal with the consequences on my own. I had decided that I was going to keep the baby. Everyone would just have to get used to it, I concluded. I knew for a fact I would be a loving mother. I didn't want to be anything like my own mother. As I was old enough to make my own decisions, I didn't need to say anything to Mum if I was going terminate the baby. However, because I had decided to keep my baby, I knew I was going to have to tell her. Timing was of the essence, and I knew that I had to wait for her to be in a good mood before I said anything. One day, soon after I found out about the baby, I discovered Mum in the kitchen washing up. I knew I had to get this over and done with if I was to keep this baby and so I summoned up all my courage to tell her everything. I sat on top of the twin tub washing machine, and mustering all my internal strength, I said, 'Mum, I have something to tell you.'

She turned around and looked at me, and I just knew she knew. 'You're not pregnant, are you?' she said, her eyes meeting mine, studying my face, frowning.

'Yes, I am,' I blurted out before I could change my mind. There I had said it! Obviously, she was very upset. This was the last thing she needed and it took her a while to absorb what I had just told her. Then she began questioning me, who's the father? Where did we have sex?

I just looked at her not knowing what to say.

'Are you sure?' Mum asked. 'Have you done a test?'

When I confirmed that there was no mistake, she automatically presumed that I would be having a termination. She also assumed she was going to have to pay for it as she was ranting about how the hell she was going to afford the operation. I told her I wasn't going to have an abortion; I'd decided to keep it. She went ballistic, screaming and shouting at me that I was too young and hadn't got a clue what I would be letting myself in for. All I could see through my seventeen-year-old, rose-tinted specs was me and my baby living in peace without Mum making my life a misery any more. Breaking my thoughts, she stood there in disbelief crying, 'What will the neighbours say?'

This pregnancy in my eyes was the key to my new life away from my mother. But before my plans got off the ground, Mum and I were in the GP's surgery and the doctor was asking me what I had decided to do. I knew my answer would upset Mum, but it was my baby and I had to protect it. I told him defiantly that I had decided to keep it. Mum started shouting, her usual mask of grounded, nurturing mother smashing to the ground in her desperation to be heard. This was not up for debate, and she backed this up by telling the doctor that I couldn't look after myself, never mind a baby. There was no way I was going to keep it because she would be the one left to look after it.

The doctor looked pityingly at me, nodding his head in disapproval. He could not see further than a stupid child having a child herself, and he sympathised with my mother who was clearly at her wits end. Putting my hands to my face, my fingers smoothing away my tears, I dropped my head into my lap in despair.

Previously, I'd been to see Leon's mother, hoping to get some support there, and she was very kind. I suppose hearing it from his mother made Leon come to terms with the fact that I was telling the truth. I had told them that I was going to tell Mum I was keeping the baby, but before I could update them, the termination was booked. The choice had been taken away from me – not even the doctor considered how I felt. On the outside I was crying, on the inside I was angry – why didn't the doctor support me? It was obvious I was fighting a losing battle, my baby's fate had been sealed, and my feelings on the matter were irrelevant – just as my feelings on all matters were irrelevant. The deal was done and it was a closed case.

In the days running up to the termination, I sat in bed at night, crying and rubbing my tummy, haunted by the fact that I'd let my little baby down. I was so weak, I couldn't fight my mother. Now my little one was going to lose its life. 'I am so sorry,' I cried, night after night, and I was so very sorry.

The morning of the abortion came, and I knew it was pointless trying to talk my way out of it. Mum had made her mind up, and my feelings didn't matter. She knew best, she thought I was a naive child who didn't know what was right for me. A kind word from her, a genuine mother to daughter discussion, was inconceivable.

We didn't have a car, so we went to the nearest British Pregnancy Advisory Clinic by bus. With my little bag held tightly in my hand, we crossed the road and headed into the clinic. I had borrowed the little bag from a friend and it was filled with the items to bring noted on the pamphlet from the clinic. A clean nightdress, a few pairs of clean knickers, large sanitary towels and a sanitary belt. I had no idea what the sanitary belt was for.

We waited in the reception of the clinic for a while, until a minibus arrived. Mum waved me goodbye, I got into the minibus with several other ladies – ladies being the optimum word as I was the youngest among them – and we set off for the abortion clinic in Leamington Spa. Feeling like a lamb to the slaughter, I held my head down in shame the entire journey, tears dropping into my lap. There was nothing I could do. I could not go back and tell my mother I had not gone through with it, as she would be so angry. One Asian lady looked at me sadly, nodding her head in pity. 'So young, so young,' she murmured. Embarrassed, I smiled at her, not knowing how to react.

When we arrived, I expected to see a hospital, but the clinic looked more like a big manor house set in beautiful grounds. Herded along like sheep, we were taken to our rooms to sign some paperwork consenting to the operation. The nurse gave me the clipboard and, as I hadn't mastered my signature yet, I reluctantly printed my name. I was left to pop on my nightdress and put on the sanitary belt, but I still didn't have any idea what it was for. I looked at the packet to see how to use it and finally pulled the elastic loop round my tiny waist. The bedroom was old-fashioned, with a single bed and a fire with a grate. There was also a little bedside table to put my toiletries on next to the bed. Alone, I lay there rubbing my belly, soothing my baby. My baby would be gone soon. I wondered if the baby knew what I was about to do? Guilt washed over me, and also a bitterness at how weak I was being, how I could not stand up to my mother. My goodbyes and last moments were interrupted as a couple of nurses came into the room.

'Come on, young lady, let's get you down to theatre,' a nurse said chirpily. We walked down to theatre and they gave me some paper shoes to pop on my feet.

As I lay on the bed, the surgeons rushing round me with their masks on doing their job, tears poured from my eyes. The last thing I saw was the surgeon leaning over me telling me to count backwards from ten as he inserted a needle into the top of my hand. 'Ten, nine...' I looked at him smiling, then it all went black.

My head hurt and I felt sick and as my eyes opened, I felt dizzy. Someone was saying, 'Wake up, Stacey.'

A blur of a face came into vision, and I didn't know where I was. Trying to sit up, I was sick and a paper bowl was held under my mouth. Looking round, I saw that I was on a ward with several other ladies – some were sleeping and some were crying. It was then I realised it had been done. The belt tugged tightly on my tummy and I realised I had nothing on under my nighty other than a huge sanitary towel hooked onto the sanitary belt like a baby's nappy. So that's what it was for! The drugs were still in my system and I fell easily back to sleep.

Within a couple of hours, we were on the minibus travelling back to the pregnancy advice clinic. Sitting in my yellow and black striped jumper, I wondered where the bus station was located, so I could make my way back to where I lived. I could not wait to get home, where I would be left alone to absorb what had happened. Finally, the minibus stopped at the Clinic and I grabbed my bag and got off. Wondering how I was going to get home, I walked limply up the high street looking for my bus stop, and then I heard my mother shout, 'Stacey'.

I looked across the main road and Mum was standing there waving at me. She hadn't mentioned she was going to be meeting me and, regardless of what I felt she had made me do, it was good to see her. She looked at me, full of love, with tears in her eyes, beckoning me over to her. I ran over to her and she gave me a big hug, and she rubbed her hands down my shoulders. She was conveying to me that she had tried to protect me from being a single parent like her. However tragic, she had meant well. She had brought my Uncle Brian with her, which increased my feeling of shame as he knew where I had been, and that I must have had sex. He had a nice new car, and it was a comfort to climb in and sit on the cosy back seat.

When we got home, Mum sent me to bed with an air that it was all over and behind us now, and there was nothing more to be said. However, over the next few weeks I felt so depressed that I had let my baby down. There was no evidence that I had suffered such a great loss, except for the leaflet I had kept from the clinic in Leamington Spa. Each night I would pray for my baby in heaven and hope that she or he was okay. My father didn't know any of this – I hoped he thought that I was still a virgin.

When I saw Leon, he wasn't really interested in what had happened, only unhappy that I had an abortion without letting him have any say. It was something he couldn't understand. There was no one I could talk to about it who did understand! We carried on seeing each other while he was on leave from the Navy. We were still so in love that it got harder and harder to tear ourselves away from each other, and it did not help that he was worried about his mum, who had decided to leave his dad. She stayed with relatives, and it looked as if the marriage was over, until one day, shortly after my abortion, Les begged her to come home, promising he would never hurt her again.

Leon was not happy in the Navy and played on the fact that he had problems with his ankle, which was weak as a result of a car accident when he was little. After assessments he got medically discharged. When he was back home full time, we went on holiday together in a caravan to Borth in Wales and had the most fantastic week of our lives. No parents there to interfere with our fun.

It was an impetuous week of laughter and reckless abandonment, in stark contrast with the usual dreary days spent back home. Tearing round the campsite in Leon's ford Escort with 'Ride on Time' by Black Box blaring out of the speakers, we were free together. We spent the days on the beautiful golden beaches, kissing on the sand and chasing each other into the cold blue sea. Conversation and laughter only stopped when we made love. When Leon lay on top of me cradling my head with his strong arms and looking into my eyes, it felt as if I was melting into a puddle of beautiful, blissful love. He would tell me he loved me and I knew he did because when I looked into his face I could see it.

It was so nice to have someone to talk to who was light-hearted and happy, and who loved indulging in Mr Kipling cakes and loud music as much as I did. We were a match made in heaven and I didn't want the week to end. Things were better without our parents, and the burden of their problems around – life was good.

We used to go to the club on the site every night, watching the entertainment and feeling like a proper married couple. The club held a Miss Haven beauty competition, and I entered and won the title. The prize was a week's holiday back on the caravan site in October for the Grand Final of all the Miss Havens around Britain. We decided to use the prize as a honeymoon! The thought of getting married and getting our own place away from my mum came so naturally. After the trauma of the abortion a year earlier, I was starting to feel I was on the right path in life.

I truly believed that once Leon and I removed ourselves from the stress that our parents were causing we would have a wonderful marriage. Young and naive, I was unaware of how much damage had already been done to our young minds. We were a dangerous combination. I was weak and had learned to be submissive to such a degree that people could treat me badly, and I would feel responsible for their behaviour. Leon was the opposite end of the scale in this abnormal spectrum – dominant and abusive. We were both products of an unhealthy upbringing. Leon was a time bomb, having grown up in a volatile atmosphere, and he needed to gain ultimate control.

The Wedding

We were nineteen when we got married in the local registry office. My mother and father were obviously against it – I think Dad knew what I would be letting myself in for as he refused to give us his blessing – but we went ahead anyway. Dad didn't pay for the wedding, but gave us a hefty cheque of a thousand pounds to get us started with married life. He did his best to talk me out of getting married, but my mind was well and truly made up.

When Leon and I split up when we were teenagers, I had been suicidal and terribly depressed, and so I was totally convinced that I had to be with Leon regardless of how bad things got, as I could never live with the pain and heartbreak again. I was also desperate to get away from my depressive mother. I didn't care that I might be jumping out of the frying pan into the fire – the fire seemed so inviting compared with the alternative. We had our wedding reception in a local pub. I was in my element but Leon seemed really distant. It didn't help matters that his mother, Diane, was sitting in a corner with my relatives and embarrassing Leon's father, Les. She was telling them the most intimate details of their relationship and how Les had forced her into sex. I don't think my aunties knew what to make of her – she was just so matter of fact about the subject. Les was obviously really embarrassed and was sinking into a bad mood, so, Leon and I left early to drive to Wales for our honeymoon.

It was strange sitting in the car next to my husband who was driving. I was over the moon, like an excited little schoolgirl, something I had been just a couple of years earlier, but Leon was very quiet and seemed caught in a world of his own. I was only just nineteen, and a very immature nineteen at that.

The journey to Wales seemed like the beginning of a new chapter in my life. No more going back under the oppressive roof of my mother's home. I was an adult, I was free. I had no idea that this new journey was about to take me to the darkest places I could ever imagine. I kept repeating, 'You're my husband, my husband,' but it was clear that Leon was not in the same happy mood. He just concentrated on the road – frowning.

Eventually, I decided to calm down a little and be quiet; I didn't want to overpower him with my excited chatter. The chances are he was still thinking about how his parents had behaved at our wedding reception, I thought, making excuses for him as usual. So, I decided to leave my poor husband with his thoughts and just look out of the window and enjoy the lovely hilly views. We passed a greeting sign, Welcome to Wales. Yippee! We were in Wales. Not long to go now before we reached our destination. Our little honeymoon caravan in Borth. The views out of the window were absolutely lovely, all the greenery, the winding roads, the vast blankets of green fields.

Finally, we arrived at the caravan, and I began unpacking while Leon sat and stretched his legs after the long drive.

'Do us a coffee, Stacey,' he ordered – and I did. He was my husband and I wanted so much to make him happy and be a good wife, just like his mum was to his dad. I'd notice how his mother would butter Les's baguette until he was happy it was just the right amount, and I concluded that this is how a wife should be in their family. So, I made the coffee, unpacked the bags, then we trotted along to the campsite shop and bought some Mr Kipling cakes. Night came and I lay in bed in all my white lace underwear, stockings and suspenders. Leon didn't really seem impressed – well, if he was he didn't say anything appreciative.

The next morning, as I was washing up and watching some very noisy geese outside our window, a car pulled up in front of the caravan and to my surprise it was Leon's parents. I wasn't expecting them. How had they found us? For a second, I felt a bit disappointed because I had been looking forward to doing some bonding with my new husband, but I quickly reasoned with myself that I was now officially a McCabe too. These were now my in-laws.

Leon and I rushed outside to greet them cheerfully. Straightaway I warmed to them being with us, I was in awe of them for treating Leon and me like adults. I was filling the little gas kettle with water when Diane stepped into the caravan and as Leon gave the orders for me to make coffees, she shouted over to me, 'Start the way you mean to finish.'

'What does that mean?' I asked her curiously.

'It means,' she said, 'if you want to be treated properly make sure you assert that at the start, because if you give in now, it will become harder to break the pattern in your marriage when you get older.' She said she wished she'd put her foot down with Les in the beginning, and maybe he wouldn't be walking all over her now.

Surely us all bonding as a family would also strengthen my relationship with Leon in the long run. It gave me a sense of security having them there, we felt like one big family.

We spent the days driving into the local towns and exploring the local markets. Leon's mother had a natural gift with style and dress sense, whereas my dress sense left a lot to be desired. So, she picked clothes off the rails in the fashion shops, suggesting what would like nice on me. Other days we would get up early and head to a tourist attraction and spend the day looking at the exhibits. Eventually we would head back to the caravan and either have fish and chips, from the camp site shop or Diane would cook something. She was a great cook. Most evenings we would all get ready for the evening entertainment, getting dressed up and heading to the local club. It was a great holiday.

After the honeymoon, we moved in with Leon's parents for a short time until the council gave us a flat. Fortunately, my mother had put my name down with the council as soon as I was old enough to be accepted, and we were given the keys to a flat pretty quickly. I loved the new path my life had taken. Leon and I went to Tesco on our first shopping expedition as a married couple, and threw everything we wanted into the trolley – cakes, fizzy pop, biscuits – without any thought about the expense.

We had instant hot water, and I made sure I had a luxurious bubble bath every single night. We had a video player and regularly hired films. It was so much better than my life at home with Mum. I appreciated all the changes immensely. Leon couldn't understand at first why I was washing up in the dusk as night descended. 'Why don't you put the light on, Stacey? It's dark in here,' he said, clicking it on. It took a long time for me to get the hang of using the electric and gas when it was needed without feeling guilty. He had to pull me up about it so many times.

Leon was working for a travel centre as a driver, and one of the perks of the job was free travel for him and his spouse. I couldn't drive and I relied on public transport, so it made sense, later on, that I collected my free travel pass. We had to go to Birmingham to pick it up. Getting myself ready for the trip to Birmingham, I did my make-up and put on a pair of big hoop earrings for the picture I would have to have taken. After all, I wanted to look attractive for it.

Coming into the bedroom, Leon noticed my earrings and demanded I took them off. He thought they looked horrible. I thought this was unfair, my earrings looked nice and I wanted to wear them for the picture. I remembered Diane's good advice on our honeymoon, 'Start the way you mean to finish,' so decided to do exactly that.

Standing firm I refused to take the earrings out.

Leon started to get agitated. In his eyes, I was being awkward and disrespectful. Normally, I probably would have taken them off, but I liked them, and really didn't see what the problem was all about. So, an argument erupted. Leon was shouting now and I froze with fear as I knew he had lost his temper. He marched over to where I was standing behind the settee where I'd strategically placed myself in a bid to protect myself. Grabbing my shaking arms, he frog-marched me up the stairs to the first bedroom we came to. Maybe he didn't want the neighbours to hear the commotion, as that room was furthest away from the walls of the house next door?

He pushed me on the bed and I bounced back up to run, but as I passed him Leon started throwing wild punches at me. The first punch caught me on my left arm, and I was so surprised I stopped running and put my arms up, trying to convey that I did not want to fight. Then bam, the next one landed right in my side. I couldn't breathe as his fists battered me, and then as I lay on the ground, he grabbed my hair and started pulling me across the bedroom, every inch scraping skin off my legs and bare arms. I was screaming and crying and trying to get hold of something to stop him and to fight him off, but it was no good, he was really strong compared to me. He flipped me up onto the bed as if I was a bag of feathers, and all I could do was put up my arms and try to protect myself. His blow were raining down on me hard and fast.

'Stop, please just stop. Leon, stop, I love you, I am sorry.'

'Don't you open your mouth and disrespect me, bitch. Do you hear me?' he screamed at me, his spit flying all over my face.

'I didn't mean anything, please, Leon, I love you,' I screamed, but it did no good, he was out of control and I knew nothing would stop him. Finally he wore himself out and slumped down on the bed on top of me.

I pushed him off and ran into the bathroom to dry my face. I was sobbing so hard. Looking in the mirror at my wet face, I gasped in disbelief as there wasn't a mark on it because he'd avoided my face in the attack, but my hair was all out in clumps and sticking to my damp face. The mascara under my eyes had blackened the skin and mingled with wet fuzzy hair strands. I looked so awful. I filled the sink with hot water, washed my face, and tried to tidy myself up, brushing my hair.

Taking myself into the living room, I sat on the sofa, crying in disbelief. What was I going to do now? I felt so scared; we were married now and he had attacked me more viciously than he had ever done before. My mind kept going over the horror of the situation, but there was nothing I could do, not in my young mind anyway. My wages as an office clerk for a local construction company was very poor, in all honesty I couldn't afford to make a go of it on my own; they were not even enough to pay for a week's rent on a cheap council flat. I simply couldn't afford to support myself. I wouldn't have known where to start anyway.

There was no way I was going to go back home to my mum. When I left that house to be with Leon and get married, I knew I would never go back, not because I couldn't but because I didn't want to. I'd endured more than I could take of living at home with her. There was no way Leon would go back to his parents and leave me in the flat either. Dad had said I shouldn't get married and I didn't want him to know it had gone wrong so quickly. My young mind couldn't see any way of getting out.

As I sat there thinking about leaving him, my mind went back to when we were teenagers and he had called my mum a whore and hit me. I remembered how it was me who had suffered because of the break-up, not him, even though he was the toxic one in the relationship. I couldn't cope with feeling like that again, spending years pining for him. I knew that if I did split up with him for hitting me, no doubt, once I had calmed down and got back to normal, I would start wanting him to hold me and love me again. I couldn't trust myself.

An hour later, Leon came in. He looked ashamed of himself. The temper had been expelled with each punch and bitter word, and all that was left now was the feeling of guilt. We didn't bother going to fetch the bus pass. The atmosphere between us was strained and I felt exhausted. The next day at work, I found that Leon had left some flowers and a 'sorry' note with the receptionist. He picked me up from work later that day, with a new tattoo of my name on his leg by way of showing how much I meant to him. He was so sorry and seemed so consumed with guilt.

It was the easiest option to put the violence behind us and make a go of our marriage. The kindness and love he was showing me was all I wanted. I just wanted a normal life. We hugged, kissed and made up; neither of us wanted to split up, and we were 'both' sorry.

Trouble and Strife in Married Life

A year after we were married Leon lost his job as a driver because he kept having time off sick. He was moaning at me to go and see my boss to try to get a pay rise, as my job as administrative assistant wasn't very well paid. I went in and saw my boss as Leon had instructed me, telling him I was now a married woman and would appreciate a little pay rise. I don't think it went down too well, but I got my pay rise – a measly fiver a week! So I began looking in the paper for something else, and eventually I came across a secretarial receptionist job for a local company.

The money was much better, so I went for it. I borrowed some smart clothes from Leon's sister for the interview and I looked and felt very professional. Blagging my way through the interview, I managed to convince the panel I was professional and, miraculously, I got the job. The trouble was my home life was going rapidly down the pan and when I got to work, I was so exhausted I could not concentrate.

As I couldn't drive, it took me an hour to walk to work every morning. Leon would sometimes drive me if he could be bothered to get up, but it was very rare. To make a good impression, it was important for me to get to work on time. Then, when I got home, I would be expected to do the tea, and catch up on the housework. It was a lot of work doing all the chores and working but it was in my nature to get on with things.

Leon was applying for jobs here and there, but he felt none of them paid enough. He was looking for a really well-paid job that didn't require much in terms of qualifications or commitment! So, he would spend most of the day visiting his family, particularly his mother's cafe, which happened to be near to my place of work. In fact, we were spending a lot of time with Leon's parents. We would visit them every single night, even if Leon had been with them all day. In addition, his mother was on the phone to him at every opportunity.

Initially, I didn't mind, as it felt nice to be part of a family. It was very kind of his parents to have us round for Sunday dinner every weekend while we were settling into our new council flat. I felt it only fair to return the favour once we had settled in, so I invited them for Sunday dinner.

The day arrived and, wanting to impress, I got up early to get the flat looking shipshape. I spent hours preparing the dinner; it was all so new to me and I wanted to get it just right. Leon's parents finally arrived and everything was going according to plan. The flat looked spotless, the table was laid and the dinner smelt beautiful. Finally, we were all seated and the dinner was dished up and I felt very proud of myself. Suddenly there was a knock at the door; we all looked at each other in surprise. We weren't expecting anybody, so I went to see who it was. When I opened the door, I was shocked to see my mother.

The first thought that entered my head was guilt, thinking that if she saw Leon's parents having their dinner she was going to resent the fact that I had asked them to dinner before her. My second thought was that if I didn't warn her before she walked in that Leon's parents were here she would feel really uncomfortable because she wasn't expecting to see them – and she really didn't like Leon's mother.

Diane on the other hand, would have been alright with my mother, but I feared my mother would have caused a terrible atmosphere. Feeling torn, I didn't know what to do for the best. There was no option for me but to tell her they were here, so sheepishly I invited her through, saying with a tense smile on my face, 'Go through, Mum, Leon's parents are in the kitchen having their dinner.' As my words entered her ears, she turned on her heel, walked out of the flat and started to run down the stairs.

'Mum, wait,' I shouted, running after her feeling awfully guilty. The last thing I wanted to do was hurt her feelings, but she just carried on. I managed to catch up with her on the street, and she turned to me, 'Don't worry about me, our Stacey, you just go back in and enjoy your dinner with Leon's parents.' This made me feel like the most awful daughter alive.

'No, Mum, you're my mother. I can manage to spread the dinner so you can come and eat with us too,' I said, but deep inside I didn't want her to come in because I knew she would just make everybody feel uncomfortable. How could I win though? I'd invited Les and Diane because they had hosted Leon and me every Sunday and I was trying to return their generosity.

Mum disliked Diane so there was no way I could have them all to dinner in the same room; it just didn't bear thinking about. Still, I didn't want Mum to feel hurt. Nothing I could say would change her mind and she marched off. Defeated, I walked back into the flat and explained that Mum had been but she didn't want to come in while we were eating. I tried to act as if it wasn't a problem. Diane looked at me concerned, 'She should have come in and eaten with us.' I tried to imply that Mum didn't want to impose. The conversation then moved on to how Leon's uncle had said there were some jobs going at a local factory. So we all chatted and carried on eating our dinner. Funnily enough, I had gone right off mine!

Later that day when his parents had gone, I was in the kitchen doing the ironing and Leon was in one of his moods. He came over to me and began analysing my technique. He began pointing out where I was going wrong. I couldn't see what all the fuss was about. Leon was a perfectionist. When I had finished ironing one of his shirts, he pulled it off the ironing board for inspection. There was a double crease in the arm of the shirt. At this, Leon lost his temper. He began yelling at me, telling me I was incompetent and I couldn't do anything right. He ordered me to do another one so he could watch how I got the double crease in the sleeve. I was terrified as I placed the next shirt on the board. When it came to doing the sleeves, I had just placed the iron onto the material when whack – Leon punched me in the arm.

Quickly, I put the iron down, as it wasn't something I wanted to be holding while Leon was flipping out, and tried to make a run for it. He cornered me by the kitchen window and began throwing wild punches at my arm. I dropped on my knees and brought my hands above my head, crouching into a ball, trying unsuccessfully to protect myself. In all the chaos, trying to get away, I reached up and scratched his face. I truly regretted it, as it incited his anger even more. Then I tried to make a run for the flat door but he got there before me and turned the key to lock me in, putting the key in his pocket. After that, he always kept the doors locked where we lived so that I couldn't escape if he started to get angry.

When he eventually calmed down, he was as usual all apologies again. He blamed it on being in the navy. He was telling me how stringent things were on all the finer details and it was something he'd carried with him into Civvy Street. He was extremely apologetic and sorry for what he had done. He had this way of excusing his behaviour with a valid reason that met his own needs, and he was always fantastic at justifying his actions. I ended up feeling sorry for him that his job had made him a perfectionist to an almost neurotic degree.

The next day we went to his parents' house and as usual we were sitting in the kitchen when Diane came in and did a double take as she noticed her son with the red scratch mark down his face. 'Leon,' she said concerned, 'What have you done to your face?'

His face did look very sore. Leon didn't answer; he shuffled in his chair, feigning embarrassment. Feeling myself blushing redder and redder I stuttered, 'It was me,' owning up to it. Leon's mother wasn't pleased and she humiliated me and told me if that was the sort of thing I was going to do I should cut my nails. Leon just sat there sad faced while she sternly told me I should be ashamed of myself. He didn't try to intervene or at least take some responsibility. I was made to feel like a psycho bitch who had attacked her poor defenceless son for no good reason. It was so embarrassing, but I was too scared to defend myself for fear of reprisals from him when we got home.

A few days later I went to visit my kind and lovely old nan. Sitting in the armchair, I looked at Nan's mahogany dresser full of lots of pictures of the family, the children, and their children, the grandchildren and my cousins, the sound of the clock gently ticking away peacefully in the background. Nan came back in from the kitchen and shuffled among the sofas with her pinafore on, holding a cup of sweet tea for me and my aunt. My aunt sat in front of the fire warming her hands and said she had something to tell me. Nan gave her a knowing look that said it was the right thing to do.

Because the flat where Leon and I lived was elevated at the top of the estate, when the lights were on, if the blinds weren't shut, pretty much everyone could see in. I didn't realise this, but one of my neighbours had seen Leon punching the hell out of me in the kitchen.

They were extremely worried and had gone to tell my aunt about it. Embarrassed at the thought of all and sundry knowing my business, I admitted he had been hitting me, but said that we were sorting things out. I made excuses about him having a bad childhood and needing my support. I told them he was trying to change.

What could they say? They could hardly tell me to go and speak to my mother or father. If, in an ideal world, my parents had been happily married and united, and Luke, Hannah and I had been the centre of their universe, then of course I would have gone home. If that had been the case though, would I ever have been attracted to Leon in the first place? If I had been brought up in a loving, stable home environment, would I have needed Leon? Wouldn't I have run a mile the first time he hit me? Maybe it was because he was so much like my mother I felt comfortable round him. After all, that was what I was used to.

Leon finally went for an interview at the factory and got the job. The money was quite good for his age. Although it was shift work, that didn't matter as it was a good job. He didn't really put any effort in with this though. He seemed more interested in trying to steal the stereos being put into the cars, or having a sleep in one of the cars being produced if he could get away with it. To hear him talk, you would think he'd had a really hard day.

In the meantime, I was making progress in my job and starting to fit in with the other staff. One day, all my colleagues at work were all talking about going to the theatre to see Jasper Carrott, the comedian, who I found hilarious. When I was asked if I wanted to go along with everyone I really felt as if I was beginning to be accepted, so, I gave my colleague the money for two tickets – for me and Leon.

When I got home later that evening, I began telling Leon all about it, assuming he would be happy to go along, thinking it would be good for him to meet all the people I work with. He told me he hated Jasper Carrott and he wasn't going. I assumed then that he would let me go – big mistake! The mere suggestion that I go out socialising without him sent him mad. He began accusing me of being a selfish bitch and firing endless questions at me, implying that I wanted to go without him because I would be sleeping with other men from the office.

He didn't trust me and my answers were falling on deaf ears; he had made his mind up I was up to no good – then he struck me. Feeling it was not worth the upset, I relented and said I did not want to go. It was more trouble than it was worth to pursue this evening out. After he had calmed down, I went to bed sobbing and feeling totally exhausted. I felt so worn out and tired, I just wanted to go to sleep. I lay facing the window and tucked my legs into my chest, pulling the quilt over my head. I was so angry with him for ruining this for me and angry with myself for having to give in to his orders, yet he always made me feel that I had caused the trouble.

Leon always used to stay up late watching television. Eventually, he came to bed and tried to cuddle me, but I tried to shrug away. I didn't want him touching me after all the arguing. I was upset and exhausted. He began demanding sex; this was the last thing on my mind after how he'd treated me. He tried to make me feel guilty by quoting one of his father's sayings, 'You should never go to bed on an argument in case one of you dies in the night!' Still, after all the trouble that evening, I wasn't prepared to just be okay and let him do what he wanted, so I continued to try to sleep.

When he realised I wasn't going to give in to him he got aggressive again. He put his hand into my knickers and yanked my pubic hair, trying to pull it out. I screamed out in pain, and he just retorted, 'Fucking slag.' Then he had sex with me anyway. I just lay there feeling hopeless at my lack of control.

When he had finished, he started being really nice to me. He said how he didn't want us to be funny with each other all night and just wanted us to be okay. He said it was wrong to hold grudges. Then he cuddled me and kissed me gently on the mouth, telling me he was just insecure and couldn't help his jealousy at times. I was too drained to argue any more.

The next morning at work, I dropped it in casually, saying that I couldn't go and see Jasper Carrott after all because we were busy that night, and my colleagues easily accepted this.

Leon would always question me when I got back from work. 'Who had I been talking to?' or 'Had I spoken to any men?' Of course I had. I had to interact with men in my job, it was impossible not to, but I couldn't tell him that. His questions were unrealistic and ridiculous and all I used to feel was fear and anxiety. Fear that I didn't want to slip up and give him the wrong answer in case the answer I gave triggered his temper.

One time, when I came home from work, he started interrogating me as usual and then he swung a punch. I don't know how I managed it, but I darted for the hall and managed to pull the flat door open – he had forgotten to lock it on this occasion. My feet reached the stairwell and I practically jumped down a whole flight of stairs in fear. I pulled the heavy fire door open at the bottom, petrified that any minute Leon was going to grab my jumper and pull me back in, but somehow I made it on to the street. Without even looking back, I ran as fast as my legs would carry me. It was raining and I was out of breath, crying and sobbing and running to God knows where. When I reached the bottom of the estate, my mind was whirling madly. What was I to do now?

Standing there in the rain, I knew that there was no way I could go back to the flat, to him, but there was nowhere else to go. The rain soaked my hair, and mascara was running down my face, and I was so tired that I reluctantly decided to go to Mum's. As I approached the house, I was in half a mind to turn on my heels and go back to Leon, but I just couldn't face him. So, wearily, I knocked on my mother's door. When she opened it, she was so happy to see me, she hugged me and acted as if she hadn't seen me for years. Obviously, she could see I was upset and she asked me what had gone on. I told her because it was plain to see that Leon and I had been arguing. Mum was very supportive. She started making plans. 'Right,' she said, 'you can stay here with me. I'll make you the spare bed up, and you haven't got to worry about a thing.'

I should have felt relieved, but all I felt was anger. Never in all my life had she been this nice to me! This woman had wanted me, and my siblings, out of her hair for years, and now she had finally got what she wanted. But there was method in her madness, this wasn't just that she had turned over a new leaf and wanted to mother me, this was because she was lonely. This was also about the jealousy she had of my relationship with Leon. I had always felt like piggy in the middle between them. They had pulled me apart over the years. They were jealous of each other and my relationship with each of them. Mum had always hated just about anybody I had anything to do with; everyone I liked she had tried to taint with her lies. She once told me my best friend from school Teresa's mother was a prostitute because I liked the woman and she wanted me to dislike her. It was only when I got older I realised this was utter nonsense.

Leon was the same; he hated me having anything to do with anyone but him and his family, everyone else according to him were 'lowlifes'. With them both demanding total loyalty from me over the years, and me not being able to split my loyalty between them equally, they had seen each other as rivals for control over me. I thought that this was another reason Mum was keen to have me home. Just like Leon, Mum's personality could change from day to day; she could easily wake up in the morning and tell me I was 'using her' and throw me out. So how was I expected to take her hospitality now without questioning her motives?

Just at that moment there was a knock on the door. It was Leon. Mum answered the door and I heard her telling him with the greatest of delight that I had moved back home with her. I could hear him begging her for a word with me, and she was just about to shut the door on his desperate face when I asserted myself, much to her surprise.

'Give me a minute with him, Mum, please,' I said. I went to the door and he was crying, saying he was so sorry and begging me to come home. Unbeknown to him, I had decided to go back home to be with him the moment I had seen my mother on the doorstep enjoying telling him that I was moving back in with her, as if she had won the trophy and he had fallen head first into a puddle.

There was no way I was ever going to be my mother's pawn again. It was too late to make the bed up for me now. What was she envisioning? That I was the prodigal daughter returning after selfishly squandering all the wealth she had given me? Yes, the fatted calf would have been out for me that night, but it would all have been thrown back in my face the next day. I was stuck between a rock and a hard place, the devil and the deep blue sea. I had endured years of my mother's tantrums, but Leon's were fresh to me and for that reason somewhat easier to take.

It was raining on my hour-long walk to work the next day and my face wasn't wet just from the raindrops. Shuddering, I pulled my coat around me deep in thought, immune to the other people making their way to work. Scurrying into reception, I ran to the toilet with my head down, as I needed to check I looked presentable. I felt so scruffy, I tidied my hair and tried to put my head into work mode. As I came out of the toilet, I walked into Andrew McFeat, the senior manager. A stiff little man, he could only have been about five foot five but what he lacked in inches he made up for with his mouth. With a superior air and speaking *at* me, not *to* me, he pushed a piece of A4 paper into my cold hands; he had a strong Scottish accent and I think among the mixture of words he was instructing me to fax the paper. Not wishing to sound dumb, I didn't ask him to repeat himself as he didn't tolerate me having difficulty with his accent. I knew this from a previous incident when I had asked him to repeat something and he had come right up to my face doing the NATO phonetic alphabet with a big dollop of sarcasm.

Michelle, my colleague, who was more respected than me, greeted me as I entered our office. I greeted her back trying to push the thoughts of last night aside. Looking at Andrew's paper, I saw it was some rough notes with a fax number across the top, so I faxed the paper, praying there would be no issues with the fax machine.

Shortly afterwards, Andrew's Scottish voice could be heard booming down the corridor as he was making his way into the office. 'Did ye get the fax across like I asked ye?'

I stood up, scurrying to the fax tray to see if it had sent. The fax had sent all right and as I picked it up he came bounding over and swiped the paper out of my hand.

'What the hell have ye done? What's this?' he said, raising his voice, his face red with anger. Confused, I started to go red myself; a few people were in the room with us and it had gone awfully quiet, with everyone waiting for Andrew's next move.

Obviously, he was really annoyed with me, and I was trying to decipher what he was saying when I realised I had sent the roughly written scrap of paper directly to a director of a company that our company were dealing with. Andrew had asked me to retype the paper and send it over professionally. Why it hadn't occurred to me to do that, I don't even know myself. My mind had been so immersed in what was going on at home that I hadn't paid attention and had just faxed the scruffy rough notes over.

My apology seemed to add insult to injury, as Andrew put his face up close to mine, tapping his head with his index finger like a frustrated woodpecker. 'Jesus Christ, are you thick? I cannot believe what you have done! They are going to read that and think they are dealing with an imbecile and the only imbecile in here is you!'

His words stung like vicious little hornets penetrating into my skin. His words, my mother's words, Leon's words, my teacher's words.

Thick and stupid.

I had not done too well at school, and as if that wasn't enough to confirm how dumb I was, I had been constantly reminded by the people closest to me who should have loved me, and now I had been exposed at work. The other office staff were probably thinking how on earth did this girl get the job out of the hundreds of candidates we interviewed. They were right, how did I?

There and then, I decided that the best thing I could do was to forget all about a career because I couldn't endure being humiliated like this again. Everyone was right; I was thick, and this had been proved today. However, the one thing I knew I could do was give love. Yes, I could give a baby lots of love. If I had a baby, I could stay at home and not have to socialise too much; it would just be my child and me. Now that was a job I felt I could do well. Wouldn't a baby be the ultimate way of proving to Leon I loved him, thus extinguishing his unwarranted insecurity?

Once again, I found myself in the toilet sobbing. I was worthless, I just didn't belong here and I needed to get home, to someone familiar: Leon. Somehow, I got through another day. That night I didn't dare tell Leon what had happened – it would just confirm that he was right about me being incapable of doing anything right, it would   shred   any   respect   he   had   for   me.

A Little Baby

Leon's family loved the idea of me getting pregnant, and they were all very encouraging. I was thrilled at the prospect as I knew I wouldn't have to work. There would be no outsiders for me to engage with who would cause Leon to be jealous. Through rose-coloured specs again, and with the naivety of youth, I had fantasies about an excited little boy coming happily down the stairs in his pyjamas at Christmas, and being greeted by his devoted and happy parents. After a lot of discussion, Leon had convinced me that he had changed and so I came off the pill. This was going to be a fresh start for us.

It happened more quickly than we expected, as I didn't see another period after that. When we did the test and it was positive, Leon was over the moon and kept shouting 'ye-haw' as if he was in a cowboy movie. Foolishly, I believed that Leon's insecurities would dissolve because I was having his child. How wrong I was. Once the novelty had worn off, his behaviour got worse.

Embarrassed that I was pregnant after everything that had happened within my relationship in such a short time, I knew people at work would judge me. All my work colleagues knew I was unhappy as I turned up crying most days. No one could understand how good we were when things were fine, and I naively believed a baby would make things better. The family around me helped me surrender to being a mother and a good housekeeper and keeping a stiff upper lip.

The pregnancy made me feel really ill, and not just from the chronic morning sickness. There was the worry of how I was going to break the news to my family. Then the shame of telling my employer – after all, I hadn't been with the company that long and I felt as if I'd been a disappointment. Then there was Leon and his insecurities.

Each morning, as I walked to work, I had to keep stopping to be sick. A few months into the pregnancy, Leon's interrogations started again, and no matter what I said or did it always seemed to be wrong. Leon still hit me, but most of the time he was careful to punch my arms, and legs or pull my hair. As angry and ungovernable as his rages were, he was careful, and in control enough, as always, to avoid my face.

One time, I got back from work and he was cross-examining me about my day. Who had I spoken to? Had I spoken to any men? The same old questions from the insane jealousy. Then he began punching me. I was petrified, especially for the baby, and, somehow, I managed to flee our flat. Leon thought I'd gone to the bathroom to clean myself up, but the door was unlocked so I had bolted down the road to his parents. I needed to tell someone. Loyalty to Leon was not my main focus now; it was my poor, defenceless, unborn child.

Leon's mother was shocked to see me standing at her door crying and dishevelled. She called Les and they both looked shocked at the state of me. I didn't need to tell them who had done this to their pregnant daughter-in-law. They were both in a state as they ushered me inside, Les shouting, 'He shouldn't be doing this to her.' He was so angry that he got his coat and stormed out of the door, saying that he was going to put a stop to this. Diane was very distressed and kept marching back and forth.

'I hope he doesn't hit him,' she said.

Then she started getting angry about all the years that Les had beaten her, and the cheek of him going up there to reprimand Leon when he had been Leon's role model and teacher. She began telling me the story again about how, when the children were younger and Les got violent, Mandy and Leon would flee the house in their pyjamas to get to the phone box to call the police. She remembered how Leon was only about four or five and he was petrified of his father. She blamed Leon's childhood for the way he acted now. There was deep sorrow in her eyes as she remembered her petrified little boy running for help in his bare feet.

This was the reason Leon was how he was; this was the point she was desperately trying to get across to me. We shouldn't condemn Leon for beating his young pregnant wife who had gone to them for help, we should pity the man who dealt the blows! That's the message that I seemed to be getting from her. At the time, I was easily influenced, still being young and naive. I trusted what these older and supposedly wiser adults were telling me. It was clear they expected me to try and help Leon.

I was beginning to feel as if I had caused the trouble, but that wasn't the half of it. When Les finally walked back through the door, out of breath and shouting about how he had just been threatening Leon and ended up hitting him, Diane hit the roof.

'You hypocrite! How can you go up there and have a go at him for something you have done to me for years?'

'What was I expected to do? Just say well done, son?' Les shouted and soon they were deep in their own fight.

The atmosphere was terrible and I started to wish that I had not involved them at all. The last thing I wanted was to cause any trouble between Les and Diane. I just wanted help, for someone to talk some sense into Leon and protect me.

Now I felt I had caused all this trouble, and I still had to go home and face the music with Leon. Also, I had this enormous guilt hanging over me because I knew Leon was scared of his father, and I didn't know what his dad had done to him.

When I did get back to the flat, I realised that Leon had been crying. He was disgusted at me for being so disloyal and involving his parents. Apparently, his dad had hit him and Leon had been humiliated and scared. He was a twenty-year-old man, and he was scared and angry. Guilt consumed me as we sat calmly for once and talked things through, the finger firmly pointed at me for all the trouble I'd caused the family. Leon promised me he was really going to try to change. I felt I owed him that chance, not just because I'd convinced myself I couldn't live without him, but because he was so screwed up due to all the violence he had witnessed as a little boy. My own feelings never even counted.

Why?

Because I had learnt from a very young age a good strategy for coping with problems in life – never put myself first, always opt for the easy life and do what the dominant party wants. Never want anything material or emotional and then anything you do get is a bonus. Always put everyone else's feelings and needs before your own. From early childhood, I'd conditioned myself subconsciously to be this way. Keep jumping the hurdles and once you're over the hurdle at least you have peace for a little while.

The beatings did stop for a time, but not for long. He always made sure after he had hit me that I had forgiven him totally before he let me leave the flat. Sometimes, I would have to pretend through gritted teeth that I had forgiven or forgotten what he'd done to me, because if Leon sensed I was bearing a grudge towards him for what he'd done this would cause another argument, and I would then be the one being 'stubborn and unreasonable'. It was so mentally draining it was mostly easier to pretend I was okay with him. It usually worked. I just had to bury my own anger towards him for what he had done, and convince myself that I was fine. That way life was more bearable. After all, I just wanted to be loved and be in a normal environment – whatever that was.

Not surprisingly, and probably due to stress, I was quite ill with tonsillitis in the first couple of trimesters of my pregnancy. I quit my job because I was too ill to go in, and would spend my days drifting in and out of sleep while Leon was at work. Of course, I always had to make sure the flat was spotless before I rested as Leon liked everything to be just so. The guilt I felt for my unborn child was immense. I cried floods of tears for him and then felt guilty for being upset as I knew it was not good for the baby – it was a vicious circle. It really hit me that there was a little baby inside me suffering because of my anguish. I felt sick to the core. What had I done? I was snowballing from one disaster into another with no guidance on how to sort my life out.

My mothering instinct was to protect, but I couldn't protect myself, let alone this innocent child. I worried that with my nerves always being in shreds the baby would be born full of anxiety. What a terrible thing to inflict on an innocent life. I was six months pregnant, wracked with guilt, and just over seven stone.

When Leon was due back from work, I would be ready to attend to him, as he was so demanding, but when he was working, I would lie on the bed, consumed by guilt for my baby. Nobody knew how bad I felt as there was no one to talk to who would understand. I couldn't talk to my family because I didn't want them to dislike Leon any more than they already did. If I opened up to Leon's family, it was obvious they were biased towards their son. I seemed to be on a merry-go-round with the moods, then the violence, then his regret, then the pity – the pity I felt for him!

Mum chose not to visit us because she didn't like Leon or his family. I used to wish that, for my sake, she would just come up and be polite with them, pass the time of day, be supportive of me, but instead she was miffed with me that Leon's family were at my house every day. She would imply that she wasn't welcome in my home, yet Leon's family were made very welcome. That wasn't the case, because there was nothing I could do about his family visiting, especially as Leon encouraged it. I would invite Mum round, but she always declined. Leon's family coming to visit all the time was very much out of my control. Some days, anxiety overwhelmed me because I knew my mother was probably looking up the road from my grandmother's house (Nan lived just down the road from where we lived) at their cars parked outside our house, feeling ostracised.

His family would turn up and settle themselves down in the living room, and it was my job to keep a constant flow of tea or coffee going for them all. No sooner had I sat down, than Leon would say, 'Do us another drink, Stacey', and they would all give me their empty cups in order to assist me. Thinking I should be hospitable to Leon's family, I tried to be the best hostess. They would all sit chain smoking and talking about different subjects, whether it be idle gossip, politics or religion. They were so enthusiastic about what they were discussing they would shout over each other and interrupt each other in an attempt to be the one who was heard. Even if I had wanted to join in, there was never a chance for me to speak – not that I did want to join in, as I had no self-confidence and felt anything I said would fall on deaf ears. I truly believed they were educated people and I admired them all, so I would listen intently to their conversations.

Sometimes I would have the whole family talking at me at the same time. I didn't know who to make eye contact with. There would be three lots of lips chuntering away at me at the same time. But they never noticed whether I was listening or not, as they were too wrapped up in what they were telling me to be aware that two or three other people were also talking to me.

Each time I went to Nan's, Mum would be there making nasty digs at me. She made me feel as if it was my fault that Leon's family were at our place all the time.

My twenty-first birthday arrived and was spent in hospital – I had gone into slow labour. My baby was on its way and I could not wait to get him out of my stressed body so that he did not have to feel any more of my heartache. The nurses had kept me in for observation and told me five days later that my placenta was not nourishing the baby and therefore they were going to have to start me off.

It did not surprise me that problems were occurring, given the emotional roller coaster my pregnancy had been. They took me into the delivery suite and inserted some special cream into me that was supposed to trigger labour. It was taking its time to begin, so eventually they put what looked like a large knitting needle inside me and tugged on the bag that had been protecting my little baby all these months. I felt a small popping sensation and the bloody water gushed out in a torrent. The pain then became excruciating and I lay on the bed not knowing where to put myself in order for it to ease.

At times, Leon and I were left in the delivery room on our own. I had been given a funnel of gas and air, which at crucial points, when the pain was peaking, I was supposed to suck through and inhale the gas to numb the pain. It made me so dizzy, it took the focus off the terrible pain. Leon found it amusing to keep grabbing the funnel off me and inhale the gas and air himself.

This was the biggest event of my life and I wanted my mum to be involved in it. Not just because she was my mum, but because if I didn't contact her and get her involved I would be cast in the role of selfish daughter again. This was the moment for us all to grow up. Leon brought the ward phone in and I tried to ring my mother in between the pains but the phone just kept ringing.

This was strange, because earlier that day when the doctors had informed us that the placenta was rotting and they needed to start the labour, Leon had called his family, and my mother, to tell them that tonight was the night the baby was to be born. I had expected that my mother would be sitting on top of the phone waiting for news, but the phone just rang continuously. In the meantime, Leon had spoken to his family again and this made me feel once again that my own mother was insignificant. It might be perceived that way by my mother, but how could I tell her what was happening when she wouldn't answer the phone?

The time had come for me to push, and push I did. I was bearing down so hard that I was groaning into my throat. I remember the midwife gently telling me not to make that noise because I was putting the effort into my throat rather than my birthing area. The trouble was I couldn't help it; the pain was like no other I had ever felt, and it totally overwhelmed me. My body was being taken over by waves of cramp and all I could hear was Leon saying, 'Stop making that noise, stop making that noise.'

I was trying not to make the noise but I couldn't help it.

Eventually, I gave one big push and I felt as if someone was ripping me open in between my legs, with the baby's head stuck at the entrance to the world. Leon and the midwife were excitedly saying that they could see the head and I totally panicked. I felt that if I gave one more push I would rip in half and I didn't want to do that. I told the midwife I couldn't push, I begged for a caesarean, anything.

She goaded me on, 'Come on, Stacey, just one last push and it will all be over. Come on, push.'

I pushed and screamed as I felt the sensation of a knife cutting my private parts. I felt the hot blood gushing out, the pressure gone, and then I heard it: the wailing of the baby, my baby.

'What did we have?' I cried, with relief and joy.

'It's a little boy, Stacey,' Leon said, as the midwife placed the tiny little baby into my arms. I was crying and shaking, sweating and deliriously happy. When I looked down, there in front of my eyes was the most beautiful baby I had ever laid eyes on. We named him Reece. He was so pure and sweet and beautiful, delicate and innocent, and totally reliant on me. He was crying a little bit, and I felt so proud.

'Look at him, Leon,' I gestured proudly. 'He is the absolute double of you.'

He was the spitting image of his father. I was instantly in love with this beautiful little baby and could not take my eyes off him. I was totally in awe.

I was feeling nauseous, so Leon took him off me so that I could be sick and then try and clean myself up. When I came back from the bathroom, I tried to call my mother again but the phone was just ringing out. I was confused, why wasn't she answering the phone? I decided to call the next best thing, my mum's older sister, Carol. I told her the wonderful news and explained that I had been trying to reach Mum with no luck. Aunty Carol was so pleased for me, but she didn't know why my mum wasn't around to answer the phone. She just advised me to get some rest.

The trouble was that I could not get any rest. When I was finally wheeled back to the ward with my tiny little bundle in tow, I realised that my life would never be the same again. I think I was still high from the excitement of this new gift God had blessed me with, because although I was exhausted, mentally I was excited. How I wanted to sleep. I knew I needed all my energy for the next few months, but it did no good. My little boy didn't want to settle either. He seemed to cry all through the night, and I was afraid he'd wake the other mums and babies on the ward. Whenever he drifted off and I put him down and felt myself dropping off in this strange place with its dim lighting, he would start crying again. Eventually, tiredness took over from the excitement and I was desperate for sleep. Anxiety was creeping in at the realisation that I couldn't just go to sleep, I had to tend to my new baby. It wasn't about me any more, it was about this little life that I was responsible for.

Some of the other mums had let their babies go into the nursery for the nurses to tend to during the night. I was so exhausted, I hoped that one of the nurses would notice I hadn't had any sleep and offer to take my little boy for just a few hours, but no one did and I struggled through the night too embarrassed to ask for help.

Morning came, with the breakfast rounds, then Leon turned up with his parents. He was in a suit with a bouquet of beautiful flowers. The day was spent getting used to my new baby, and when he finally did go to sleep for a little while I decided to go up to the phone and try and get hold of my mum. No one had heard from her still!

In my maternity nightgown, I hobbled sorely along the corridor until I reached the phone. The phone rang and rang but then, at last, she answered.

'Hello, Mum,' I said, full of emotion. A silent minute passed. 'I've had a little boy,' I said in a wobbly voice. Her response was so cold and hard it took me aback. First, she retorted that she knew I had, in a tone that implied that she had had to hear it from someone else, and was the last to know, as usual. Imploring her, I tried to explain that I had been trying desperately to contact her. She cut me short and finished her little speech with, 'You've made your bed, now you can lie on it.'

As I hung up the phone, with all the emotion and hurt pent up inside me, I took in a deep breath and let the river of tears burst out. I sobbed like a baby. My mother was hurt, and I had hurt my mother. Hobbling back to the ward I could not stop the tears and grief. I tried to hurry so that I could get back to my bed to hide away and pull the covers over me to release the pain and distress through my sobs.

A midwife caught sight of me in the corridor, as I was wandering back to the ward. She was a short, stiff Irish woman, with brown bobbed hair and a wise old face. She approached and asked me what the matter was. I tried to mutter I was okay, when I clearly wasn't, and headed into my ward. With tears flowing down my face and all the other mums looking at me, I climbed into my bed, so ashamed, so sad and so depressed.

The midwife who'd seen me in the corridor came up to my bed. 'Now you've got this beautiful child,' she said firmly, in her comforting Irish accent, 'what on earth is there for you to cry about?'

Trying to pull myself together I began explaining how I had been trying to get hold of my mother, and how when I finally did she had been very cross with me. The midwife took in what I was saying and gave me some valuable advice, which really changed the way I thought about my mother. It wasn't the advice I would have expected as I had been told continuously to respect my parents.

'Your mother spoke to you like that when you have just had a baby? Well, I tell you something my dear, the important person in your life now is this little boy. He is relying on you and you have got to be strong for him. If your mother talked to you in such a harsh manner with no regard for the fact that you had tried to contact her, and have just had a baby, she isn't worth worrying about.'

It was a relief to hear such words, especially coming from someone as respectable as a midwife, who had my best interests at heart and wasn't trying to manipulate me. This was a woman with no agenda other than what was best for me, and, if I analysed the situation, she was absolutely right. That was the turning point in my relationship with my mother. In that moment, I left behind the girl and became a woman. However, there was still a very long road to travel.

Surprisingly, Mum turned up at ten o'clock that evening when visiting time was well and truly over. She had got a lift to the hospital from my uncle who was very boisterous and loud. She had turned up at a time that had suited her, but the nurses said she could have a few minutes. She approached my bed, all smiles, with no trace of how she had spoken to me earlier that day. She was in the mode of the good mother who had saved the day. She and my uncle stayed for about ten minutes, fussing over the baby and slightly embarrassing me with their loud tones at such a late hour. Then she gave me a big kiss, I guessed probably to show the surrounding spectators she was such a caring mother, and then they left.

At least she was speaking to me.

Taking Baby Home

Eventually, it was time for me to go home, and to be honest I couldn't wait. It was difficult to sleep on the ward, and I kept worrying about Reece disturbing the other babies and sleeping mums at night. The house was freezing cold, it was winter, and we didn't have any central heating, so we kept all Reece's clothes in a cupboard in the living room, where there was the only fire in the house.

I finally got to sit down with my newborn son on my lap – alone because Leon had gone to visit his parents. I studied his innocent little face, his tiny little features. He was oblivious to the environment I had brought him back to. A wave of guilt washed over me – what had I done bringing a child into this situation? I silently prayed then that Leon would be good and grow up for his son's sake, but I knew deep down that I wouldn't be able to protect Reece from Leon's angry shouts and violent jabs towards me, for I couldn't protect myself.

I felt so sorry for him and so guilty to have chosen to bring a child into this, as I finally realised the pitfalls of that decision. He was such a nervous and unhappy little thing. He was a colicky baby and all he seemed to do was cry; the slightest noise had him jumping out of his skin.

I realised that I had fooled myself into thinking that the baby would be like a magic wand that I could wave and the trouble would stop. When Leon had been nice to me it had seemed the most natural next step to have his child, but seeing the tiny baby in my arms in that cold living room I knew he was no miracle – well, he was my miracle but not in the saviour sense.

Later on that evening, Diane, Les and Diane's friend Shirley turned up. Shirley was very foul-mouthed and went everywhere in her slippers; she never washed her hair and for this reason they nicknamed her Lurpak, after the butter, because her hair was so greasy. I was a little dismayed at them turning up; after all, Leon had been with them for most of the day.

Every time they came round, they stayed for hours. That night, however, I was tired, I didn't want to sit talking – not that I ever got a word in – and making tea. I wanted to relax with my new baby son and adjust quietly to being a mum. The usual routine started, as they all got comfortable in their chairs, chain smoking and shouting over each other while Reece lay in his Moses basket sleeping in the living room among us, and the smoke.

The photos from the hospital of us all had been developed and Diane was passing them round the room for us all to see.

'Here, look at this one, Stacey,' she said, pushing a picture into my hand. It was a photo of Leon sitting on the end of my hospital bed staring down into his lap and frowning. The picture had captured him looking worried, and in the background was me, pale and blotchy from the trauma of the labour, with the baby in my arms.

'Doesn't our Leon look like he has the weight of the world on his shoulders in that picture, Stacey?' she said, looking at me, worried.

He certainly did and I had no choice but to agree with her on that point. However, there was a little voice inside me saying, what does he have to look so worried about? He has a wife who loves him and tends to his every need, yet he is never satisfied. Then he has this beautiful little baby son, and the only problem that will be caused to this innocent child will be when he is in one of his angry moods and that poor child is subjected to the tense atmosphere he will create, and the shouting and horror of violence. Leon could quite easily have had a smile on his face, he was the master of the situation and he could stop us all being unhappy by keeping control of his anger. Never mind her son, what about my son?

Being tired and seeing Reece asleep, I decided to go to bed and take him up with me, out of the smoky environment. It was freezing cold upstairs, but I tended to Reece and made sure he was tucked in, nice and warm. Lying in bed, I could still hear them shouting downstairs over an hour later. It was hard to sleep with all the noise and I was getting irritated lying there.

For God's sake, I had just come out of hospital, why did they always have to stay for hours? Where was the consideration? Then I began worrying that if Mum went past to go to Nan's, she would see all the cars outside and think I was shunning her, yet again. I didn't want them all here. I wanted to go to sleep.

As they were talking so loudly, I heard my mother's name mentioned, so I bolted upright and my ears pricked up as I listened angrily. They weren't interested in me, or the baby, they just wanted somewhere to sit and smoke, and drink tea and gossip about my bloody family. Feeling my temper rising, I snuck out of bed and went to the top of the stairs, leaning over the banister. I could quite clearly hear Shirley and Diane saying that they could not believe how cold my mother was towards me. How dare they, how bloody dare they?

Why couldn't they have some decency and keep their thoughts to themselves? She was still my mother, whatever had happened. How could Leon's mother discuss my business with some woman who had no connection with me at all, and in my own home? I just erupted, my hormones doing somersaults, and before my brain had time to get into gear, my mouth was already in action, shouting, 'I can hear you all talking about my mother, you know!' As the angry accusation tumbled out, I instantly regretted what I had said.

They all went quiet. I heard some shuffling as they paraded to the front door to leave. Whispers rose up the staircase to where I stood, mortified. Leon came to the bottom of the stairs and shouted, 'What did you just say?'

'You heard,' I shouted back, and at once, as I started to calm down, I thought, *Oh shit, I'm in for it now.* Then Diane shouted to Leon, for my benefit, that they were all leaving, and Leon shouted up to me, for the benefit of his family, 'Nobody has even mentioned your mother, Stacey, so I don't know where you've got that from.'

Then I heard him imploring them all not to go, and I could hear his parents retorting they weren't going to stay where they weren't wanted. *Oh my God*, I thought, confused, *were they talking about my mum?* But I was sure they were. I quite clearly heard it, otherwise I wouldn't have shouted downstairs.

Dread filled me as I heard the front door shut. Leon came bounding up the stairs like a raging bull. 'What the fuck are you on about? Nobody mentioned your fucking mother, you fucking idiot.'

I knew I had heard it, I also knew I was in deep shit, because none of them were going to admit it. It would all be quite convenient to make me look like a raging looney, and them like the decent honest folk they liked to think they were. I wasn't going to be told I had imagined things. I was sure of what I had heard, but how can you argue with a liar?

Leon insisted that I had imagined it, and then made a meal of the fact that I had humiliated him in front of his parents, and made them feel so embarrassed I'd driven them out, after everything they had done for us. Inside, I was thinking they had done so much that my family hadn't had a look in. Then I felt confused because that was my family's choice. Still, my feelings had got the better of me and I could not have sat upstairs listening to people gossiping about my mum. I grimaced, realising I probably did go about things the wrong way, but then I hadn't invited them round anyway.

Leon was just shouting me down. He could always win the argument and he made me feel as if I was neurotic and bad minded. He insisted I phoned his mother to apologise. I wholeheartedly refused. I was still quite sure of what I had heard, and I wasn't going to apologise and support their idea of me being neurotic.

Leon could see I wasn't going to back down and so he lost his temper. He smacked me really hard round the face then, grabbing my hair, he came right up to my face and said, 'Nobody mentioned your fucking mother, now you get on that fucking phone now and call my mother and apologise for making her feel so uncomfortable.'

Worried that Reece would hear his father and be frightened, I knew I needed to get Leon to calm down and, beginning to doubt my own mind, I dialled his mother's number.

When she answered, I told her I was ringing to apologise and she went into a long-winded speech about how nobody had mentioned my mother, but she was prepared to forgive me based on the fact that I had just come out of hospital and probably had post-natal depression and that's why I wasn't thinking straight. So that was that. I just wanted things to calm down for little Reece's sake, so it was best to let it drop. I was fighting a losing battle anyway.

The next day, I saw Leon's parents as Leon insisted I go around there with him. I felt humiliated. Being so young and unworldly – combined with the negative impact of being brought up by someone who made me say sorry for everything whether I was right or wrong, just to keep the peace – I didn't have the skills to enable me to deal with this type of situation. Also, the fact that Leon's parents were totally biased towards Leon didn't help. However he treated me, I was always expected to be more understanding of his frustrations; after all, he grew up watching his father beat his mother.

Once we arrived, I sat with the three of them, while they discussed me and their vast, in-depth knowledge of post-natal depression. In a way, I was glad that they had come up with an excuse for my outburst because for me to try to defend my honour against these three fiercely strong characters would, no doubt, result in my total humiliation. Also, there was the added bonus that because we were all seemingly getting along so well, due to the fact that I had backed down and gone along with things their way, Leon was being extremely nice to me.

He was acting like a proper father to Reece and everything felt truly peaceful and comfortable, once I'd put out of my mind what I had heard the previous night. In fact, when it was time to go home, Leon carried the car seat out to the car and we seemed like a happy little family. When we arrived home, I settled Reece, made Leon a drink, then we sat up for a while discussing how we were going to decorate the house. Leon seemed so positive and things were looking up. They stayed on a nice, normal note for a couple of weeks. This was bliss for me – my husband and I getting along like a happy little family. It was all I had ever wanted.

As usual, it didn't last. Leon's moods started to creep back like a big black cloud. I was doing everything in my power not to rock the boat and keep him happy. It was so hard with a crying baby, and in-laws that were round most of the time giving us advice or criticising my mothering skills.

It was also around this time that I mastered the art of breastfeeding. I had been successfully breastfeeding the baby for about six weeks. My breasts had been awfully painful as Reece had tried to latch on, but I'd persevered through the pain, and finally I was enjoying feeding him and the bond it was creating.

One day, I'd run myself a bath as Reece lay sleeping in the bedroom. It was a rare occasion that I had the opportunity for a nice, undisturbed soak in the bath. Leon was banging about the house looking for his brown leather belt. The cause of his irritation was not that he had lost his belt, but quite clearly that I was enjoying myself. He didn't seem to like it when I relaxed.

He came into the bathroom, asking me if I knew where his belt was, his irritated presence making me feel uncomfortable for lying there relaxing while he was stressed. However, I was really tired and trying to enjoy my bath, so I didn't jump out of the water to look for the belt, as he obviously expected me to.

This clearly agitated him, and he began saying I was lazy, a fat slag, and I should get out of the bath and help him look. I retorted with words to the effect of, 'Can't I have five minutes to myself without being disturbed?'

To this, Leon turned around, his face contorted with anger, and the next thing I knew he had roughly grabbed hold of my left breast. My breast felt like a house brick as it was full of milk, and the pain seared through me as he viciously twisted my swollen gland. The pain was excruciating, and I screamed in shock and horror. He then walked off downstairs quickly and I started to cry. Reece had woken up and started to cry, so I lifted myself shakily out of the bath. I had to try and pull myself together. My head in a spin, wincing, I picked my son up to comfort him hoping he would not sense my pain. Needless to say, my breast went black and my milk dried up within a few days, so I had to give up breastfeeding.

Leon was deeply ashamed of what had happened and was full of apologies, as usual. He cried and begged my forgiveness, and, as always, I did forgive him – anything to make him be kind to me again. He always seemed so genuinely upset and sorry for his actions that I always ended up feeling sorry for him. It was clear he hated himself and wanted to change! The desire to leave him had entered my head a few times, but I couldn't see how I could do it. I was twenty-one and immature. I relied on him financially, and I didn't have anyone I could turn to. I couldn't tell my dad what was going on because he was working away from home, and why worry him? I hadn't got the energy to even think about planning to leave. Battling to get through each day and tending to Reece, plus keeping the house tidy was just about all I could cope with. I really couldn't see any further than that.

Leon's parents were round at our house every day now because Leon was off work on sick pay. This was another suggestion put into his head by his father. Les would brag about how he had fiddled loads of time off work over the years by pretending he had back problems. He made it sound so good, getting paid to do nothing. It wasn't a good idea in my view, but I daren't voice my opinion – it seemed I was the odd one for always thinking of the moral viewpoint. 'You work to live, not live to work,' Leon would say.

Leon's family were the only people I socialised with, so I began to question my own thoughts. Maybe I was too uptight, maybe they were right and I was just unrealistic? Anyway, the problem was that Leon had a good job at the factory and his father had talked him into taking time off sick, which seemed a great idea to Leon because he hated going to work. So, he took his dad's advice and went off sick from work for quite some time.

One day there was a knock on the door and it was two officials from Leons work place, visiting Leon to find out when he was coming back to work. Leon quickly positioned himself on the chair and tried to look as if he was in mild pain, as I let them in. It was obvious looking at Leon that there wasn't anything wrong with him, as he lay there exaggerating his back pain. He was a young, fit man just making a fool of himself.

I felt such a fake and so humiliated to be part of this poorly acted display of suffering. Every time they looked at me, I blushed – it was as if they could see right into my head and knew we were deceiving them. But it was Leon cheating them, not me. If it was up to me, he would still be at work; having him at home and around me all the time was wearing me down, and was certainly not my idea of how a man should be behaving when he had a young family to support.

They asked Leon questions like, 'When do you think you will be back to work?' Looking down at Reece, I felt bitter that this was the role model he had to follow.

When they eventually left, I let out a sigh of relief and Leon started moaning at me.

'What's the matter with your face,' he snarled.

It seemed to me that, whatever the situation, I couldn't win; not only had I had to endure the humiliation of looking like a liar in front of two strange men who could plainly see through our little act, now I had Leon's mood to contend with. It was hard for me to act pleased about what we had just done, and Leon didn't like me having a mind of my own one bit.

In the usual build-up to an argument, questions and accusations were being thrown at me by my angry husband. He was shouting at me and making digs about how useless I was, and how I was a selfish bitch who just cared about myself. Something snapped inside me under all the pressure, and I couldn't hold back.

'What the fucking hell sort of parents have you got encouraging you to take time off from work and put your job at risk when you have a baby to support?' I spat. 'How fucking humiliated do you think I just felt watching you, a young fit man, lying in the armchair pretending to be ill in order to con the company you work for, just so you don't have to go to work? Anybody with half a brain could see that there is nothing wrong with you, really.'

I had overstepped the mark speaking up for myself, and I knew it, but I had no control over the frustration that had brewed. At that, Leon ran towards me and I knew he was going to batter me. Panic took over me and, with Reece in my arms, I turned on my heels and ran out of the living room door. God knows how he didn't catch me at that point.

Followed closely behind by a raging Leon, I ran as fast as my legs could carry me with the baby in my arms. My feet were clambering up each stair like lead weights as I willed them to go faster, fearing that at any minute Leon was going to grab my ankles and pull me down the stairs. In my blind panic, I accidentally banged the top of Reece's head on the wall, and he began to cry.

I felt sickened, but I couldn't even stop to comfort him, as I had to get away. I ran into the bedroom and tried to push the door shut, but Leon was so close on my tail it was impossible to do so. Exposed like a deer in a large open field with no trees for camouflage, and no distractions, I just stood at the end of the bed with Reece screaming in my arms, as Leon bounded towards me like a hunting lion. There was nowhere left to run, and in my fear, I begged, 'Please don't hit me, please don't hit me.'

Leon pulled his fist right back and punched me full force in the face, with no regard for the fact our baby son was cradled in my arms. I fell back onto the bed, ensuring Reece stayed on top of me. As I fell, I tried to avoid hurting my baby. I hit the bed and I knew somehow that there wouldn't be another thump to follow, because this time he had hit my face, and he never hit my face. Lying there with my poor baby in my arms, I was sobbing, but not for me, for my poor boy who had just had his little head banged on the wall.

Cuddling him close to me, I told him that I loved him and everything was going to be okay. My poor innocent little baby must have been terrified and I couldn't protect him. He had been subjected to this whole horrible incident, and the guilt just engulfed me.

Leon came creeping over to us. 'Oh my God,' he started crying, 'What have I done? Stacey, what have I done to you? I am so sorry.'

He was sobbing like a little boy, and I knew he must have made a serious mess of my face as he was obviously very worried. Plus, I could see with my own eyes my jaw jutting out. Leon was trying to hug and kiss me and the baby. Pushing him away, I placed Reece in his basket and walked to the bathroom mirror to see what had happened to my face. The right side of my jaw and face was very swollen and black.

Leon was worried he had broken my jaw but wouldn't take me to the hospital for fear of reprisals. Under Leon's influence, I hibernated in the house for more than a week until all traces of the bruising had gone. Leon kept begging my forgiveness and promising me that he knew this time he had gone too far, and it would never happen again. I told him that it wasn't just for me he had to stop, it was for Reece too, because this was not a good environment to bring a child up in and I didn't want my son to suffer because of the violence. This was his last chance I told him, and Leon seemed so genuinely upset that I believed him when he said he would never risk losing Reece or me again.

However, things were spiralling. It seemed the more I let him get away with, the worse he got, and still everything seemed to be my fault.

When Leon and I were getting on, I had foolishly confided in him about my feelings towards my mother. It was something I'd had to get off my chest. However, it gave Leon the perfect excuse to order me to stay away from her. He reasoned that it was her causing the difficulties in our marriage because she was always causing me problems, which were pulling us apart. In an effort to be loyal to Leon, and because what he had said had made sense to me, I kept my distance from her.

Once my face had healed up, I was eager to get out and, one day, when the weather was just lovely, I put the baby in the pram and went to see Nan. Just my luck, Mum was there, but at least she was in a really good mood. It was a beautiful sunny day and I was planning to take Reece into town with me to pick up something for tea. Mum invited herself along, and quite frankly it was a delight that she was being so nice to me, so I didn't mind.

We were walking through an alley at the bottom of my nan's road, a common footpath people used on the estate to get on the road to town. A lot of my husband's family lived in the same area as most of my family so it shouldn't have surprised me when Leon's aunty Sharon came walking towards us. Inside, I was panicking because I was with my mother and I knew if word from Sharon got back to Leon it would cause me some serious aggravation.

We exchanged pleasantries; she made a fuss of Reece, then continued on her way. Worried now that Mum and I had been spotted, I started going over in my head how I was going to explain to Leon that I had defied his orders. Mum, noticing I was preoccupied with worry, kept asking me if anything was the matter, but I lied and said everything was fine.

By the time we got into town, I had convinced myself to stop worrying. It wasn't as if Leon's aunty Sharon would phone him to tell him she had seen me with Mum – first, because she didn't really have that much to do with Leon anyway, and second, she didn't know that Leon had issues with me seeing my mother so she would probably just forget it.

When I got home later, Leon was there and I prepared tea for us all. Then Leon decided he wanted us to visit his parents. We went in and were invited into the kitchen. Leon's mother was so house proud we hardly ever went into the living room because she didn't like the cushions messed up. We would all squash ourselves into the tiny kitchen and sit on stools. We stayed for about an hour then left. In that time, I was slightly on tenterhooks in case his mother had seen Sharon and she knew I'd been with my mother that day. Thankfully, nothing was mentioned. At home, everything was fine and I wanted to get Reece prepared for bed so I took him upstairs to give him a little bath. Leon decided to go back to see his parents again.

A couple of hours later, Reece was settled upstairs asleep and I was sitting watching the television. Leon arrived home and straightaway I knew he was in a bad mood. My stomach began churning, wondering what had happened this time. He went into the kitchen, and then he ordered me to him. 'Stacey, I need to speak to you now. Get in here.'

Heaving myself off the chair, I reluctantly went to him. He was quiet and frowning. I felt a tense atmosphere brewing.

'What's the matter?' I asked him gently, trying to break the tension.

He stared at me, his face distorted with disgust as he looked me up and down. 'I don't believe you,' he sneered, 'haven't you got something to tell me?'

Something to tell him, I thought, *but what?*

'I don't know what you mean,' I murmured, conscious that everything I said from this point on sounded pathetic. Whatever I had done, it had really wound him up.

'Don't know what I mean?' he sneered, mocking me. 'Why are you lying to me?'

'Please, Leon,' I implored him, my heart thumping. 'Honestly, I don't know what I have done.'

'What have you done?' he yelled. 'Where have you been today?'

That was it, the penny dropped, he knew I'd been out with my mother. Now I really started to panic because I knew he had the perfect excuse to start an argument.

'Why did you lie to me, Stacey?' he said.

'I didn't lie, I just didn't tell you. I didn't want to wind you up. I just didn't think it was worth telling you,' I babbled, hoping that he would let it drop.

'So, you deceived me then. You decided to lie to me and make me look a dickhead? If you can lie about this, what else can you lie about? You deceitful bitch. I told you to keep away from her and what you do, you defy me, go totally against me. I am trying to look after you, and this is how you fucking repay me.'

'Sorry. I am so sorry,' I said, getting really anxious, waiting for him to explode, panicking, and trying to find a way to calm him down.

'How do you think it feels for me to know my own wife has been deceiving me?' he spat out angrily.

Feeling hurt that he would think I would deceive him I defended myself. 'No, no, it wasn't like that,' I cried. 'Please let me explain.'

'Well go on then,' he shouted angrily. 'Explain, explain to me, Stacey.' He walked away from me towards the kitchen door, then punched it, making me jump with fear. Then he started pacing up and down, churning himself up.

'Come on then, liar, let's hear it,' he shouted.

He pulled a chair up and sat down on it with his arms folded, legs apart, awaiting an explanation. Trembling, I got a chair and sat down opposite him gently grabbing his hands, half affectionately and half to protect myself in case he raised them to me.

'I went to Nan's and Mum was there. I mentioned I was going to have a walk up the town because it was such a lovely day, and Mum invited herself along. I couldn't get out of it really and couldn't really see it was a problem as she was being nice.'

'So, your loyalties lie with that old bag, and not me, your husband,' he screeched.

'Of course not,' I retorted, 'they lie with you, of course. I just couldn't get out of it.'

'So why didn't you come and tell me this straightaway? Why wait for me to find out?' he shouted angrily.

The subject of the argument was irrelevant really, because Leon had a knack of turning the tiniest thing that was displeasing to him into something very bad. He could make mountains out of molehills. Unfortunately, verbally, I couldn't compete; he just had an answer for everything, and made me look like the bad, ungrateful wife. When I did make sense and he was losing control, he would get violent. He made the rules and I was supposed to follow them. Assuming, of course, that he always knew what was best for us!

'I repeat,' he said huffing angrily, 'why didn't you come to me and say "Leon I have been up the town today with my mother?"'

'Because I didn't want to upset you. I was scared and that's the truth.'

'The truth is you have been caught out for deceiving me.'

He marched over to me, his whole presence overpowering my frame, leaned in, and shouted into my ear, 'Why didn't you tell me the truth then?' Hopelessly, I let out a sigh of despair as I knew that whatever answer I gave him, it would be the wrong one. 'Are you deaf?' he shouted, and I started to cry, knowing what was coming next.

The anxieties churned inside me because I knew I couldn't just say what I wanted to say, which was, 'Look, I have had enough, we'll discuss this when you've calmed down.' The truth was, I was petrified to move and I didn't want to antagonise him.

'You have been with me all teatime,' he continued shouting, 'and you haven't said a word to me. You outright deceived me, didn't you?'

Then he grabbed my face in his hand, squeezing it hard, before pushing my head sharply against the wall.

'Stop fucking crying, I hate it when you fucking cry. Oi, Stacey, did you hear me? Now answer my question, you deceived me, didn't you?' he shouted, as if I was some sort of idiot. Exhausted and desperate to put an end to his questions, 'Okay then,' I shouted, 'but I never meant to.'

'It's all coming out now, the truth, isn't it?' He nodded, justifying his actions to himself. I walked over to him crying, my head was all over the place and I tried to hug him. I just wanted him to hug me back and calm down. 'Get off, slag,' he said, pushing me to the floor. Landing with a thud, I cried 'No, no,' in disbelief. I couldn't believe this had got so out of hand.

As I pulled myself up, Leon looked at me in disgust and marched out of the kitchen, banging the door. 'You silly cow, you make me sick,' he shouted as he stomped up the stairs.

Grabbing a chair, I sat myself down, trying to stop my crying from becoming out of control.

Going over the whole horrible episode in my head, I wondered how it had all come to this. How did he know I'd been out with my mum? Something struck me, the only place he had been tonight without me was his mother's again. Funny, because we had both been to visit his parents earlier that day and nothing was said.

'Oh my God,' I said under my breath as the truth dawned on me. 'She knew it would cause me trouble, she knew Leon didn't like me to have anything to do with my mother.' She must have waited to see him when he was on his own to drop me in the shit. She had stuck the knife in, knowing what he was like with me.

Realising the facts of the situation, another emotion began to come over me – anger. All this trouble again because of his mother, who had obviously done this on purpose otherwise she would have mentioned the fact that she knew I'd been with my mum when Leon and I had been visiting her earlier.

When I went into the bedroom, Leon had the quilt over him and was staring angrily at the wall. 'Well,' I said, 'I hope your mother is happy with herself that she has caused me all this trouble!'

'What's my mother got to do with it?' snapped Leon.

'Because she waited until she saw you on your own to tell you that I had been seen out with my mother today. She knew full well you would be angry with me. Why did she have to go and say anything and cause all this trouble? I tell you something, I am never going to speak to that woman again.'

This was like a red rag to a bull. Leon sprang out of bed and ran at me. I tried to dart out of the door, but this time he was too quick.

Shoving me up against the door with his body, he pushed his face into mine and with his face all screwed up he growled, 'Don't you dare talk about my mother like that.' Then he pulled me viciously by my hair. I was trying not to scream, conscious that our child lay sleeping innocently within a few feet of us. He pulled me to the ground and punched me a few times hard in the back and the kidneys – basically anywhere that would not show in public. Then he marched off downstairs to have a cigarette.

Calling the Police

My poor baby started crying and I went over to him, gently soothing him. This was ridiculous, my poor innocent son having to suffer yet again because of Leon and his family. My mother was not the best of people to get along with, but still. So, I decided that enough was enough. It was true that I could not leave, but why should I? Why should it be me who had to go? I knew that I couldn't go on like this any more, and for the first time thought that I might be able to make Leon leave. I was going to fight back against him and his family, for my son, and for me for that matter. I was going to try and achieve some peace in our lives. Picking up the phone, I quietly dialled 999.

'Hello, I need the police, please. My husband has just assaulted me.'

Within a few minutes, the police arrived. The look of shock on Leon's face when I let them into the house was indescribable. He obviously couldn't believe I had done it. Of course, he went straight into denial. 'Stacey, what are you talking about? I haven't hit you,' he lied, in front of the police officer.

He tried to insinuate to the police that we had just had a little argument, but the police could see straight through him and they began to lead him out of the door. He looked over at me and I could see the fear in his face, and I started to cry. Yet I knew I had to see this through; I simply couldn't take any more. Shuffling into the living room, I collapsed onto the chair, sitting there numb for what seemed like an hour, feeling more confused than ever.

A knock at the door startled me out of my thoughts. *Oh my God, who can that be?* I thought, hoping it wasn't him. Right now, I needed time on my own to get my head together and decide where to go from here. The police had told me he would be spending a night in the cells, buying me time to think. Slyly peeling the curtains back, I peered out on to the street. Diane and Les's car was parked on the road outside. My insides somersaulted; suddenly I felt guilty. I had just had their son arrested. I wasn't sure if they knew what had happened and that's why they were here. Why else would they come around again?

As I pulled the door open, they both began to take their shoes off ready to walk in, chattering away that they had just come back from visiting Lurpak. My face must have been crimson, I was blushing with guilt so much, as it dawned on me they obviously were not aware that I'd just had their son arrested for assaulting me. Luckily, they were so wrapped up in talking to me they hadn't noticed my sheepish body language.

Wearily I escorted them into the living room and made an excuse that I'd be back in a minute because I was going to put the kettle on. Anything to get away from them for a moment to pull myself together, as I knew that I was going to have to tell them that Leon was in a police cell. They must have assumed Leon was in, because his car was still parked outside.

Then Diane called to me, 'Where is he, then?'

My heart nearly stopped. I knew I would have to leave the safe haven of the kitchen and go in to them and explain. Thinking I was going to have a panic attack my heart was beating so fast, I put the kettle down, took a deep breath and, bracing myself, walked into the living room. They must have guessed from my sombre expression that something was wrong. They looked at each other, confused, then back to me, and Les asked, 'What's happened?'

'There's no easy way to say this, but Leon has been arrested,' I said, feeling that I wanted the ground to just swallow me up.

'Why, what's happened?' his mother asked in a high-pitched screech as she got to her feet. The inner conversation with myself saying that I had nothing to be ashamed of and that I was completely in the right didn't help me at all. His parents would not see it that way.

I began to tell them that he had assaulted me – ironically, they didn't ask me why he had done it or how I was. I was glad they didn't because even I, coward that I was, knew it was all his mother's fault he had hit me, and that must have been the reason why she didn't ask.

'Where is he? How long ago was this?' Diane demanded.

I explained to them where he was, and, walking out of the room without giving me a second glance, they rushed into the hall, put their shoes on and went to rescue their son. Sitting there, somehow, I felt racked with guilt, almost as if I had set some poor innocent man up for a crime he didn't commit. Try as I might to tell myself that I had no need to feel guilty, the looks on his face and the faces of his family told me the opposite. Crying, I picked the phone up and called his sister, Mandy. I knew she wasn't as biased as the others, and I didn't have anyone else to speak to. Mandy arrived straightaway and I explained to her what had happened; she agreed that I'd done the right thing and he had to be taught a lesson.

A while later, the phone rang and it was Diane. The tension hung heavily between us down the phone line.

'Listen, I hope you know what you're doing? First of all, you do know that the police will probably be giving Leon a good hiding tonight, don't you? That's what they do to people who hit women.'

The irony of it, I thought.

'Second, if he is lucky enough not to get a prison sentence, he will get fined at least a thousand pounds for this. Then if you two do decide to get back together, which you probably will, how the hell are you going to afford that? If you go up to the station tonight and drop the charges, you can try to sort things out properly without all this unnecessary trouble.'

Naive as I was back then, even I knew that the point she made about the fine was utter nonsense. But it indicated to me that she would say anything to get Leon off the hook, regardless of what he was putting me and Reece through. There was no apology either for her telling Leon I had been out with my mother and causing all this trouble. That was probably why she was so desperate to get me to drop the charges, because deep down she knew she had sown the seed for what had happened.

For once in my life, I stood up for myself and politely told her that I was going to leave things the way they were. However, when the police came back for me to make a statement, I had worried myself so sick about coming face to face with his family again, and thinking how they would twist it all round to everyone we knew, reluctantly I decided I just couldn't go through with the confrontations.

Feeling intimidated, I told them I didn't want to press charges. This was in the early nineties and in those days a victim of domestic violence could decide not to press charges and that would be that. The police advised me that he would still spend the night in the cells in order to give him something to think about; however, he would be released in the morning.

The only option for me now was to take Reece and leave. There was no way I ever wanted to see him or his family again.

So, in my despair, I called my old school friend Teresa. She still lived with her mother, who had also suffered domestic violence in her life and had chosen to leave and go it alone. Luckily for me, they kindly insisted I took the baby and went to stay with them. Reluctantly – as it meant I had to leave my home – I packed a bag for myself and Reece and caught a cab down to Teresa's.

When I woke up the next morning in a strange house, the events of the previous night hit me like a ton of bricks. Immediately, I felt homesick, and I worried about how Leon must have felt waking up in a cell. Still, I had to put those kinds of thoughts to the back of my mind as I tried to convince myself that my priority was Reece's and my safety. Reece and I were sharing a bed and there wasn't much room. It was hard going because I hadn't brought any of his baby things and the house wasn't child friendly. Reece was an unsettled child at the best of times, and with me feeling so depressed and him being so uncomfortable, I just wanted to be in familiar surroundings. Teresa and her mother were extremely kind and did their best to make me feel at home, but it wasn't home!

Later that day, Reece had such severe diarrhoea it went right up his back and all through his baby grow. He was absolutely plastered in it. I took him upstairs to the bathroom, but the bath was full of laundry so I couldn't bath him in there. I didn't know where to start to get him clean, and he was screaming and crying. Feeling so low and homesick, I started crying too. If I had been at home, I could have stripped him off in the bath and sorted him out. Everything seemed so difficult, like trudging through mud, being here without my own things to hand. Then I began to wonder how Leon was feeling, arriving home to find us both gone. This made me feel sick inside. I was actually starting to miss him, I suppose because he was all I had. I tried to be strong and keep in mind how he and his family had treated me, but it still didn't stop the bellyache that longing for him gave me.

Margaret, Teresa's mother, kindly offered to take me into town so that I could get some nappy cream and necessities for Reece. I hardly had any money and wondered how I was going to manage once the small amount of money I did have ran out. Also, I felt as if Reece and I were in the way, even though Margaret was doing her best to make me feel welcome. Reece's constant crying was so depressing, and I worried it was getting Teresa and her mother down. I didn't like to put anybody out, and that's what I felt I was doing. Driving into town in Margaret's car, all the worries were going around in my head.

As we went to pull into the garage, a car screeched in front of us and blocked us, preventing us from turning. 'What the hell is going on?' Margaret shouted, snapping me out of my daydream. Then I realised it was Leon – he must have seen us. Before I could even think about what was going on, he was walking over to the car and opening the back door. He leaned into where I was sitting and he looked awful, a strange yellowy colour.

'Please, Stacey,' he pleaded, 'please come back home, I am so sorry. I miss you so much. I have been so bad to you.' His chin started wobbling as he told me, 'I love you so much. I can't be without you. Bring the baby back home, please.' He was begging me to come home with tears running down his face – and in front of Margaret too. This in turn was making me cry, because deep down inside, I had missed him too and I did want to go home, not just for him but because I wanted to get Reece settled and I couldn't do that at Margaret's.

Maybe this time I really had taught him a lesson. I agreed to go back home, and no sooner were the words out of my mouth than Leon was opening Margaret's boot and getting the pram out to put into his car. Margaret looked concerned and totally unconvinced. While we had a quiet minute, she said that she hoped that he had learnt his lesson and that if I had any more problems, I was welcome to call her again. Saying goodbye to Margaret, I felt like such a user. I felt that I had imposed on her and now I was off on my way, but I was really grateful to her and Teresa. It was just that I wanted to get back home, give Reece a nice bath, settle down with my family and try again.

Over the next few weeks, things did settle down and Leon did make more of an effort with Reece and me. He got himself back to work and even admitted that he should consider my feelings more, rather than listening to his family's advice. Everything was rolling out as I had imagined in my dreams as a little girl. It wasn't perfect, but as perfect as I had ever had it in my life. I was very contented. Leon was like my best friend for the next year or more – there were no ructions or problems, he was just loving and considerate. We had been so loved up, I started to really trust him.

As a girl, I dreamt I would grow up and have one boy, then one girl. The boy would be first because he would be able to protect his younger sister. So many times, I had wished that I had a big, strong brother who would have stuck up for me against Leon. I wanted the children close together in age in my idealist family fantasy, so we decided to try for another child. I didn't want Reece growing up being an only child, I wanted him to have a sibling to play with.

Things had been good between me and Leon, and I really thought the bad times were behind us now that I had proved I would not stand for any more violence. He was treating me with more love and respect and seemed a dedicated family man. Reece was nine months old when I conceived, and with hindsight the timing wasn't great I was struggling to cope with him because he was a demanding baby. Naively, I thought if I had my children close together it would be easier in the long term as I could have my freedom quicker than if I left a big age gap between them. Little did I know that caring for two children is exceptionally harder than caring for one.

Baby Number Two

Leon and I wanted to find a nicer area to live now we had children to consider. We had been looking at bigger properties and so decided to buy. Driving seemed to run in the male side of Leon's family so, taking his father's advice, Leon put in for his HGV licence and passed first time with flying colours. It wasn't long before he found a job delivering foam for settees to furniture factories. It was 1993. We got a mortgage and bought our first house.

It was a little terraced house, sold to us by an old couple who had cleverly painted over the damp patches, and forgot to mention it came with a woodlouse infestation. To me and Leon, it was a step in the right direction – we were finally on the housing ladder.

It was during this pregnancy that Leon began associating with one of his old school friends and discovered cannabis. He would come back from work, roll a spliff and become all happy and chilled. I hoped it would just be a phase he was going through, but over time he came to rely on it.

This pregnancy was different because I was happier, and things finally seemed to be going okay. I looked after myself better, but I did pile the weight on. I didn't mind though, as I saw myself as blooming and that being a good sign that the baby was healthy. As I got bigger towards the end of the pregnancy, Leon seemed to be less attracted to me. In fact, he didn't want to go anywhere together, and I got the distinct feeling he was ashamed of me. He was invited to a work's night out and didn't ask me to go too. He said it was just for the workers and not partners, but somehow I didn't believe him. My confidence was sinking, but I kept hanging on to the fact that once the baby was born I could work at losing the weight and make my husband desire me again. Don't get me wrong, he didn't go off sex – he never went off sex.

Summer came and in mid-June the familiar cramping pains woke me from my sleep – I was in labour. We quickly got my bags into the car and dropped Reece off at his nanny Diane's. I think this was the one occasion when she had him overnight. The labour was quick and hard, but fortunately it was easier in the sense that I knew what to expect this time.

Finally, I gave birth to a beautiful baby girl. She was six pounds in weight, bang on, identical to her brother Reece. Anxiety hit a little once Leon had gone home and I was left on my own with her. I kept trying to sleep while she slept, knowing I needed to get my rest, but I couldn't relax. I was expecting her to keep waking up and crying like Reece had done. However, this baby was entirely different. She slept well and seemed a lot more contented, and she wasn't nervy either, like poor little Reece. She was a very settled baby from the onset, giving substance to the saying, happy pregnancy, happy baby.

Leon brought Reece to the hospital to meet his little sister, Sophie. He was eighteen months old at this point. When he saw me with this new baby in my arms he grew hysterical, throwing himself all over the floor and refusing to come to me and meet her. This worried me immensely. I certainly didn't want him feeling left out. Leon insisted I came home so we could try to settle as a family immediately, so I discharged myself after the doctor had checked me over.

It was quite overwhelming having two babies to look after, and Reece was finding it difficult not receiving my full attention, as he had before. When the midwife came to see me, I couldn't stop crying, feeling out of my depth.

'How am I ever going to get him to accept her?'

It was very difficult to cope, but the midwife somehow made me see it wasn't the end of the world and in time Reece would get used to his new sister. He did eventually get used to her, but it was still a chore to stop him being awkward with me because of her.

Leon was going out socialising more, as I was immersed in motherhood and cleaning. If he wasn't at work, he would be out and about visiting friends and going for smokes or popping in to see his parents. My life was just one big rota of feeding the children, bathing the children, changing the children, getting the children ready so that I could go shopping and take them both with me. The responsibility lay heavily on me. Leon wouldn't help me in any way. My idea of child rearing was that it was totally my duty to get on with it with no help. Nobody seemed to notice I was struggling and that I was depressed, but I had made my bed, so I just had to lie on it.

Life at home was just one round of tending to the needs of my children and my husband. Had he showed me any affection for my efforts it would have made it so much easier, but I felt as if I had turned into his mother too. I tried to make myself look attractive and admittedly the weight was falling off me, but inside I felt like an old lady.

One day, Leon came back from work in a really bad mood. This was the last thing I needed, considering there was nothing to look forward to in my life at the moment apart from bed and sleep. He began picking fault with the cleanliness of the house. I hadn't seen him in such a bad mood for a long time.

In between the little living room and dining room there were glass-panelled doors with little squares of frosted glass in them to let the light travel through the old house. Leon started criticising the house and making an issue of the kids' fingerprints on the glass panels. Feeling wound up myself because I was constantly on the go, trying to keep on top of things, and he had the cheek to moan about marks on the doors, I retaliated. He told me to clean the doors and I retorted that I was too busy and that if it was getting to him that much he should clean them himself.

This seemed to be the trigger that fired up his old temper – the one that had disappeared for more than a year – and he came roaring over to me. *No, no*, I thought, knowing what was coming next. It wasn't so much that I knew he was going to hurt me. I was panicking because I didn't want the children to be subjected to this environment. Before I knew it, he was punching my arms and yanking my head, my hair entwined in his big hands.

'Now look what you've made me do,' he yelled, as he unexpectedly restrained himself after a couple of minutes.

Why did things have to go like this again? I thought, as the tears rushed down my face. I was doing my best and it still wasn't good enough, and now the poor children had to hear all the shouting. Somehow, I sensed that he wasn't going to hurt me again because he knew he had overstepped the mark, so I took advantage of it and shouted at him, 'Why do you have to be so horrible and always cause upset to me and the children?' The tears were streaming down my face and I hoped that somewhere inside him he could find it in his heart to be remorseful.

'Do you want me to leave then?' he asked. This was quite an unexpected response.

I was thinking to myself, I don't know why he bothers asking me that because he knows damn well he wouldn't leave me. Well, it wasn't really about me, it would be more about the house, 'his' precious house that 'he paid for' – which I was quite often reminded of!

Of course, I felt that it would be a relief if he just left; at least we would have a roof over our heads without the children being uprooted. Anything would be better for me, and the children, than to keep having to be subjected to his moods and violence. Other women seemed to get on okay on their own, and I was practically doing everything anyway, so it wasn't as if he'd be a great loss. Financially it might be difficult, but right then I didn't care. I wasn't a great spender of money anyway. Leon was so tight I never had anything new, and the children's clothes were from charity shops, so I couldn't see things getting any worse.

All these thoughts were rushing round my head as he stood there waiting for an answer.

'Yes,' I said finally, 'I would like you to leave.'

All the time I was thinking how silly this was because I knew there was no way he would let me and the children have his house, but he surprised me and began marching up the stairs. I was a little relieved but suspicious enough to know he had something up his sleeve.

This walking off and leaving me be was totally out of character for Leon; he usually didn't stop until things had snowballed out of control. Eventually, I heard him coming down the stairs and as he stepped into the living room he had a suitcase in his hands. He looked at me and asked me again, 'Are you sure you want me to leave?'

'Yes,' I replied, my heart thumping with delight and disbelief. At that, he calmly picked the case up and walked out of the back door. Then I heard the car start and the next thing I knew, he was gone. At first, it was lovely that we had the house to ourselves and the violence hadn't spilled over into the night. Making the most of it, and feeling guilty because the children didn't deserve to have this going on around them, I sat and played with them. It wasn't as if I could relax though, because I kept thinking he was tricking me, and that at any minute he would walk through the door. Even though he had gone, he still had control over me because every time I heard a car coming down the street I had to look up at the window to check if it was him. Yet, he didn't come back all night.

Instead of relaxing as I would have loved to have done, I was confused. There was something more to this than met the eye. The fact was, though, I knew Leon would be back because of the house, and wherever he was, I wouldn't be fortunate enough that he would stay away forever. After all, who would wait on him hand and foot like I did? Leon had always made it clear that the house, the possessions, the money in the bank, and the car – and me – were his. I knew he wouldn't leave it all behind, so my mind was constantly analysing the strangeness of it all. The majority of the time I was perched on the chair looking out of the window, expecting his car to pull up.

It took two days for the penny to finally drop. Once again, I had been so naive. Everything finally started to make sense. The argument that had erupted out of nothing had obviously been pre-meditated. My sister's boyfriend Sean and a few more of his mates had hired a caravan and gone to Rhyl, North Wales, on holiday for the week. That was it, I thought. Leon had planned it all in order for me to respond by throwing him out. I remembered he actually asked if I wanted him to leave; he was making it my choice. He knew I desperately wanted him to leave so that I could try and make a normal life for my poor babies. He had been so manipulative; I was livid.

If anyone needed a bloody break it was me, with a six-week-old baby and a toddler to look after. The selfishness of what he had done was beyond comprehension. At least when he returned he would have to be humble, knowing I had sussed out his conniving plan. I decided that I would tell him he wasn't welcome back, and hopefully then he would have the decency to leave me be. This was Leon though; I knew he wouldn't give up on his possessions without a fight, but I wasn't going to let him defeat me over this.

Exactly one week later, as I predicted, Leon called and I didn't waste any time telling him not to give me any excuses, that I knew where he had been and the lengths he had deceitfully gone to in order to get there. He didn't deny it, but then again, how could he? He knew I could ask Sean and he would confirm it.

Leon was being so nice, begging and pleading with me to just let him explain, but I slammed the phone down on him. I didn't want to hear his excuses; he had behaved so appallingly. That didn't stop him coming home though. He let himself in with the key and I couldn't physically stop him.

Pent up with a week's worth of anger and disgust, I let rip at him. I really didn't want a battle with this selfish man, I wanted him to just accept that it was over and leave me in peace – but he wouldn't. He was trying to insinuate that everything had got too much for him and he needed to get away. That he thought he was doing me a favour by walking away rather than staying around and arguing with me.

The cheek of it, him needing to get away! At least he had an escape from the house and the children. He could go to work or go visit his family and friends, leaving me with the children. There were no relaxing breaks for me from the routine.

Leon just sat there looking remorseful and nodding in agreement with me – which was unusual because usually he would twist things to make it seem I'd caused the trouble. Then he started saying how much he had missed me, and that the break had made him realise what me and the kids meant to him, that he was going to help me out more with the kids and start taking me out more. Then he said he wanted to take us to McDonald's, to go out as a family. Defeated and tired from trying to get him to leave, the offer of going out to eat and having help with the children was too tempting to refuse. Not just that, I knew that eventually Leon would tire of my whining, then let his sorry act drop and start getting aggressive and I couldn't bear that. He helped me to put the kids' coats on and get them in the car – their dad there to tell them if they started being naughty. A break outside these walls and something nice to do for the kids was all I wanted, so I didn't think about his week of freedom. We had a great time out as a family and, for a while, he behaved like a good dad again.

A Little Independence

Leon was job hunting again as he had tired of delivering the foam. He heard about a job going driving for a local company, went for the interview and got the job. It was quite well paid and things seemed to be looking up. It was a real struggle for me getting about with a toddler and a baby, so I had been learning to drive. Since leaving school, my driving lessons had been few and far between due to finances, and it seemed only a dream to me even to pass my test, let alone to have the luxury of getting about in a car.

All the women in Leon's family had their own cars, so Leon allowed me to take lessons when we could afford it – which was hardly ever. However, just when I seemed to be nearing the stage to put in for my test we either couldn't afford the lessons or my nerves were so bad due to desperation to pass that I would fail my test. When I had failed my fourth test I was absolutely heartbroken. It didn't help that before each test Leon would tell me that if I failed this time, he wouldn't be paying for any more lessons.

Thankfully, Dad stepped in and paid for a crash course for me as it seemed the only way I would ever pass: a week of intensive lessons followed by the test. The driving instructor seemed a little soft with me and came around in his own time to give me extra lessons for free. Leon didn't mind because he was an old man and no threat to him physically, plus I think he was thinking of the money he was saving. That final fifth attempt came and the night before I had nightmares that I couldn't take my test because it was snowing so badly. When I woke up, I was so nervous that Leon insisted I had a Valium to relax, so I took half a tablet and, hey presto, I passed!

It was a waste of time though. For some reason, Leon wouldn't let me have the car and kept saying I wouldn't be safe in it. Leon's work was about half a mile down the road from where we lived. Each morning he would take the car to work, leave it in the car park and go off to do his job. This was so frustrating for me knowing the car was sat there all day, not being used. Some days, I would be walking from the town with the double pram and bags of heavy shopping and I'd get caught in the rain and arrive home soaked to the skin. Time and time again, I begged Leon to let me have the car to save me struggling up the hill every day. It seemed madness that the car was parked outside his work when I could be using it, but Leon always put his foot down and refused.

One day, when I knew he would be popping back for dinner, I left him a note on top of the fridge. It was a long letter explaining how frustrated I was that he could see me struggle each day and wouldn't let me take the car. In the letter, I used a little psychology about the fact that his sister and mother had cars of their own and they didn't have two little babies to take everywhere. I also mentioned that if it was him in my position, there was no way I would see him struggle with the children while the car was left standing.

Pushing the pram into town later that day, I heard a car pull up alongside me. To my surprise, it was Leon. Being quite angry with him that he was nice and snug behind the wheel and I was on foot, I continued to walk and ignore his presence.

'Stacey, Stacey, come and jump in the car.'

I just ignored him, so he pulled over and jangled the keys in my face.

'Come on then, Stacey, are you going to drop me back to work then, or what?'

I couldn't believe what he was asking me, he was going to let me have the car! You bet I was going to have it. I couldn't fold the pram up quickly enough. Strapping the children in the back, Leon drove the car to his work and, as we pulled up, he gave me a lecture about driving carefully. Then he got out and walked into the warehouse, leaving me ecstatic.

When he was finally out of view, I jumped into the driver's seat and just sat there buzzing with excitement. This was going to be a new lease of life for me. Slowly I adjusted my seat and turned the engine over. Pulling out of the car park in control of this vehicle, I felt like the cat with the cream. Cruising down the road, watching all the houses zipping behind me, I imagined how long it would take to do this route on foot. This was so easy. I could go anywhere in no time at all – so I drove into town, then I went to Nan's. It was a day I had dreamt about for so long, one that seemed impossibly out of reach, and now it was here. I was so happy.

Leon and I were getting on really well. He was still smoking the cannabis and had pressured me into taking a few drags now and again. Eventually, it had grown on me and a few drags led to us smoking a spliff together each night once the children were in bed asleep. We would talk and play music all night long and I noticed how much better it sounded when stoned – you could hear individual notes, as if the music came from your soul. Everything seemed to be going so well. Leon and I were really happy and life was so much easier now that I was driving. The evenings would be a time for us to look forward to now, so that we could smoke and get close to each other.

In time, Leon was offered the night shifts at work. We knew we would miss our nights together, but the money was better and we wanted to upgrade our home, so we decided it was for the best that he did it. Once he got into a routine with the night shift, it meant he didn't get home until about six thirty in the morning. We began to see less and less of each other. It was putting pressure on our relationship because it meant Leon had to get his sleep in the day and he expected me to keep the children quiet downstairs, which was difficult with two toddlers.

In a bid to let him sleep, I tried to get out and about with the children each day. The strain was getting immense and Leon was becoming grumpy again. Sometimes I felt that he envied the fact that I didn't have to go to work.

But my life had totally been hijacked with the arrival of the children and having Leon's rules and regulations to contend with. My life was just one big Groundhog Day – get up, get the kids ready, tidy up, go and get food. The majority of this time the kids would be screaming and playing up. If I needed to go to the shop, it was an expedition in itself. I had to make sure they didn't need changing, or were due for a feed, then get two lots of coats on. Nothing in my life was simple. Sadly, during what should have been the best time with my little children, I felt like a slave to my family.

One Saturday, Leon had been out and bought himself an electronic chess set and had sat most of the day playing with it. He had been in quite a reclusive mood all day. Late afternoon on this winter's day, we were all in the living room settling down for the evening. The lamp was on, the curtains were closed, and Leon was sitting on the chair with his arms folded, chewing his top lip with a frown on his face. He had a habit of chewing his lip when he was in a mood. I was walking on eggshells, trying to keep the heaviness out of the atmosphere. Sophie was in her baby walker, and she and Reece were playing with some toys on the top of its tray.

Something happened, I can't even remember what it was as it was so trivial, but it made Leon lose his temper big time. He picked up the chess set and threw it at the wall in anger. The pieces went flying everywhere. My heart started to thump, and I was helpless to stop the situation escalating in front of my poor children. Inside, I was screaming. I just wanted it to stop at this, but I knew it wouldn't. He had all the control.

The children were frightened and started to cry, and my heart was in my mouth. I was panicking, but I had to get him to calm down because I did not want to have my children subjected to this. How could I have brought children into this relationship thinking it would make things better? How deluded I had been thinking love would win through when I was dealing with a man who only thought about his own feelings.

Going to the children and telling them it was okay, although it clearly wasn't, I tried to distract them by laughing and making some sort of puppet show with their toys. Leon then began ranting and raving about his chess set and the pieces being lost. Being already on my knees to comfort the children, I began crawling round the floor, quickly picking up the pieces that were strewn everywhere. 'It's okay, Leon,' I said, imploring him to calm down. 'I can see them. I'll pick them up.'

The children were still crying, and I so wanted to pick them up and take them out of the room, but I knew he wouldn't let me. I knew I had to find the pieces to the chess set to stop him getting crazier. Scurrying round the floor on my knees, I was trying to sound in control. 'Here we are, here's another,' I kept saying chirpily, dropping the piece into the box. I was almost done, except there was one piece missing and try as I might I couldn't find it. Leon, who had temporarily calmed down, was getting wound up again now. 'You better find that fucking piece, Stacey. I am fucking warning you!'

'Okay, okay, I am looking,' I said, desperately crawling round the floor, scanning every inch of the area to find the blasted chess piece. Inside, I just wanted to scream at him and tell him to get off his lazy fucking arse and find it himself, the bullying bastard. Causing all this upset to the children and me, just because he was in a bad mood. I hated him so much, but I had to repress it because I knew it would make matters worse if I started shouting back at him. All that would achieve would be the kids getting upset again and me getting a smack. So, I had to maintain self-control and focus on finding the chess piece.

Half an hour later, I was still crawling round scanning the same spots, knowing full well I wasn't going to find the blighter. I was desperately waiting for permission to stop looking so that I could give my kids some love and comfort. It was quite obvious now I wasn't going to find it. I was crying with frustration, but I couldn't let the tears fall freely because I knew Leon hated to see me cry – he always said it made me look ugly. Still, the tears were spilling out against my will. Eventually, the voice of power spoke, with what he had decided was the solution, 'You will have to take the chess set back to the shop, Stacey, and tell them there was a piece missing. If you go now, you will probably catch them before they shut.'

Oh God, no, I thought, anxiety fluttering in my stomach at his unreasonable demand. My face was swollen and red from crying, my head in a mess because of all the stress. The children needed their mum, not me going out to sort this stupid chess set out. Dishonesty was something I didn't practise very well. The thought of going into the shop looking as rough as I did and taking the game back that had been packaged before purchase, and then lying to the staff was just petrifying to me.

Yet, I knew there was no point in arguing and the only way I would restore peace to this household would be to come back with a new chess set – and time was ticking on before the shop shut. So, I tried to tidy myself up a bit, then left the house. I got in the car, worried sick about taking the game back, so I drove around the corner to a quiet spot round by the park where no one could see me release my pent-up tears.

I could cry freely now and let all the anger, the sadness and the frustration out. I sat there screaming in frustration – I hated that bastard. Right then, I just wanted to end it all. My life with him was unbearable, it was one test after another. Then I thought about the children, my poor little babies who needed me so much. Who would take care of them? What would it do to them if I killed myself? Would they grow up and follow in my footsteps? I thought about their poor little faces as their father was losing his temper, how I wanted it to stop. I didn't want them exposed to all this violence.

Then I thought about having to go into the electronics shop with my ugly face that was swollen from crying and having to lie, to stand there humiliated among strangers, and hope that they would exchange the goods! It was all too much.

I hated him.

I hated him.

I revved the engine and drove the car back round to the front of the house, crying, and then I sat there banging the horn like a maniac. *I'll show him a nutcase*, I thought.

The curtains moved and his face came into view, frowning. His previous outburst had expelled his anger so I knew there would be no repercussions.

He was trying to look as if he was puzzled and was not sure what I was doing and why. He was feigning the look of someone confused and alarmed, so I screamed, even though he probably couldn't hear me because the windows of the car were shut. I screamed and stuck my two fingers up; I screamed how much of a bullying wanker he was, and how much I hated him. He just stood there looking perplexed.

I suppose that was for the benefit of the neighbours who were looking to see what this crazy woman was doing sitting screaming in her car and thumping the horn.

Then I sped off before he could come out and try to get me inside. I knew I had overstepped the mark now and that I'd probably made things worse for myself, but I did feel a little better for letting my frustration out. The only thing I had left to do now was to go to the shop. So, I parked the car by the shop, looked in the mirror at my ugly face, with my big red swollen nose and thought, sod it.

I got the stupid game and walked into the electronics shop. The men behind the counter just stared at me, but by now I was too angry to be embarrassed so I marched over and didn't even attempt to act normal – that would have been a waste of time considering the state of my face. Placing the chess set on the counter, I requested matter-of-factly, 'Could you please swap this game for me for a new one? My husband tells me there is a piece missing. If you don't exchange it and I have to take the old one home, my husband is going to hit me.'

There were two young men behind the counter and as I spoke they stared at me in amazement. I could almost see their jaws hit the floor. Not one of them commented. To them, I probably looked more like a demented druggy who was wild for a fix. Fortunately, they just got me another game and handed it over. Walking out of the shop, I felt relieved. I hoped that by the time I got back he would have calmed down. Now that I had his new game, I had achieved what he had ordered me to do, so maybe it would be okay?

When I got home, Leon had calmed down and he had found the missing piece, and now he expected the whole episode to be forgotten. It was a terrible situation to be in. I so desperately wished that I lived alone with the children, but I couldn't see a way out of it. When bedtime came, I was so exhausted from the drama that evening, I just wanted to sleep. Leon had other ideas and I was too exhausted to argue any more. What was the point? He would probably just get angry again and it was the poor children who had to suffer hearing him. So, as usual, I just lay there and let him have his way with me. He was kissing and cuddling me, and I found that quite comforting.

There certainly were two sides to Leon and that's what caused all the confusion for many years. There was dependable, logical, sensitive, loving Leon, who was calm, charming and made me feel treasured and secure. We could get on like a house on fire, talking, laughing and making love all night long. Even his smell comforted me – it must have been his pheromones. If it could have been put in a bottle, it would have soothed and lovingly engulfed me.

On the opposite side of the scale came bad Leon. When he was in a bad mood, or lost his temper, he turned into a totally different person. He was frightening to say the least, insulting, abusive, intimidating, aggressive and violent. The problem was that I was so in love with the good side of Leon, because he seemed like my comfort blanket, it somehow made me forget about the bad Leon. Good Leon was clever, he could turn his hand to anything – fixing cars, DIY, there was nothing I had to worry about with the car mechanically and the house cosmetically; he took care of everything, making me feel cared for. When we did get along, we really did. You see some couples sitting in a pub together with nothing to say to each other, but Leon and I were never like that, we never ran out of conversation, we had a fantastic rapport.

When bad Leon came out, he not only abused me but he would spend hours bullying me, mentally torturing me and wearing me down until I couldn't get any lower, so by the time he had released all his anger and the good Leon came back, I was glad to be comforted and clung on to his kindness. It was like living with two different people – and quite similar to living with my mother.

It was hard to believe that they were the same person, but pinging between the two egos seemingly made it impossible for me to leave. It screwed with my head so much I didn't know whether I was coming or going. Logically, you would presume that anyone would get the hell out of a situation like that, but Leon was extremely manipulative and charming.

By this time, my life was totally controlled by Leon and his parents. It was no use rebelling against Leon's bullying tactics and asking them for support because they made it seem as if I was somehow to blame.

He was so house proud; everything had to be perfect and unreasonably in its place. My father's side of the family were upper-class people, and Dad wasn't doing too badly for himself either. He lived in a lovely big house, but he had never asked me to take my shoes off before entering his home as Leon's mother did, and expected me to in my home. I found it embarrassing asking Dad and Helen to take off their shoes when they came to see us, but if I ever brought it up, Leon, who imposed this rule on me, would lecture me on how he paid for the carpets and he didn't want dirty shoes on them. I had to apologise to Dad for making them take off their shoes, but he was kind and said, 'Stacey, if I had to come to visit your house naked in order to see you and my grandchildren I would, so don't stress about it.' But stress about it I did. Life was evolving into rules and regulations, all the policies of Leon's family, which was okay if you were one of them, but not so easy for me.

The repercussions I endured, should something not be up to the expected standard, left my nerves in shreds. Everything had to have its place and be clean and tidy. I was extra vigilant not to make any careless mistakes that could cause an argument. Painting or doing crafts with the children was out of the question, even when Leon wasn't there, as I just was so fixated on keeping everything tidy. It was sad. I never got to enjoy my children or my home in a normal way.

Something Amiss

Something was different that morning when I woke. Leon wasn't back from his night shift, although he usually got home around four in the morning. It was seven thirty, with no sign of him, and I was beginning to worry when the phone rang. It was Leon.

'Where on earth are you?' I asked. 'I'd just started to worry you'd had an accident at work.'

Leon sounded strangely calm and quiet, 'Listen, Stacey, I'll be back in about an hour and a half; I am still at the motorway services.'

I sensed that this wasn't the truth; my intuition was strongly telling me he had been with another woman. Then I dismissed the thought as being ludicrous. When would he get time to meet another woman? He was always on the road, or at home, or at his mum's.

The thought was still there though, and, as if in a dream, I went onto autopilot. I had an hour and a half to become the perfect wife when he walked through the door. I gently got the children out of bed and prepared their breakfasts. Then I made myself up as best I could. I tidied round and got the children in the bath. Perfectly timed, Leon came walking through the back door and into the kitchen. The central heating was on, the house was nice and tidy, just how he liked it, and our children were playing angelically in the bath.

It was an idyllic home setting, derived from my sense of inadequacy.

Acting as if I was concerned that he had had a hard night, I put the kettle on for him and noticed how he was absorbing the perfect family environment. I was intent on showing him what a wonderful family we were and how lucky he was to have us. At my most pleasant, I did him some breakfast and got the children out of the bath. However, the voice in my head said, *How dare he think he can do better than me.*

Everything was unusually in perfect order. Leaving the children playing, I ran Leon a bath. He had a long soak and I went in to talk to him for a while. There was definitely something amiss about him.

It was strange how I all but knew it, even though nothing had been said.

Leon went to work that night and was late again in the morning. Still, I went along with what was happening with no questions. This made me feel in control of the situation, as Leon was taking more risks in order to do what he was doing, thinking that I was totally unaware that anything was going on. He seemed to sink into a low mood when he was at home. He would lie on the bed staring into space, hardly speaking to me. I began to question what was really going on. Was he falling into a major depression? Feeling ashamed that I had presumed his out-of-character behaviour was due to an affair, I began convincing myself he had depression. Sitting at his side on the bed one day, I gently stroked his hair, telling him I was worried about him and begging him to open up to me. As much as he had caused me suffering I still saw a vulnerable little boy at times when I looked at him.

'I know something's wrong, Leon, please talk to me about it.'

It was no good, though, he wouldn't talk to me, so I begged him to go and see the doctor. I was really concerned that he was heading for a breakdown, he seemed so distant.

A few days later, on his day off, he unusually sprang out of bed really early and quickly started getting dressed.

'What are you doing?' I asked, confused because it wasn't like Leon to get up this early if he didn't need to.

'Listen, Stacey, it's best for you that you don't know,' he said.

'Don't know what?' I retorted. 'Where are you going?'

'I've got to go on some business and it's best that you don't know anything about it. The least said the better and then you won't get into any trouble,' he said, pulling on his trousers.

Now I was really confused, but Leon never answered to me; he never had, and he never would. So, I just gave up asking and sadly watched him go. The car pulled off and he was gone. That was it. I didn't hear from him all that day or the next. Worried sick, I called his parents. Knowing he was particularly close to them, I concluded that if anyone would know what was going on, they would. But that was a dead end, because they seemed as concerned as I was.

I didn't know what to think, but his behaviour was awfully strange. My whole world was consumed with thoughts of where he could be, and what he was doing. Finally, the car pulled up on

Sunday evening and he came strolling in through the back door. He kept his head down and quietly went into the living room, where he collapsed on the sofa.

'Where have you been?' I asked frantically. 'I have been worried out of my mind.'

The not knowing made me understand the yearning people go through when a loved one goes missing. It is endless limbo.

Lying there, looking absolutely shattered, he answered, 'I needed to get away, Stacey. It was all getting too much for me.'

He did look really exhausted. 'Stacey,' he said, 'do you mind going out and picking me up a McDonald's? I haven't eaten.'

Me being me, as usual, I couldn't do enough for him. 'Of course, I will. You just rest. When I get back, we can talk about it.'

That was the trouble with me, I always tried my best to please him. I wanted him so much to love me. When I returned half an hour later with his food, I wanted answers. 'So, what happened then, and where have you been sleeping?'

'I just needed to get away, Stacey, like I told you. The mortgage, the kids, everything is getting on top of me, so I just decided to go for a drive.'

'So where did you sleep?' I asked, as he was stuffing a Big Mac into his mouth.

'Motorway services,' he mumbled, chomping away at his burger. 'There are toilets in there and showers, so I had a wash there then kipped in the car.'

'You could have rung me, Leon. I have been worried sick.'

'Here you go again,' he replied. 'I told you I needed to get away, I couldn't face calling you. Then on the way back the car ran out of fuel, so I had to walk miles to find a garage. I was so tired, and it took me hours to find a garage and sort the car out. Now I just feel totally exhausted,' he said, looking ready to crash out on the chair.

So, I left him to have a sleep as I tried to keep the noisy babies quiet.

The next day, his behaviour was even stranger. After lying on the bed for hours, staring at the ceiling as if in mourning for a lost love, he called work and told them he wouldn't be in for the rest of the week. Trying to talk to him was getting me nowhere and I was seriously concerned for his mental health.

After a few days, I even went to see our doctor about Leon's behaviour but he told me that Leon would have to come to the surgery to talk things through himself due to patient confidentiality. When I asked Leon to see the doctor, he refused. He was so odd with me; he would look right through me as if I didn't exist.

When I got back from the doctor, I saw Leon standing on our neighbour's drive. This neighbour was a car trader who Leon spoke to now and again because Leon was always changing our cars. At the time, we had a rover metro.

Strange, I thought, as I entered the house. The next thing I heard was our car starting. When I looked out of the window, I saw Leon taking it to the car trader's over the road. Maybe he was just showing it off? But that's not what had happened. Leon had sold the car to the car trader for a lot less than it was worth.

'You've done what?' I cried in disbelief when Leon came back, searching for the logbook and telling me he had sold the car. Now I was really worried about him, wondering what had possessed him to sell it. We relied on the car for everything and it wasn't as if we had another one to replace it with. This was complete madness. Something wasn't adding up. I had a niggling feeling he was hiding something from me. Unless he was he going mad?

'Are you seeing another woman?' I asked him.

'Don't be ridiculous, Stacey. How would I get time to meet another woman when I'm always out on the road driving? I just wouldn't get a chance.'

That sounded logical enough to me.

However, he then got the yellow pages and began looking at car hire companies.

'Why are you looking at those, Leon?' I asked, confused.

'You'll see,' was the only answer I could manage to coax out of him. Was that the sort of thing a person did while having a breakdown, look up car hire companies? Eventually, he went into the other room with the phone and I listened by the door. I couldn't believe my ears when I heard him arranging for a car to be delivered. My mind was running through all sorts of scenarios; maybe he was going to take us all away. All I could do, while it all unfolded, was wait, because Leon refused to talk to me.

Eventually, there was a knock on the door and a very attractive young lady was standing there holding the car keys and some paperwork. This was getting utterly ridiculous, I thought. I was actually coming out of the denial stage and realising that whatever Leon had planned, it didn't involve the children and me. The woman was chatting away to Leon about the car hire and I was becoming increasingly paranoid, to the point where I even thought that the woman was involved in what was going on, that she was his other woman, and that she had brought the car round to rub my face in it.

Moving the net curtain to look out, my temper fired up when I saw this great big executive-looking car outside the house. Very flash indeed, and definitely a luxury we couldn't afford. My anger was getting the better of me, so I began to question Leon in front of the sales lady in a manner that embarrassed him. 'What have you hired that car for and why are you being so secretive?'

Sophie was in my arms and was crying a little, and Reece was pulling my legs to be picked up too. My agitation was mounting because I knew that whatever was happening I was trapped, I had to look after the children. Sensing that I was upset was making the children worse.

Leon didn't seem so much in a trance now that the sales lady was sitting there shuffling with embarrassment on the chair.

'It's for business, Stacey,' he said in a condescending tone, and I wondered if that was for the sales lady's benefit. The sales lady got the papers signed and I heard her say that the car had to be back on Sunday afternoon by one o'clock. I noticed the badge she wore with the company logo, Lye Hire – a local company. Then she politely left our house as quickly as possible, leaving Leon and me alone.

'What's going on? Why have you hired that stupid big car?' I pleaded.

I felt so helpless. Something was in the pipeline for him again and, as usual, I was going to be the one left holding the baby – or rather, babies. Leon continued to ignore me and went and went upstairs. Sometime later, the door opened at the bottom of the stairs, and he came through with a small suit case he had obviously just packed in preparation to leave.

Finally, he broke the silence and spoke to me.

'Right,' he ordered, 'I need you to come with me. Get the kids ready.'

It was no good asking him why, so I got the children ready as quickly as possible, curious to see what was going to happen next.

Although I was sobbing because he was leaving, when he told me to get the kids ready, somewhere inside me I was naively thinking that it was all a big surprise, that he had hired the car to take us away and was trying to keep it to himself until the last minute. It was cruel the way he had gone about it, but if it turned out that he was just teasing me I would have been so happy. After all, I was desperate for a break.

Finally, we were all in the luxury car cruising down our little road. All my questions to Leon were falling on deaf ears. Eventually, we pulled up in town in the high street and Leon got our savings book out of the glove box and gave it to me.

'I need you to go into the bank and withdraw all the money,' he said. There was about six hundred pounds in there.

In my head, I concluded that this money was for me and the children, because he was leaving, or that it was for the secret trip he was about to take us on. So, I did as he asked because by now I was curious as to where this little venture was going to end up. When I got back into the car with the money, he snatched it off me and put it in his wallet.

'Just one more thing I need you to do for me, Stacey,' he said as he pulled up outside our local social security benefits office.

'What are we doing here?' I asked in disbelief.

'Listen to me, Stacey, I want you to go in there now and tell them that your husband has left you. Take the kids with you, and tell them we have a mortgage too. They may give you some forms to take home with you but fill in as much as you can when you're in there to get it sorted as quickly as possible.'

To get what sorted? I thought, confused.

'If you can't fill the forms in, show my mum and dad when you get home and they will help you.'

My head was in such a whirl, and in between the children crying and demanding my attention, and the car hire and our savings being withdrawn, I was just going with the flow of things. Whatever was happening, Leon had obviously got it thoroughly planned, but right at that moment I couldn't see the wood for the trees.

As if I hadn't been degraded enough, I found myself sitting in the social security office making a claim while my husband was sitting pretty outside in the car park. Looking round at all the people who were struggling on welfare benefits, I concluded that I blended in quite well. The children were moaning, gripping my jogging bottoms trying to be picked up, and my face was red from crying. Grabbing a ticket, I sat down and waited my turn, staring at the floor in total disbelief as the children climbed all over me. After about twenty minutes, my ticket number was called and I reluctantly approached the counter.

The lady behind the counter asked me what the nature of my claim was and from there I just went onto autopilot, answering all the questions.

It was so humiliating, but in a way, I felt that I didn't have any dignity left after all that had been happening. The children were crying as I tried to give the lady the information she needed, and I was crying because I felt so low. I was so fed up and the lady looked at me as if I was just another rundown single parent.

The irony of it was that I didn't want to be there, and I didn't want to be a single parent. I wanted to be at home with a nice husband and children, not going through all this drama. Eventually, she dealt with my claim in so far as she could and she then gave me the forms to fill in for the mortgage claim and so on.

When I went out to the car to Leon, he was sitting there as cool as a cucumber. I was quite surprised he didn't have the audacity to moan at me for taking such a long time to sort the claim out. Pulling into our street, my stomach dropped because I knew then that I had to stop kidding myself that this was some lovely surprise holiday.

Leon calmly came in the house and picked up a few more bits and bobs, all the time ignoring my frantic questions. I shut the children in the living room in front of the television and continued to pester him to tell me what was going on.

Eventually, he replied that now I had been to the social security office he was sure that we would be okay for money.

'I am leaving you, and never coming back,' he said, as if it was just normal.

I felt as if my insides were being strangled with anxiety. How dare he hire a big posh car? Was he trying to impress someone? It was madness to take all our money and walk out of our lives in such a nonchalant manner, as if he were popping to the shops for a paper.

At that point, I became hysterical. It wasn't just the fact that he was leaving me, it was the fact that he was going to leave me in limbo, because really, he hadn't given me any idea of what had happened, or where he was going. I knew that from then on my days would just be staying in, with the children misbehaving, and looking out of the window every five minutes wondering where he was. He was leaving me now because it suited him, instead of leaving me when he had overstepped boundaries and caused chaos in our home.

The absolute cheek of it was that if the selfish bastard had got another woman, I could guarantee without a doubt in my mind that the novelty would wear off quite quickly and he would come back home to us, tail between his legs, and pressure his way back into our lives as if nothing had happened.

That was what was so frustrating, that and the fact that it was breaking my heart and he was still prepared to go. In a desperate bid to stop him from leaving, with all my emotions yearning for him to stay, I grabbed his shirt and screamed and cried, 'You're not going, you can't leave me here with the children and no money.'

He just smirked at me and shook me off him as if I was a piece of dirt.

In my anger, I screamed to him as he walked out of the door, 'If you're putting me through all this pain to go and be with another woman, I will never have you back, you mark my words, I'll never have you back.' I meant every word of that too, because I didn't want him back. Leon went riding off into the sunset leaving me as usual to deal with the aftermath. Putting a smile on my face, I went back into the living room to the children. 'Right, who wants some tea?'

As I had suspected, my days were spent sobbing and looking up at the window every time a car came down the street. The frustrating thing about it was that if I had had a guarantee that he wasn't coming back, and I at least knew where he was, even if it was with another woman, I could have quite happily moved on with my life.

Although I constantly wondered where he was, the atmosphere in the house was a lot better. The pressure to clean and please Leon was off, and the children and I could please ourselves. So as not to upset them, I tried to keep their routine as pleasant as possible. We had visits to the park of an afternoon, where they could run and play and let off steam. Even when sitting on the park bench watching the children playing, I half expected him to turn up. Then, when we set off for home, I was half expecting his car to be there and him to be in the house waiting for us. My thoughts were constantly of him and where he was and if he going to walk through the door in the next minute.

Of course, Leon's parents came round every day, worried out of their minds – not for me or the children but for their poor prodigal son. They came up with all kinds of suggestions as to where he could be; his mother even said that she thought there was another woman at the back of it. It was impossible to move on with my life because I knew that eventually Leon was going to turn up like a bad penny. Why didn't he at least have the decency to phone me and let me know if he was okay? It was horrible living in this constant limbo.

That first Saturday night, as I lay in bed tossing and turning, an idea formed in my mind. It was such a good idea because it meant that I could actually catch him red-handed with his fancy bit and then he couldn't lie his way out of it, as no doubt he intended to. The car hire place. I remembered the logo and I knew that the car had to be back there tomorrow by one in the afternoon. I figured that if I hid near the car hire place, I would see him arrive back with the car and the chances were that the woman would be with him.

Excitement bubbled up inside me as I imagined his shocked face as he was finally exposed and was unable to deny what he had been up to. Then my fantasy went on deliciously to how I could humiliate him by telling her that she was welcome to him because he was nothing but a spineless wife beater who had abandoned his wife and kids.

Then sadness took over, because I realised I had no one to look after the kids if I went to confront him. I knew his parents wouldn't have them; they would want to know where I was going for a start and there was no way they would get involved with catching their own son out. After all, I could be gone hours if I had to be waiting there first thing in the morning in order to catch him, and he didn't arrive until one o'clock.

If I took the kids with me, they would probably get fed up, be tired and cold, and make so much noise they would give me away as I hid. So here was my golden opportunity to catch him. My stomach did somersaults as my mind kept going over it again and again, but, as usual, being left with the children had restricted me in what I could do, and there was no way I could go and catch him in the act. It just didn't seem fair. I never seemed to get any justice. In a way, I couldn't wait for the children to grow up so that I could be a bit more independent because at the moment they were the bars to my life in this prison. For the time being, my priority had to be the children.

Sunday afternoon arrived and I was like a cat on hot bricks. I had got up really early because I couldn't sleep. Then I'd cleaned the house from top to bottom and got the children ready. I spent most of the day sitting on the window ledge of our bay window looking through the curtains waiting to see Leon returning home. It was cold and boring sitting at the window, but I couldn't tear myself away in case I missed his return.

The day turned into night and Leon still hadn't come back. My heart sank, not because I missed him so much but more because my mind had been driving me mad with questions and scenarios about where he could be, and I desperately wanted answers. After all, he had walked out and taken every penny from the car and our savings and left us with nothing – not even an explanation.

Leon's parents made a regular habit of coming down and sitting with me in the evenings, but they never took the children to give me a break. There was a fine line between being looked after and being monitored,   I   suspected.

The Other Woman

It is said that things turn up when you least expect them, and I was least expecting it the next day when I heard a car revving up outside our house. Looking out of the window, there in our parking spot was a silver Mazda, and who was behind the wheel steering it into the space?

Leon.

He let himself in, looking all dapper and happy. 'Come and look at this,' he said, as if he had never been away. In a state of mild shock, I didn't say a word and just followed him outside as he pointed at the big car. I didn't like it one bit. This was a car that had been bought while I had been at home with the children, going out of my mind with worry. For all I knew, it could be his other woman's car.

'Look at the number plate,' he laughed. It contained the initials SFC. I knew some sort of put-down was coming now by the fact that his private joke had amused him so much. Still, I just stood there without saying anything, staring at the car. As an icebreaker Leon said, 'The car, well I bought it because the registration reminded me of you. Stacey Fat Cunt.'

This wasn't amusing to me at all, and I just turned round and walked back into the house. Leon followed me back in and the children were both really excited to see him. 'Daddy, daddy,' they chorused, vying for his attention. He picked them up like the doting father that he wasn't and gave them both a big hug. Waiting for him to give the children their five minutes' worth of attention, I went into the kitchen and leaned against the worktop.

Eventually, he followed me in and was trying to hug me with a smug grin on his face. For once, I was having none of it. He had left us for almost a week, led me to believe he was having a breakdown, taken all our money with no explanation, and now, as I had predicted, expected to slot back into our lives.

'Where have you been, Leon? Don't you realise what you have put me through? I have been going out of my mind, wondering and worrying about where you were. It's got to have been another woman because you look fine to me. Now the least you can do is tell me the truth and put me out of my misery.'

'The truth is, Stacey, I needed to get away. I think I was having a breakdown because the last few days have been a bit of a blur. Today, for the first time, I wanted to see you and the children. I missed you all so much today, I just had to come home. You are my life, don't you see that? I am sorry I have put you through all this, Stacey, but my head hasn't been right. I feel much better now. Please forgive me and I'll make it up to you and the kids.'

His excuses were the same, and again he said that he had been sleeping at the motorway services. He had used the hire car to go and look at the Mazda in Birmingham. Something didn't ring true, but he seemed so sincere and so sorry. The children were so happy to see him and the house felt like a happy home. What could I do but give him the benefit of the doubt? What if he had really been ill? What sort of wife would I be? I thought, naively, that to start being nasty to him now just as he was in a state of recovery might tip him back over the edge. 'Come on,' Leon said, 'let's go and take the kids to Tipton Park and feed the ducks. They'll love that.'

The kids were screeching with excitement as I helped them get their coats on. It was so happy and exciting. When we got to the park, and Leon treated me as if we were first loves all over again. He put his arm round me protectively. He played with the children, pushing them on the swings. Then we sat on the bench watching them and he cuddled up to me, kissing my forehead and telling me how he had really missed me and how much he realised he loved me.

It was all I ever wanted. I was quite content to let the previous week go, just to have me and the children contained in this bubble of love and contentment. We had such a wonderful afternoon and I hoped that things would stay like that forever. On our way, home the Mazda roared up the hill – it was so powerful, although I still didn't like it. Leon indicated to the left and manoeuvred the car ready to pull into our street. Suddenly, he turned the wheel sharply and swerved back out again on to the main road.

'What are you doing?' I asked confused.

'Going to Mum and Dad's. I think it's only fair that I let them know I'm alright,' he said. That was fair enough, I supposed. We arrived at his parents like a happy little family, all united again, and his parents seemed delighted to see him. They also swallowed his excuse that he had been escaping reality for a while.

While Diane and I were chatting, I heard Leon in the background asking his father to pop outside with him to have a look at the car. Diane and I continued talking and I thought nothing of it, until half an hour had gone by and they still hadn't returned. When we looked out of the window, the car had gone.

'Where have they gone now?' Diane said.

'They've probably gone for a drive in the new car,' I replied. Another half an hour passed then they returned, confirming what I had thought.

When we finally arrived home, Leon seemed quiet and on edge again. There was something strange going on. That evening his parents came round and we all settled into the living room. They arrived looking very solemn as if they had been given some bad news. Going into the kitchen to make drinks, I wondered what was going on. When I had finished passing the drinks out I sat down and Diane said, 'Stacey, we need to talk to you.'

Now I was getting really worried; they all knew something I didn't, and it was something that was about to rock my world.

'It's Leon. He has been seeing another woman.'

I looked round at them all staring intently at my face, waiting for my reaction. My gut reaction was to burst out crying. Then I got up, ran into the bathroom and sat on the floor, sobbing my heart out. This was a living nightmare. It was one thing him having an affair, but he hadn't even got the guts to tell me himself, he'd got his parents down here to tell me. He probably thought that I would contain my emotions in front of them.

I wasn't going to this time. The last few weeks ran through my head, all the degradation of being dropped off at the social security office and being left without a car, but the main knife to the heart was the way I had grabbed Leon's clothes as he had tried to walk out of the door to leave me and the children. Then my words rang in my head, 'If you're putting me and the kids through all this just so as you can be with another woman, I will never have you back.' Those words boiled inside me like a private pact I had made to myself. This was my oath and I was not going to budge on it. It was an oath fuelled with anger and indignity for all the shit I had put up with.

At that moment, Diane knocked on the bathroom door. 'Stacey, can I come in, love, and talk to you for a minute?'

'Yes, you can,' I said, preparing myself for whatever she had to say to back up her son's behaviour. This was one time they had not got a leg to stand on. The little girl who didn't like to upset people was now overwhelmed by the hurt and deceit that had ruined her life. Diane came in and sat down on the floor beside me. She said she understood how I was feeling because she had been through the same thing with Les.

'Who is she?' I asked, thinking that as Diane was aware of this sordid affair maybe she knew all the details too.

'I think it's someone he works with, but I am not sure,' she replied.

'Well, whoever she is she can have him because there is no way I am having him back now. This is the final straw. When did he tell you about it anyway?' I asked, curiosity building up in me.

'It was today I found out, Stacey. You know when you all came to the house to visit us earlier and Leon and Les nipped out for a drive? Well, they went to see her.'

'Why, does she live locally or something?' I asked. It wasn't that at all, though. It turned out that when Leon and I had been to the park with the children that afternoon, the other woman had been sitting outside our house waiting for him. Diane said she wasn't going to cause any trouble for me – that was an understatement considering what I was feeling now! She just wanted to catch him on his own and ask him why he had left her. So, Leon had left her in the lurch for me this time.

Leon had started to turn into our street but seen her in the car sitting by our house and panicked, then drove to his parents. He had then spilt the beans to his dad, who had gone with him down to our house and told her to go away, that it was over.

So they all knew, and now they were breaking it to me as a team, instead of Leon being man enough to have the courtesy to tell me one to one.

'Well, he needn't have bothered' I said annoyed. 'I'm not going to have him back now after everything he has put us through.' Recalling it all in my head, I continued, 'I cried and I begged him not to leave and he walked out on us, focused on going to be with her. He didn't care about us at all, and I warned him that if he was leaving me to be with another woman, there was no way I would take him back. And I won't.'

Instead of supporting me in what I had just told her, Diane said, 'Look, Stacey, that girl obviously really loves Leon. She sat outside your house for hours today in tears, hoping to sort things out with him and to get him to go back.'

'So what?' I said exasperated. 'Am I supposed to feel sorry for her? Am I supposed to feel grateful that he wants to be with me and not her?'

'Well, if I were you, Stacey, I would think about this carefully; after all, our Leon is a good-looking lad, you know.'

That really was a corker. As naive as I was, I couldn't believe the way she had just insulted me. She was as busy spinning the web to keep me trapped as her son was. Still, I couldn't find it in me to tell her how she had made me feel. It was easier to let them all think that what they were saying to me was sinking in. If I had let them know how far ahead of them I was in their plans to monopolise my life in their son's best interest, I would lose the battle. They were so manipulative, I could see where Leon had inherited it from. However, now wasn't the right time for me to try and debate with them. It was safer for me to hide behind the worn out, dizzy, blonde exterior.

Sensing a little of my attitude, his mother left the bathroom adding, 'Just think about what I have said and don't be too hasty. It may seem like the end of the world right now, but it really isn't.'

As I listened, I heard them saying goodbye to Leon, and before they had chance to step out of the door, I ran into the living room. 'Leon, I think it's best if you go home with your parents tonight,' I said, desperately hoping he would.

They all deserved each other. I was amazed that they all assumed that Leon could just walk back in after leaving me – as if it was still his home. I had to make a stand now because otherwise he would worm his way back in as usual and I would be swamped again. The kids and I didn't need him, and I didn't want him anywhere near me.

Diane piped up, 'You're in a state of shock, Stacey. It's best that you're not left on your own tonight.'

Since when had any of them really cared about me? In other words, they didn't want to have Leon back living with them, and they knew Leon intended to reclaim his house now that the novelty of this other woman had worn off.

They both left and I slumped on one of the big old comfy chairs in the dining room. For the first time in my marriage, Leon asked me if I'd like a cup of tea.

'Yes please,' I muttered. This was the moment that had been building up for weeks, the moment of truth. The lies had started to come out now and there was no going back. Leon would have to answer my questions.

Sitting crying in the chair, I felt as if my heart had been ripped out. There were waves of anxiety rippling coldly through my ribs, heart and stomach. It was bad enough to be hit and treated like a slave, even though through it all I still loved him. But now this man, my husband, walking into the dining room with my drink, had suddenly become a complete stranger.

It was almost as if I was in mourning for a husband who had passed away, for this man who sat opposite me, who I'd thought I knew. I didn't know him at all.

'Who is she then? What's her name? How did you meet her?' I was really curious, I wanted answers.

He told me that she was a girl who worked at the transport offices where he worked, and that made it all the more real, making me feel all the more sick. She was a real person, this woman my husband had been fucking and putting me through hell for.

'How old is she?' I asked. It was strange because as much as I wanted to know everything, each answer would strike another blow to my damaged heart.

'She's thirty,' Leon replied. This made me feel even worse, because I was only twenty-three and a thirty-year-old woman to me was wise to the world, and no doubt very experienced and enticing in the bedroom department, whereas I felt like a naive and uninteresting stay-at-home mum – a nothing in comparison. Looking into Leon's eyes as the tears dropped involuntarily from mine, I could have sworn he was trying to stifle a smug smirk. Worn out from crying and arguing and not wanting to hear any more, I went up to bed. As I mounted the stairs, I shouted down to Leon that it was best he slept downstairs. That was the first time I had ever had the nerve to say that to him, and any other time he would have hit me for it.

113

Lying in the dark, staring at the ceiling, I tried to absorb all that I had learnt that night. It was torturous going through it all, imagining Leon with this older woman. Then Leon came upstairs and climbed into bed beside me. Shuffling to the edge of the bed in the darkness, I turned my back on him to make it clear I didn't want him near me, but Leon, not being one to ever consider my feelings, just shuffled up to me and put his arms tightly around me.

It felt nice and protective, and I softened as he planted little kisses on the back of my head. For a moment, it all seemed like a bad dream as he gently pulled me onto my back and continued kissing me on the mouth. I almost wanted his love, until he started to be intimate with me, because as he got closer to me, everything came flooding into my head.

What he was doing to me was what he had been doing to her. I just wanted him to get off me, but I knew he wouldn't. So I just lay there praying he would hurry up and finish. Once he had finished, he went to sleep in no time at all; he was obviously exhausted.

For me, it wasn't that easy. I lay there crying. There was no way I could sleep. I wanted to sleep. I was so tired but all I kept thinking about was him being with her. Looking at him snoring away, I hated him. It was okay for him, dead to the world. I didn't even have the luxury of switching off from all the pain.

Lying there, I began to piece all the information together that I had gained that evening and my mind went into total overdrive. I had to see this woman for myself; I needed to know the whole truth. I needed to see what she was like and how he had treated her. Did she know that he was a violent bully and a control freak? Did she know he was married with two little babies? There was only one way to find out.

Daylight streamed through the curtains. Lying awake all night had left me feeling tired and exhausted. In the night, I had concocted a plan to get all my questions answered. Little tasks had plagued my mind, like finding the logbook in the Mazda and seeing if the owner of the car actually came from Bell Green. When I had asked Leon where Bell Green was he told me it was in Birmingham, which was odd, because I had never heard of it. So I looked in the map book and it was in Coventry, where the headquarters of the company Leon worked for was situated.

I figured this woman must work for the Coventry base of Leon's employer. So I picked up the phone and nervously dialled the number for the Coventry branch, not sure what I was doing really, but too stressed to give a damn. A lady answered the phone, stating the firm's name and asking how she could help. My heart leapt into my mouth. Was this the woman, I wondered? Then I steadied myself with the thought that, even if it was, she was the one who should be nervous, not me.

'Yes, you may help me actually, I would like to speak to the lady who is seeing Leon McCabe.'

'Right,' she replied with a hint of surprise, 'I'll just try to connect you.' She didn't dismiss me or ask what I was talking about, so maybe I was on to something, I thought mischievously.

Then another lady answered and I asked her the same thing. She asked who I was. 'It's his wife!' I replied, almost smug in the fact that the whole of the office would know what was going on and they were all in a panic wondering whether to put the call through or not.

I spoke to three different ladies and knew they were just buying time because his mistress would be trying to get her explanation together. Finally, another lady answered, and I put forward my request again. When this lady spoke, I had a gut feeling it was her. She replied quite flatly, 'Yes, it's me.'

There was a moment of awkward silence as I wondered how to deal with this woman. Then I continued, 'Did you know he was married with two young babies?'

'Yes,' she answered.

Yes! I couldn't believe she'd admitted it. I suppose I was half expecting her to deny it, because if it had been me I would have felt thoroughly ashamed of myself, and even more so to admit it. Stuck for words, I decided to cut to the chase.

'What is your name?' I asked her, feeling that I had the right to know after what she had done to wreck my life even more.

'Cheryl' she responded.

'Will you meet me, please?' I asked. I was aware that Leon would be up and about any minute and I didn't want him to know that I was making plans to meet his mistress because he would no doubt have found a way to stop me. Surprisingly, she agreed to meet me.

The only landmark I could think of suggesting for a meeting place was a local museum. We arranged to meet there at one o'clock. She told me she would be in a white escort with a CB aerial on the top – another revelation that put another bit of the jigsaw into place. Leon had bought a CB radio a couple of months ago, telling me it was useful for getting traffic tip-offs from other drivers. Even then, I had subconsciously sensed there was more to it than that.

That morning, Leon was at my beck and call and for once I could call the shots, so I was going to take full advantage of it. I told him I was popping to the shop, and I left the children with him for a change while I walked out and left him in limbo. Of course, I had no intention of going to the shop, I was going to Mandy's for a makeover. I wasn't going to meet his mistress looking all dowdy.

She had been the seductress over the last God knows how many months, there for my husband's pleasure, always one step in front of me as she knew there was a wife involved. Whereas I had been unaware of the situation, swamped with screaming babies, changing nappies, washing, ironing and housework, totally oblivious to the reality of the situation, and probably just looking worn out half the time.

At least I knew I could scrub up exceptionally well when I made the effort. I wanted her to see his wife, and not in the light Leon had probably painted me. So, I headed to the girl who had style: Mandy.

Although Mandy was Leon's sister, she had always been very supportive of me. In fact, I don't know what I would have done without her. She was not manipulative like the others. She always tried to help me as much as she could but still maintained a friendship with her brother. This was good for me, because I didn't want people to start disliking Leon and I knew I could offload my worries on to her and there wouldn't be any comebacks.

She offered to come with me as a support, for which I was truly grateful. When I got to her house, we looked though her wardrobe and came up with an outfit that was very smart and with a hint of glamour. It was certainly not the kind of thing I would wear for every day, but Cheryl, Leon's mistress, wasn't to know that, was she? Some people may have thought I was mad to want to meet her, but I felt as if I was going crazy with all the lies and deceit around me. At least if we met, she would be able to fill me in on the missing pieces of the puzzle.

Mandy and I waited by the museum, mesmerised as every white car came onto the horizon. Eventually, an old white escort came past with a CB aerial prominent on its roof. My stomach was doing somersaults. As Cheryl got out of the car, I took in how she looked. She was a similar build to me, but where I was blonde and fair skinned, she was a brunette. We nervously made our way into the pub and Mandy made polite conversation with her.

It turned out that Leon didn't treat her anything like the way he treated me. She filled me in on the whole affair; how it had started the very morning I had suspected he had another woman when he was late back from work; how he had pursued her endlessly, waiting outside work for her and paying her compliments.

He had given her the clichéd story of the wife who didn't understand him. One thing that made me quite angry was when she showed me a note he had left her while he was at her house and she was at work. It read something like, 'Can't wait to see you tonight. I have bought us a nice bottle of wine.' This was hypocritical considering he didn't like me to drink. He always said women drinking round him reminded him of the drunken slags who would dance round him in bars, making utter fools of themselves, when he worked abroad.

Now here he was telling this woman he had bought her alcohol – charming! Also, I found out that she was only twenty-seven – a few years younger than Leon had told me. Knowing Leon like I did, I knew it was to make it sound as if he had pulled a mature woman of experience – just another cruel way to dig the knife in.

There were many facts I found out about my husband from Cheryl, and he certainly didn't sound like the man that I was married to. When I filled her in a little about what he was really like, she was absolutely shocked. I can't be sure if she thought that I was just the jealous wife, trying to put a wedge between them, or if she felt that I was genuine. That was frustrating, really, because I wanted her – especially her – to know what a bully he really was. I told her that if she wanted him she was welcome to him. I meant it, too. After what they had done together behind my back, I certainly didn't want him any more. She was tempted by the rotten fruit and as far as I was concerned, she would be doing me a favour by taking him off my hands. Obviously, she wasn't quite so keen once I had spoken with her.

In order to confront him, I asked her to come back to our local park with me, where I intended to set Leon up. The plan was to get him to meet me in the park. I hoped he would turn up thinking I was alone, only to be confronted by his wife *and* his mistress. Then I planned to humiliate her and show him up for the liar he was by asking him to choose. Because one thing was certain, I knew he would choose me.

However, when Leon approached the park to meet me and saw us both, the coward turned on his heels and ran off the other way. Maybe the meeting of the two separate worlds and the two different characters inside him would have made him explode.

Smug is a very good way to describe how I felt. I thought I had all the ammunition I needed to get the worm out of my life. What I didn't bank on though was that he would grind me down again until I had no choice but to let him back in. That evening, I told him to leave and that I didn't want to be with him any more, but he refused to go. What could I do? I couldn't throw him out physically. The anger I felt inside was immense. How dare he? He went off and had an affair and, just as I predicted, he got bored and wanted to continue playing happy families.

The sheer anger inside me pushed me to fight my corner. Unlike Leon, I had two demanding babies to look after, plus his interfering parents to contend with. It didn't matter that I was within my rights in not wanting to be with him, I knew that it wasn't going to be easy. Even his parents would see it as poor Leon losing his house.

When he went out, I tried locking the back door, but he just kicked it in. This caused great upset to the children, so I called the police, but he told them to get out of the house because it was his house and there was nothing they could do. Because this time he hadn't actually hit me, they didn't seem to have a leg to stand on, so they left me to it. Sticking to my guns, I kept reiterating that I wasn't going to have him back so it was best that he should leave.

Leon refused to leave, he said it was his house and he was going nowhere. He told me if I didn't take him back I would regret it.

'Do your worst,' I said through gritted teeth, because nothing was going to change my mind. So, he marched upstairs and pulled all my clothes out of the wardrobe. Then he got the scissors and started cutting them up and ripping them. Being stubborn and knowing I couldn't get the better of him physically, I stood there watching, but I made sure that the expression on my face was one of indifference.

He could tear all my clothes up but I wasn't going to have him back. It was quite ironic, because usually in these types of situations it's the person who's had the affair who gets their clothing cut up, not the person who's been cheated on. When he had finished with my clothes, he got my make-up bag and filled the sink with water and threw the entire contents in it. He even broke every prong on my afro-comb. There was literally nothing left that belonged to me by the time he had finished, apart from the clothes I was wearing. Still, I stood my ground and told him that there was no way I would have him back. Then he marched out in a mood.

He hadn't been gone long when there was a knock on the door and I found a strange woman standing there. She looked me up and down and said, 'Excuse me, dear, help a fellow woman out, and buy a tablecloth off me.'

She was a Romani traveller, and I just looked at her and laughed slightly, 'I haven't got a stitch of clothing apart from what I have on my back right now, so a tablecloth is the last thing I'm going to want to buy, sorry.' It was totally out of character for me to be so sarcastic with anyone, but I felt triumphant in a way that I had risen above all the chaos Leon had created for me and still stuck to my guns. I felt indestructible. The lady walked away slowly, giving me a bit of a frown. I thought that perhaps I'd upset her for not buying one of her tablecloths, but it didn't matter in that moment as everything was crumbling around me. After all the heartache, Leon had repeatedly bulldozed his way back into my home and my life and I couldn't see an end to it.

The pride I felt in myself gradually faded as Leon continued to put pressure on me to take him back. Mentally exhausted and desperate for peace, I knew I could not win this battle. Under pressure, I took him back and tried to sweep it under the carpet. I hadn't got the strength to keep fighting.

New Home, New Start

Leon found a continental job driving for a local company that delivered to France. The money was really good and it had the saving grace that Leon was away from home for many days at a time. That was a positive, because as we saw very little of each other, we were getting on better. It took the heat off me with keeping the house to Leon's liking, and it meant that the children and I could be more relaxed. Before he was due home, I would have plenty of notice to get the house looking immaculate. Also, because the money was really good, it meant we could afford to move to a better home. We put our little terrace on the market and it sold quickly – and all its bad memories with it.

Things seemed to be looking up. Leon was socialising with men who also had young families and it was rubbing off on him to be the provider and the family man. The violence even stopped for a while, although I was still under the control of him and his family. However, the fact that it was often me alone with the children meant our lives really improved. I could deal with Leon and his family on the odd occasions that they were all at the house.

Our beautiful new home was in a better area and about ten miles away from Leon's family. It was a big, three-bedroom, detached house on the end of a quiet suburban cul-de-sac. We even had a nice new car. The children got settled in a lovely school that could be reached by walking along the canal each day. It was idyllic, and I thought happily that maybe the hard times were finally over.

Not long after we moved, Leon said that he wanted me to go back to the social security office and tell them that he had left me again. I couldn't believe what he was asking of me. How greedy of him. He was on a really good wage and I simply didn't want to live that way – the way his parents had taught him to be. There was no need for us to do it, and I told him it was pure greed.

Leon did not like me having an opinion and he went mad. 'It's okay for you,' he shouted, 'you're not the one who has to go out to work. We can't afford this mortgage and we are going to end up losing this house. All because of you and your fucking morals. Is that what you want?'

I tried to argue my point that it was committing fraud and was too risky, and I didn't want to live constantly looking over my shoulder. As usual, he turned it all round on me again. He got very aggressive and started smashing things up.

'Look at the pressure you're putting me under, Stacey. Why don't you just do as I ask? There's no need for any of this.' In the end, I relented for a quiet life. I felt as if I had no choice. I was frightened he was going to hit me, and he was scaring the children, so I agreed to go up the next day and sort it out. He always managed to wear me down into submission.

Of course, to add to the pressure, when his parents came round that evening they agreed that it was a very good idea, once again making me look as if I was just being plain awkward. In fact, I did have to question myself, was I just plain awkward? Because it seemed the majority of things they deemed okay, I silently disagreed with.

Social security started paying the mortgage and Leon was fitting the image he had always desired, driving round in a brand-new car and living in a big house. However, our quality of life was not good. I was constantly trying to broach the subject with Leon that I was paranoid about what we were doing. After all, I used to go the local post office with the social security book to cash the money, and people knew Leon was working and had a nice house and car; it wouldn't have taken much for them to put two and two together.

Every time I complained, he ended up getting violent, so I learnt to keep my worries to myself and just muddle on. I felt so ashamed when I was in the company of my father or other members of my family. What would they think if they knew what I was doing?

It was hard to keep up with the Joneses, and Leon wanted the best of everything. And he had his ways, through me. Leon and I didn't go out much as a family. There was the odd Sunday after lunch when we would go for a walk in the country with the children. I thoroughly enjoyed these walks, as they seemed like good family time. The children were in their element because Mummy and Dad were happy together. It was too much to expect things to keep running smoothly though, and bit by bit, the violence began to creep back in. Everything seemed to be on my shoulders.

When Leon was in bed in the morning, and I was downstairs, he would stamp on the floorboards as a signal to me that he had woken up and I had to go up to him. When I did, it was always to order me to bring up his cigarettes and lighter, and a coffee. I hated him stamping on the floor like that.

Reece was quite hyperactive, and Sophie seemed to wind him up with everything she did. They were always arguing and fighting, and it really got me down. By the same token, I was quite soft with them really because I felt such a lot of guilt that I had let them down. Very often, if they weren't at school and Leon was at home, they would be made to sit in front of a movie all day long. This was so that Leon could take me into the kitchen to interrogate and bully me over whatever random thing he had decided that day had annoyed him.

Leon wanted me to have another baby. He'd often said he wanted 'a football team of boys' but the naivety of youth had been erased by the reality of being a parent, and no matter how nice he was at times, I was never seduced into his idyllic fantasy. I made damn sure I kept taking my pill; there was no way I was bringing any more children into this.

When I knew he was going to start, my first concern was for the children. I didn't want them being exposed to it. So I would always say, 'Let me just put a cartoon on for the kids then we can go in the kitchen and talk.'

In other words, I was pleading, 'Please let me protect the children from your aggressive behaviour and get their minds on to something else, then I am free for you to pick on and bully at your leisure.' That's how it felt to me anyway.

I will always remember being in the kitchen and Leon going on and on at me, asking me questions. I can't actually remember what the questions were about now, but no doubt he had made something trivial I had done into a big deal. He would be up in my face, spitting and demanding answers, shouting, pulling my hair, and angrily banging my head on the kitchen cupboards.

All I can remember is seeing the twisted expression on his face, and not really being sure what answer to give him. Sometimes I would smirk due to nerves, even giggle, and this antagonised him even more, but sadly I couldn't help myself. Because I was frightened to death of him, I used to pray inside that it would hurry up and be over. Tears would fall involuntarily as I tried to maintain a normal expression, and this used to get him even angrier. He often demanded that I stopped crying and feeling sorry for myself, but I really couldn't help it.

Everything was a trick question. Everything I answered was something that would give him the excuse to hit me. I would attempt to cook the kids' tea, but he wouldn't stop badgering me. For instance, I would have potatoes on the boil because the children had just come back from school, and he would grab the boiling pan and fling it into the sink, potatoes and all, and shout at me to pay attention, when all I wanted to do was just be a mum to my kids and make their tea.

Often there would be a knock on the kitchen door and their little voices would say, 'Mummy, can we come in?' I'd ask Leon to give me a second to sort the children out, then I'd peer through the door, forcing a smile, and tell them to go and sit down in front of yet another movie, reassuring them and hoping that I wouldn't be much longer. Although I always was longer, because I had no control over the situation and couldn't say to Leon that I had had enough and I wanted to be with the children.

Then there was the fact that, as nasty as he could be, he could be just as nice. He seemed to have a split personality, a Doctor Jekyll and Mr Hyde. The nice side of him used to come out in front of his family and friends. I used to think that Leon was in easy-going mode when this happened, because he would act so laid back in front of people. Sometimes, for example, I would study him when he was in the company of his friends, and he would talk so quietly, and come across as gentle and articulate. It would make me so angry inside to think how he had treated me the night before. I used to wonder what his friends would make of it if they saw a video of what he had put me and the children through the evening before.

He was so false and everybody seemed to fall for it, apart from my family, that is. Possibly they could sense my unease and tension when he was about. He used to think he knew it all too, and he would capture people in one of his conversations and nobody else could get a word in.

He wasn't the sort of man who would just settle for beans and toast for tea either. Everything had to be the best for him, as long as I was the one delivering. One day, I had spent ages preparing and cooking a lovely curry. The children were watching television, and everything seemed nice and comfortable. When we all eventually sat at the table, I brought the food in. We were all eating away and Leon was in one of his moods, for whatever reason. I don't know what I said to him, but something made him flip. All of a sudden, he just stood up, shouting, and pushed the bottom of the table in temper, flipping it up into the air and onto the floor.

The poor children just sat there petrified and wide eyed. Thankfully, they had moved out of the way just in time.

All the food, drinks and crockery went all over the carpet and splashed up the walls. The children just stood there paralysed with fear as he went after me and I ran around the table. The absolute worst thing about these times of violence was the fact that the children were there. It used to make me feel so sick and helpless because I desperately wanted to protect them from it, yet I was absolutely powerless.

As he was chasing me round the table, which was now on its side on the floor, and the children were screaming, all I could think of was how to get him to calm down so that the children didn't have to see this. 'Okay, Leon, okay, please calm down and let me sort the children out. Please, then you can do what you want,' I shouted, confused and despairing of the whole madness of the situation.

He grabbed my hair and flung me spinning onto the floor. All the time I was trying to retain control and act calm because the children were witnessing this. As I tumbled over, I was still saying, 'Okay, please just stop for a minute.'

He loomed over me panting for breath and, desperately trying to play the situation down, I said to the children, 'It's okay, Mummy's okay, go upstairs and play in your rooms.' The children scuttled over to the chairs and Leon shouted, 'Now look what you have done, you stupid cow. Look at the state of the carpets, they are fucking ruined.'

I replied quietly, trying to remain civilised for the children's sake. 'Okay, Leon, it's not a problem, I will get a cloth and clean it up.'

Then he swung his foot at me trying to kick me back over as I crawled on all fours over to the plates and forks on the floor, trying to tidy them up. 'You fucking better hope these carpets don't stain,' he shouted.

I scrambled to my feet and into the kitchen to get a dishcloth to get working on the stains, before he had another excuse to hit me and upset the children.

All the time this was going on I was aware of myself muttering quietly to Leon over and over again, 'It's okay, it's no problem, I will get it sorted, you just calm down.' Then I got down on my hands and knees and began to scrub the floor, praying that the stains would come out of the carpet.

Inside, I wasn't calm at all. I was so angry and full of hatred. If I could have gained the strength of a super being, I would have taken him out of that room, after calming the children down, and beaten the shit out of him. The selfish bully, putting the children through all of this just because he was in a bad mood.

Back in the living room, I picked the table up and took all the items into the kitchen to be cleaned. I scrubbed the walls and the carpets, until it all looked spotless again, and all the time I just wanted to soothe my children. While I was washing up, he came into the kitchen and, as usual, turned the whole situation round and made it seem as if it was my fault. He said I gave him a funny look at the table and asked me why I always had to start.

From childhood onwards, I had developed a massive guilt complex. I worried about everything that happened and surmised that it was somehow my fault. My mother and my husband knew exactly how to tap into that and use it to their advantage. When you are constantly being criticised and put down, picked on and bullied, your perception of what is right and what is wrong becomes distorted.

I was so low within myself that I doubted my own mind and took notice of Leon, who seemed to be the one who was strong and logical. I wasn't functioning the same way as a person under fairly normal circumstances; my self-esteem had plummeted, and great stress was a regular occurrence, so I became very vulnerable.

Just to get through the day, keep the house tidy, and look after the children took so much effort, there wasn't no strength left in my mind to get my head straight and fight what was going on. An abuser is like an emotional parasite; they feast on all the strength you have to help them thrive, chipping away at your confidence until there is nothing left of you and you are totally reliant on them.

As he blamed me for the situation, I found myself apologising to Leon and he hugged me tightly and told me it was all okay now. Those little moments of displays of affection meant the world to me and kept me going on this strange merry-go-round. I would be so relieved he had calmed down and I could see to my children. I'd be so glad to get back in the living room with them and sit with them and try to talk to them about normal things, like what was on television or what they had done at school. Over time, this became more difficult because the longer I was in the marriage, the more I was cutting myself off from reality.

The majority of the time, I was in a trance-like state, functioning on autopilot. I used the coping strategies I had learnt as a child – to absorb the other person's anger in order to make them feel better, and to put myself second as long as the other person was happy – to deal with this abusive marriage. I continued to see my life as a series of hurdles I had to jump, and every incident I took the brunt of, I saw as another hurdle I had managed to overcome. The calm after the storm was my reward for my endurance.

Troublemaker

It was always difficult going to the post office to cash my social security, knowing that I was committing fraud. I was extremely paranoid about getting caught. Let's face it, we were a young family in a nice house, in a lovely area, driving round in a nice car. We hardly looked the stereotypical types to be claiming benefits. However, it was a no-go topic of discussion with Leon. It just made him lose his temper if I brought it up. Leon was very much an image conscious person. He had nice clothes, nice shoes, and was always groomed immaculately. The only thing I can remember having new was a dress for his friend's wedding. That was only because all the people going to the wedding were wealthy and he wanted us to fit in with them, making sure that I looked the part just as much as he did.

One Monday morning, we were going out somewhere and Leon insisted I put the dress on. I felt utterly ridiculous because the majority of the time I was just a jeans-and-trainers type of girl. I always felt self-conscious dressed up. The children were at school and we weren't doing anything special. Still, as usual, I did as I was told. If I always did as I was told, I figured I couldn't get the blame for anything, although it took me years to see that it was never that simple.

So we went to the post office that was in a little precinct of shops near where we lived. Pulling up in our car at the shops, Leon sat behind the wheel, as I tottered off awkwardly in my high heels and dress to cash the social security money. I felt awfully self-conscious, not to mention such a fake, and I couldn't wait to get back into the shelter of the waiting car.

There was a queue in the post office, and as I was waiting and the queue was moving very slowly, I was looking around at the sweets and magazines on display. I felt somebody looking at me, and I checked to see who it was. My eyes met the eyes of a woman about my age who was glaring at me angrily. Feeling embarrassed, I blushed and looked away quickly, wondering why she was staring at me like that. Did she know me? Had I done something to upset her?

Then I thought maybe I had made a mistake and misread things and she wasn't really staring at me. Maybe I was being overly paranoid. So, I thought I'd take another look just to check. Sheepishly, I turned around again and tried to take a sly look at her. Without a doubt this woman was scowling at me still, so I quickly turned away again. I could almost feel her eyes boring into the back of my head, sending a shiver down my spine

As I was cashing my money, I was panicking and making plans for how I was going to get out of the shop without passing her and having to see her again.

Unfortunately, the only way out of the post office was to walk right past her. *Right*, I thought to myself, *you can't let this woman intimidate you, Stacey, just walk past her as quickly as you can and don't look at her. It will only take two seconds then you'll be out of the door.* It was just another hurdle to jump. When the cashier had served me, I took a deep breath to pull myself together and made my way to the exit. However, as I passed the woman, she purposely elbowed me, slightly pushing me off balance. I knew that no matter how scared I felt I couldn't let her see my fear. So I shouted, 'What's your problem, ay?'

She shouted back, 'I'm not the one with the problem, you are!'

People were stopping what they were doing and staring at me and this woman. There was no way I was going to stand and have a slanging match in the local post office, so I marched out. At least I had made it clear that she couldn't get away with it, I tried to console myself.

Shaking like a leaf, I approached the car where Leon was sitting with the window open, music playing and his sunglasses on. I got in the car beside him and told him in disbelief about what had just happened, hoping that the man of steel would go back into the post office and deal with her. After all, I was sure he would be better than me verbally and it would have been nice to think he would stick up for me. He did no such thing though, he just sat there watching me get upset and didn't say a thing. All he was concerned about was that I was to go back into the shop for him and get him his favourite paper, the *Daily Sport*.

Not wanting him to sense that I felt totally intimidated, I got out of the car and went to fetch his paper. I was half expecting that nasty woman to appear again and say something, and I was relieved when she didn't. I quickly got what I needed from the shop so that I could head back to the safety of our car. Jumping back in the car, feeling glad that my mission was accomplished, I felt the relief wash over me. However, as soon as my bum settled in the passenger seat, Leon said to me, 'You, wait!'

'What?' I uttered in disbelief.

'You know why,' he answered, but I didn't. I started panicking, but I was slightly angry too that there was going to be trouble for me – yet again.

'What have I done?' I whined in confusion. I couldn't believe it when he told me that while I had been in the shop fetching his paper, the woman who had had a go at me in the post office had come over to the car where he was sitting and told him that I had been ogling her boyfriend.

'No way,' I shouted in disbelief, 'she didn't even have a boyfriend with her, in fact I never even noticed a bloke in there.'

'Well, that's funny,' Leon retorted, 'because he came over to the car with her and he didn't say anything, but she was having a go at him too.'

'But I didn't even see a man in the post office. What was he like?' I asked anxiously, convinced he was making it up.

'He had a black leather jacket on and black hair,' Leon replied.

Scanning my mind in a replay of my time in the post office, I thought back to who I had seen in there, and, very vaguely, I could remember a man standing slightly behind me in the queue with a black leather jacket on, but I certainly hadn't been looking at him.

Looking at another man indeed; more like I was feeling like an idiot being in the post office in a party dress cashing my social security cheque. I had felt uncomfortable being dressed up, looking as if I was going to a wedding when I was actually scrounging money. I'd got enough to cope with in my life dealing with Leon and his violent outbursts to have the capacity to think about admiring other men.

'Take me back to that post office now,' I yelled in anger as he began driving back home. Fury was bubbling up inside me. This woman had obviously seen me looking smart and concluded in her jealous little brain that I was giving her boyfriend the eye. The ironic thing about it was that my life was a living hell. I was being bullied day in day out by my husband, and this woman had just caused me to have yet another undeserved battle.

I was begging Leon to take me back to find this woman because I wanted to prove to him that I was not guilty of this pathetic accusation.

Frustrated, I shouted, 'Some husband you are, not sticking up for me. I bet that woman is laughing her head off at me now, thanks to you. Instead of doing the loyal thing and telling her to wait there until your wife comes out of the shop to speak for herself, you played right into her hands and let her think you believed her. If someone had come up to me and said the same thing about you I would have said, "Well, you wait there then until my husband comes back and we will see what he has to say about it!" How could you let me down like that, I'm your wife for God's sake, and you took a stranger's word over mine.'

Leon took me straight home and amazingly he didn't hit me either, so I think he knew I was telling the truth.

Nights Out

Leon had started to go out regularly on a Saturday night. These were the odd, rare times that I saw him in his easy-going, happy mode when there was just me and the children about. Typical Leon, as long as things were going his way, we were allowed to be happy.

He would come down the stairs dressed in his new clothes, looking very dapper – bearing a slight resemblance to an olive-skinned Peter Andre. His entire aura oozed vanity, but he did look very handsome and smart, and he knew it. The thing that used to annoy me about it was that I never had a night out, even though I would have loved one.

The only time I did go out with him, he ended up spoiling it by walking out of the club early and accusing me of not wanting to be with him. That was just because I went to have a dance with my friend, and I was not glued to his side.

I must admit that deep down, much as I thought I was in love with him, I secretly hoped he would meet someone else on one of those nights out and leave me for her. It was the only way I could see myself being free. Sadly, I knew that would end in tears for me because he'd only stay with a girl until the novelty wore off and then expect to come back to reliable old me.

On one occasion, he stayed out all night and I heard him sneaking in at about eight o'clock in the morning. The funny thing was that I actually felt happy about this. *Maybe he has slept with someone*, I hoped, because I expected that would lead to him eventually leaving me. He seemed very surprised when I came downstairs and didn't even question him about where he'd been. Merrily, I hummed my way into the kitchen to make him a cup of coffee. When I took it in to him, he made up some feeble excuse that he had stayed over at his friend's.

It was obviously a lie, but because I wanted to encourage him to do this more often, I acted like the gullible wife I very often was and told him to get himself to bed for some rest. Although I should have known better. Leon would never have left me and the children and that house for anyone else when he could have his cake and eat it.

My sister Hannah suggested that if Leon was going out regularly, I should have a night out too. She told me she was going to the Tower Ballroom in Birmingham with a group of friends and asked if I'd go with them. Typically, I told her I would have to check with Leon, and to my surprise he reluctantly said I could go. But then again, how could he say no when he was out every weekend?

The plan was that he would have his night out on the upcoming weekend, and then he would have the children for me the following Saturday evening so that I could go out with my sister and her friends.

It was all well and good on Leon's night out, as he got dressed up as usual to go out with his mates. In a way, I didn't resent him going out because I thought that at least he was playing fair and letting me have a night out too. Once he had had his night out though, his mood changed. By the Friday before I was due my night out, he had a truly miserable look on his face.

My night out approached and I was happy, although I tried to act fed up in case he suspected I was looking forward to it and got jealous and stopped me going. This would be my first night out in years and I couldn't wait. The nearest I got to a nightclub was putting on Radio One on a Saturday evening and listening to the dance charts. On my own in the living room, I would dance my legs away. Now it was really going to happen for me, and I couldn't wait.

In the week leading up to my night out, I had a recurring dream. It was the evening of the big event and I needed to call my sister to make sure she could come and pick me up. In the dream, I would dial her number, but annoyingly I kept punching in the wrong digits, so I would spend endless hours trying to phone her and not get through. In my dream, I panicked because the hours were passing and, in the end, I missed the night out – all because I couldn't dial the number correctly.

I suppose that was quite metaphorical of my situation in real life because I was dying to have a good night out, but it always seemed impossible for me.

Then Leon made my dreams come true, but not in the way a girl dreams of her love doing. The evening before my night out, I was putting the washing away in the bedroom when he came upstairs to me. He was in an evil mood and began throwing accusations at me. 'You only want to go out clubbing so that you can go off shagging!'

Astounded, I turned to look at him with a feeling of dread; this was an absolutely ridiculous accusation. I tried to tell him not to kick off but he started pushing me and getting in my face. 'You just want to meet someone else, you fucking fat-arsed, ugly slag. Who would want you? You're a goofy-toothed bitch with a fat fucking arse,' he yelled.

'Please keep your voice down, Leon, the kids will hear you. I don't want to meet someone else. I just want a night out with my sister,' I replied, tears brimming in my eyes, knowing his intentions were to put an end to my plans.

'You're not fucking going, so you can forget it, and don't start fucking crying,' he shouted. His angry words cut into me deeply, making me feel worthless and ugly. Here I was, again being stopped from having a life of my own. I knew it was no use arguing with him. In fact, if I had tried to argue he most certainly would have concluded that I was desperate to go out, which would have made him even more jealous, so it wasn't worth me even trying. Foolishly, I thought that if I didn't make a fuss that maybe he might change his mind and let me go – but of course he didn't.

Stomping on my plans wasn't enough for him, he wanted me to pretend to be okay with it, so he tried to creep round me and was trying to kiss me. Of course, I was really angry and tried to ignore him. He pushed me on the bed, kissing me. I didn't want to respond but found that I was responding for fear of making him angry again. Then he started tugging my clothes off and I panicked, because I didn't want to have sex.

He must have sensed me getting tense and he shoved me off the bed, saying, 'What the fuck's the matter with you now? Don't you want to have sex with me?'

Of course, he knew I didn't want to have sex with him, but he continued ferreting away until he had pushed himself inside me. I just lay there looking at the ceiling, hating every thrust, tears falling down the side of my face, which I discreetly tried to wipe away before he saw them. When I cried it only fuelled his rage and I feared he would think I pitied myself again. As soon as he had finished with me, he tried to be tender, stroking my head and telling me he was sorry for the way he had been. He said he loved me so much he couldn't stand the thought of me going out without him in case somebody chatted me up. He said it wasn't me he didn't trust – it was other men.

The only reason I was coping with my life now was because Leon was working away from home most of the week. The time alone was great, but when he came back and started arguments, he always stood by his motto of 'never go to sleep on an argument' – his excuse to have sex no matter what he had done to me. He always managed to somehow get me to be okay with him before he went off to work again and gave me those few sweet days of peace and normality on my own.

When he was gone, I would fantasise that he had left me and the children and the house was just ours. It would have been the ideal situation for us had he left permanently. I stayed because it was easier. I could not face all the upheaval to me and the children of moving somewhere else. Plus, he had control of the money, and he frequently made a point of telling me that there was no way I would ever manage on my own financially with the children.

Leon's Fantasy

Things had become too comfortable for Leon the way they were, and thanks to his father's influence, he began having more and more time off work claiming he was sick again. Unfortunately for me, this meant he was round me all the time. Our sex life wasn't normal, although at the time I didn't realise it because I hadn't known any different. I could never say no to Leon when he wanted sex, or when he wanted a sexual 'favour' performed. Because I was so naive, he convinced me when I was young, that if he got an erection, it was excruciatingly painful for him until it was relieved, and it was my duty as his wife to relieve him whenever he had one, so I could not say no – there was never a choice in the matter. It was awful, because he had an extremely high sex drive.

As I was so busy looking after the children, and jumping to Leon's orders, plus trying to keep the house in show-home condition, sex was the last thing on my mind. Any attempt to complain that he was getting too demanding would always end up in a big argument, and he would conclude that I was not affectionate. The main arguments we had were because in his eyes I was not loving; but the truth was that I was too tired for sex or not in the mood because he had been picking on me. Even if I had lived the life of a lady of leisure and had a cook and a cleaner, I still don't think my sex drive would ever have matched Leon's.

When I wanted to go to bed at night, I would have to ask Leon's permission because he liked me to stay up with him. Whenever I slept, I felt more comfortable turning my back to him and lying in the foetal position. Leon didn't like this and would nudge me to stroke him to sleep. I used to have to gently stroke his skin until he nodded off – even if my wrists were aching and tired. Or he would snuggle up to my back whether I liked it or not, and push himself into me. I would just lie there and wait until he had finished. It wasn't worth me saying that I didn't want to have sex with him because my feelings didn't matter, and he would have turned it round and made it seem as if I was being awkward.

When he was working abroad, he would regularly come back with hardcore pornography that wasn't available in the UK. I didn't have a problem with it as I was always immersed in housework and caring for the kids. However, it was starting to have an effect on our sex life. Leon thought our sex life was too mundane and began pestering me to do things I considered were not the norm and were often very painful for me. Two of the things he had become fixated with were anal sex and our having a threesome with another woman. I thought it was okay for him to fantasise about both these things, but actually doing them was quite another thing.

However, the other woman fantasy became an obsession with him. Every time we had sex, he brought it up. He would keep on and on at me about how it would bring us closer, because we would be being totally open with each other. I felt like saying, 'Well, would you be as willing if we had a threesome with another man?' But I never dared to utter this in sarcasm, as I knew better than to antagonise him. If he had any inclination that I was interested in another man, which I wasn't, he would probably have hit me, although it would have been clear to anyone that I would only have said it to him to point out how selfish his suggestion was.

He would go to sex shops and purchase magazines. He was constantly pressuring me about copying what he read, and I thought that if I played along with him a little bit, looking at these magazines, maybe eventually he would tire of the idea and go on to something else. When I gave in to him, Leon became nicer towards me and so at least I got something out of it all. If there was any way I could find to get my husband to treat me nicely, I would do it. Otherwise, life was intolerable when he was around. As time went on, it wasn't enough for Leon to fantasise about it, he wanted the real thing. This started to get me down; I didn't want to take things that far.

One evening, I was lounging on the settee trying to watch *Coronation Street* and he was sitting at the dining room table reading one of his magazines. I was trying to relax and enjoy the soap, but every so often in the background, Leon would shout over to me, 'Stacey, come over here, come and look at this woman. What do you think of her?' This was so annoying because I thought I had given him enough of a hint that looking at women for threesomes was the last thing I wanted.

Leon was like a dog with a bone. 'Stacey, are you interested or not?' he shouted over.

Quite plainly I wasn't, but I knew better than to tell him that. So, I'd trot over to the table to him and have a look at the advert, pretending to be interested. He would point out a lady and I would say something like, 'Oh no, I don't like the look of her, she looks rough.' Or any excuse I could come up with.

In the end his patience wore thin with me and he started to get angry. 'Why have you got to go and fucking spoil things, you miserable bitch? Do you want to cause arguments again? What's wrong with us having some fun? You always have to go and wreck things, don't you?'

'It's not that,' I replied. Inside, I was thinking that this situation was getting out of hand, so I decided it was best to be up front and suffer the consequences. 'It's just that, it's okay as a fantasy but I don't really want to bring another woman into our sex life. I just don't feel comfortable with it.'

That was like a red rag to a bull and he started to smash the room up and go mad at me. 'You know you're fucking trouble, don't you? You're fucking frigid, you are. Any other woman would do what their husband wanted to spice up their sex life, but no, not you. You've got to be boring and ruin things, haven't you?'

Scared that he was going to wake the children up, I told him what I thought would calm him down and pacify him. 'Look, Leon, I'm sorry, I am just tired tonight. I am not ruling out the idea, just give me a bit of time to get my head round it.' That was enough to calm him down. Then he asked me to get him a coffee and instead of leaving it alone he followed me into the kitchen, as I prepared his drink, with the magazine in his hand, still making suggestions. It was as if he'd dismissed everything I had just said about how I felt, and he was behaving as if I was all for it too.

This whole warped desire of his had been taking over my life. While he was keen on the idea to the point of obsession, I was frantically worrying how I was going to put a stop to the situation escalating into reality. I even wrote a letter to a problem page, but I purposely left it in an unsealed envelope as if I intended to post it, knowing Leon would find it in the kitchen drawer and read it. The contents of the letter to the agony aunt were along the lines of 'my husband is pressuring me into a threesome'. I went on to say how the only time he seemed happy and treated me okay was when I gave him the impression there was a possibility I would go through with it. Then when I opened up to him that I really did not want to do it, he got angry.

I wanted Leon to see how stifled I felt by his demands, and I hoped he wouldn't push me into it any more. If Leon did read the letter – and he more than likely did – he never mentioned it. He just carried on talking about it.

It had been a couple of weeks since he had last mentioned the idea, and I was getting ready to go and pick up the children from school, when he started talking about threesomes again. Because the children weren't there, I thought it was a good opportunity to try and tell him again that I just couldn't go through with it. That way, if he didn't like what I was saying and lost his temper, the children wouldn't be witness to it.

He was sitting on the chair, avidly flicking through a magazine, when I knelt down in front of him. 'Leon,' I said nervously, 'we really need to talk,' gently putting my hands on his knees and looking him straight in the eyes. 'The thing is…'

Leon knew me so well that before I could go any further, he said through gritted teeth, 'I hope to fucking God you're not moaning about this threesome again.' I knew I had to remain firm because it was only a matter of time before he arranged things to act out his fantasy and I could not go through with it – it was not who I was and it did not interest me at all.

'Leon, please,' I implored, 'I love you and I just can't bear the thought of sharing you with another woman.'

Never mind the fact that I simply did not want to do it.

His eyes were wide with anger and he leaned back on the chair, and pulled his knees up tucking them into his chest. It all happened so quickly. He kicked out and catapulted me backwards onto the floor. As I fell back, he looked at me in disgust, 'Look at you,' he said through gritted teeth, 'you make me fucking sick. We sort things out, get on okay and then you start causing trouble again. What's the fucking matter with you, you frigid bitch? Why do you have to be so boring?'

Pulling myself off the floor, I knelt up again in front of him. I needed him to know how desperate I was. Inside, I was hoping that his conscience would get the better of him and he would realise that he was being totally unreasonable. I was crying now in desperation, pleading to his better nature. 'Please, please, Leon, I just can't go through with it. I am sorry if I let you down, but I just can't.'

His eyes were sticking out in fury, almost as if they were on stalks, and I knew he was going to hit me.

'Okay, calm down,' I pleaded. 'Forget I said anything, please.' Then I realised it was time to go and fetch the children from school, so I managed to plaster over things again and tell him I would probably do it, given time.

Getting in the car, I looked in the mirror and realised that my face was red from crying. It was a common for me to collect the children from school looking as if I had been sobbing. I was immune to the stares of the other parents because I always had so much on my mind.

When I arrived home with the children, Leon was surprisingly very happy.

'Hello, kids,' he said, with a big smile on his face.

I went into the kitchen to do the kids' tea. An hour or so later, the children were settled and watching television and Leon piped up that he was off to the gym for a couple of hours. When he left the house I sat on the sofa and kept going over things in my head. There was no way he was going to let up on this threesome idea. I was so depressed and there seemed no way out. I actually contemplated suicide. But I couldn't ever consider it seriously because I worried about what would become of the children if I killed myself, and how my family would feel. I truly felt terribly trapped. There was no one I could talk to, and nowhere for me to go because I relied on Leon for money. Plus I was so worn out with worry, conjuring up the energy or brainpower to plan to leave was way beyond my capabilities.

The children sat there contentedly, but inside I was screaming. I couldn't take any more of the mental torment. Then an idea entered my head; there was a way of escaping this life without killing myself. I leapt up and went into the kitchen, grabbed the big bottle of vodka sitting on a shelf and poured myself a large glass. Drinking one glass after another, I quickly became totally intoxicated. Then I managed to drag myself into the living room and plonk myself back on the settee. The room was spinning round and round and all my troubles had merged into a big blur.

Looking back, I remember a feeling of shame washing over me as the children kept coming up to me and asking me what was the matter. The guilt combined with the vodka made me retch, and I sat there being sick all over myself. I could barely move other than to heave and be sick. Then I remember the door opening and Leon walking in. I half expected him to hit me and go mad, but he just stood there laughing. 'Look at the state of you, bloody hell, Stacey,' he chuckled.

'Come on,' he said, picking my limp drunken body up in his big strong arms. I could hear him muttering to himself as he was carrying me up the stairs. I think it was the only time in my marriage I had ever known him to take care of me. He stood me in the bath and switched the shower on. He was trying to strip off my clothes, but I was so drunk I couldn't even stand up straight. He got my clothes off and began to shampoo my hair. 'Come on you,' he said affectionately, pulling me out of the bath and wrapping a big towel around me.

Once again, he took me in his arms and carried me into the bedroom. I remember him throwing me on the bed and fidgeting about trying to pull the quilt back. He was drying me off with the towel and all the time he seemed amused by my paralytic state. Then he grabbed me and manoeuvred me onto my stomach. I had not got an ounce of energy in me and I just lay there drifting into a dizzy sleep.

Then all of a sudden, I felt him climb on top of me. The weight of him was stifling me and I couldn't breathe. I tried to move, but I couldn't. Then I felt a stabbing pain in my back passage. I tried to scream but my head was pressing into the pillow and it came out as a muffled cry. I felt as if I was suffocating, and the pain was like nothing I had experienced before, even with the anaesthetic of intoxication shielding my body from the full force of it. I tried to struggle, but he was too heavy, I could not move. He did what he had to do then he got off me and left me to go to sleep.

The next morning, I woke up and lay there, shocked at Leon's appalling behaviour – this was terrible, even for him. I confronted him about what he had done. As always, he turned it around on me and made it about how disgusting I was for getting that drunk in charge of the children. To a degree he was right, I should not have got so drunk around my children. I deeply regretted that and felt sorry for them being left with their own mum doing that. I should have been caring for them, as the responsible adult, but reflecting on how the pressure had ramped up in my head, and how badly I needed to escape from the situation I found myself in, I knew I had to cut myself some slack or I would have gone mad.

Suffer Little Children

When Sophie was about two and a half, we were hit by a virus that turned into tonsillitis and she and I were both terribly ill. When babies are ill, they become incredibly clingy and Sophie only seemed to get comfort from my hugs and love. This particular night, when bedtime came, the poor little mite was crying and reaching out for me not to leave her. Being so ill myself, I knew that if I slept in the single bed with her, it would get too hot. So, understandably, I asked Leon if there was any chance that he could sleep in Sophie's bed just this once, then she and I could share the double bed and have more room.

'You must be joking,' he replied, and that was that. I was surprised he actually allowed me to sleep with Sophie though.

In her sleep, she kept snuggling up to me and as much as I wanted to have her close to me, I tried to keep some distance between us as we both had temperatures. It was so uncomfortable. Eventually, I drifted into a distracted sleep and was woken by strange murmurings coming from my little girl. Crooking myself up on my elbow, I gently asked her what the matter was, but she wasn't making any sense. When I felt her forehead she was burning up really badly. Switching the light on, I picked her up to go and get her a drink to try and cool her down. That's when I saw that she was a very odd colour.

She was deathly white, with red blotches covering her cheeks. Immediately, I took her into the bathroom where it was lighter and tried to get a better look at her. She seemed totally oblivious to my presence and was staring vacantly at the ceiling, rambling on about gobbledygook. Panicking, I began to shout for Leon because now I feared the worst – meningitis. He sprang out of bed, took one look at her and told me to call an ambulance. Running downstairs, I grabbed the phone and dialled the emergency services. As I was talking to them on the phone Leon began shouting, 'Tell them to hurry! She's stopped breathing!'

Panic surged through me and I threw the phone to the floor to get to my baby. Leon was wrong – she was still breathing. Before I had a moment more to think about it, there was a knock on the door and two paramedics rushed in.

Sophie was in my arms and they saw she was still breathing. One of the drivers seemed extremely annoyed, as he had obviously been under the impression that it was a life or death situation and raced to us to find it wasn't quite so bad.

He asked, 'Who said she had stopped breathing?'

Leon didn't answer and rather than ignore the paramedic I feebly told him that 'we' thought she had. Leon had obviously been exaggerating.

The paramedics said it looked as if she was having a febrile convulsion, so they were going to take her to the hospital to get her checked over. Leon went in the ambulance with her and I stayed at home to look after Reece. Eventually, he called me from the hospital to tell me that she was okay.

It turned out that because she was very young, her body didn't have the ability to sweat like adults do, therefore she had grown hotter and hotter with no way of releasing the heat. Being in bed so close to me had not helped. Then, because her body couldn't cope with her temperature any more, she had a febrile convulsion, a type of fit, just as the paramedics had said. The hospital staff had managed to cool her down and get her comfortable, and Leon was going to stay there overnight with her. Relief washed over me that she was going to be okay, but I couldn't thinking that if Leon had let us have the big bed, this might not have happened.

The next day, he returned from the hospital for some breakfast and a sleep because apparently the mattress the hospital provided for parents wasn't very comfortable.

'You'll have to stay with her tonight,' he ordered. We went back to the hospital once Leon had freshened up. Our little girl was fast asleep and looked quite comfortable. I still felt incredibly ill with tonsillitis and I knew that I shouldn't have been on the children's ward, with all these sick children round me, because I was actually contagious, but I had no choice. Leon went after about an hour and I sat by Sophie's bed talking to her and trying to get her to drink. My throat was so swollen I could barely talk myself.

Night came and I got the hospital mattress out to lay it on the floor. I couldn't wait to sleep because when I was sleeping I couldn't feel the discomfort, and I knew I was healing. The nurses gave me a thin blanket to put over me and I tried to get comfortable. It wasn't easy being so close to the floor, with staff walking up and down all night and me feeling so ill. The next thing I knew it was light and I woke up absolutely drenched with sweat. My head and throat were killing me, and I felt so weak and ill. Sitting up, my wet hair was stuck to my head and I tried to scramble to the bathroom before anyone could see the mess I was in. My clothes were clinging to me as if someone had put me in the shower with them on. When I looked at myself in the mirror, I was red in the face and there was dry skin all round my cracked lips where I had dehydrated so badly. I knew I needed to get home; I did not have the energy to get showered or changed. What energy I had, I used to get to the phone.

The phone rang for ages. When Leon finally answered it, I could barely talk because my glands were so inflamed. 'Leon, you are going to have to come and get me, I am in a right state. I'm drenched through, and I really need to come home now, please.'

'I can't come now I have hardly had any sleep myself; you'll have to give me a couple of hours at least,' he said.

A couple of hours! Wearily, I made my way back to the shower and freshened myself up as best as I could. Then I sat in a chair and waited, and waited and waited. Eventually, he turned up looking as fresh as a daisy. He told me to go home and sort myself out while he waited with Sophie but said that I would have to stay there with her again that night. My life felt like a trial of being constantly pushed to the limit, but it wasn't in me to rebel. I was too weak and too conditioned.

Finally, Sophie got over the worst of the virus and was allowed to come home. I started to pick up too. Some weeks later, while Leon was working away, the phone bill arrived. Out of curiosity, I began analysing the numbers, and then I noticed a bunch of strange numbers. Worse still, they were all numbers that had been called the nights I had been staying in the hospital with Sophie. Something told me to check if they were the same as the numbers for escort agencies and swingers' clubs listed in the back of Leon's weekly paper. Without going into it too much further because it made me feel sick, I could see that some of the numbers tallied up!

So, while our daughter was in hospital and I was very ill, my husband, who had refused to give up the comfort of our bed, was also calling other women. It was just more confirmation of how

144

selfish this man really was. When he returned from work that night, I confronted him about it. Of course, he couldn't deny it because the proof was there in black and white. He tried to minimise the situation, and he even apologised. He admitted he had called the numbers, but he said that it was merely for titillation. Being as reasonable as I could be and knowing that it was an argument I could never win, I decided it was best to sweep it under the carpet. In my head, I thought that now I had shown him how reasonable I was, maybe he would start being a little more reasonable with me. I couldn't have been more wrong.

Falling to Pieces

It wasn't very often I had anything to do with my mother. It was just easier that way, given her personality. Now a mother myself, I had enough problems dealing with similar personality traits in my husband. Leon made it difficult for me to have a relationship with my mother. She, I suppose, had ironically given him the perfect excuse to demand I didn't see her, because of her behaviour towards me.

She was aware that Leon was violent towards me because people had witnessed him hitting me, but Mum's attitude was that I had made my bed and I could lie on it. She was willing to be a mother to me but only if I completely excluded Leon from my life. The trouble was that I was in the middle of a battle of wills when it came to Leon and my mother because they had such similar personalities.

There were times when the children were toddlers when I felt I really couldn't cope. Those days were very hard, and I would curse my mother because she never offered to help me with them.

She had, on one occasion, knocked on my door when Leon and I lived in our first old terraced house, around the time he was having an affair. She asked to see her grandchildren and it was clear she was in a very unpleasant mood. I tried to ignore that, and politely invited her in, regardless. Her whole persona was very dismissive of me and she declined my invitation, telling me she was quite happy to stand at the door and talk to them for a few moments. She stood at the door talking to them for a minute or two, then quite abruptly turned on her heels and took herself off down the alley at the side of the house, leaving me feeling quite bewildered.

She made me feel incredibly guilty, as if I had rejected her in some way or made her feel unwelcome. Now that I was getting older, I began to see things in her that I hadn't seen before. I realised that I had nothing to feel guilty about because I had politely invited her into my home on many occasions and *she* had chosen not to come in.

That time she left me standing bewildered on my doorstep I had wondered what it was all about. It wasn't about seeing the children. It was about making me feel bad again, and upsetting me. After all, what interest had she ever shown in them? She had never helped me with them. She had never offered to babysit them or take them out for the day. Even when I had been desperate for help with them, I had never felt comfortable enough to approach her because she would have thrown any help she gave me back in my face.

The tide had slowly turned with my mother and I realised it was best to keep my distance from her. I still loved her, but I could not deal with her moods. Of course, when I had discussed this with Leon in the past he was quite happy that I felt this way towards her. Leon had to go the extra mile though, and forbid me from having anything to do with her, claiming that it always ended up upsetting me. I naively saw this as him protecting me, but in fact it was just another way of controlling me. So, over the years I did see my mother when I visited my lovely nan and she was there too, but I tried not to get too involved with her as on the rare occasions I did, since I found her too demanding and it always ended up with her falling out with me over something trivial.

Leon arrived back from one of his driving stints in abroad in an even worse mood than usual. The children were about three and five now. He was wearing his red checked lumberjack shirt; he looked grubby and dishevelled as if he hadn't slept for a few days, and he smelt of stale cigarettes. I was trying to juggle sorting the children and doing the tea and, of course, trying not to do anything wrong that might make Leon turn nasty. Well, nastier than he was being in any case, so I was quite on edge, to say the least.

Pottering around, I happened to glance outside and noticed a car pulling up right outside the house. My stomach dropped when I saw it was my mother. It was typical of her to turn up without calling first. It wasn't actually that which I minded so much, but rather that she was probably in Nice Mummy mode, just like Leon's easy-going mode. This mode had caused her to pay us a visit, but she couldn't have picked a worse time with the mood Leon was in!

I could hardly turn my mother away because he was in a mood. Also, she didn't really turn up that often – not like Leon's family – and, after all, she was still my mother. Even so, I was filled with dread as I had to give Leon the news that she was here, and I knew he would take it out on me. He was on the settee staring into space when I approached him timidly, 'Leon, my mum's here.'

He glared at me with so much hatred I thought he was going to hit me there and then. 'Well, get rid of her then,' he growled menacingly, his eyes bloodshot from lack of sleep.

An icy fear crept over me and my stomach turned over; she was knocking at the door now and I hadn't time to think of a plan to get out of this terrible situation. So, I turned to him and whispered pleadingly, 'Look, I'll do her a quick drink then she'll go. Don't worry, I'll sort it.' My head was in a spin because I didn't know what his next move would be.

Answering the door, politely smiling with my head still full of the memory of Leon's growl that I had to get rid of her, somehow I managed to pretend that there wasn't a problem.

'Hi, Mum, do come in,' I said, opening the door to let her in. As I followed her into the living room, I expected Leon to still be in the chair, but he wasn't. The chair was empty apart from a few scatter cushions. I could hear Mum talking to me in the background, but my mind was fretting over where Leon could have gone. I thought hopefully, *Maybe he went up the stairs behind me as I answered the door, and got into bed.*

'Would you like a drink, Mum?' I asked, trying to get the drinks out of the way so she would hurry up and leave, because the longer she was here the more he would be boiling up. Mum asked for a cup of tea and continued talking away, not that I could hear a word she was saying. Trotting into the kitchen, I flicked the switch on the kettle and then, out of the corner of my eye, I saw a dark shadow on the floor, huddled by the side of the fridge Oh my God, I thought as I realised it was Leon. What the hell was he doing sitting on the floor like that?

I quickly pushed the kitchen door shut in case he started shouting, and I didn't want my mum to hear him and feel uncomfortable. Plus, it would give her more ammunition against him in the future, and she was not much better than him in her pursuit of control.

'What are you doing there?' I asked, bewildered.

He looked up at me and his eyes were red and bulging with temper. 'Get rid of the fucking slag,' he spat through gritted teeth, as if trying to stop himself from shouting it.

This really was too much. I couldn't let him lose his temper with my mum and talk to her like that. 'Please, Leon,' I pleaded quietly, 'let me do her a drink now, then I will get rid of her. I can't just tell her to go, can I?'

He looked at me and seethed over and over again, 'Get rid of the fucking slag.'

I was absolutely terrified that she would hear him, and what made it worse was in the background I could hear her and the children chatting happily away, oblivious to this intolerable scene going on in the kitchen.

I made the tea as quickly as I could, afraid that with every minute my mother was here, Leon was getting closer to erupting.

When the tea was ready and I took it in to her, my mother asked me, 'Aren't you having a drink, our Stacey?'

'No, no, I am okay. I haven't long had one,' I lied, just wanting to hurry this horrible situation along. If my mother had noticed I was distracted, she didn't let on. Maybe she hadn't noticed anything. It was amazing that I was acting so calmly, I suppose. Suddenly, Reece rushed up to his nanny, unaware of the cup of tea that sat at her feet, and before I had time to react, the cup fell over and the tea spilt all over the clean, mint green carpet.

For a second, I was paralysed with shock, staring at the big stain. I would have to go into the kitchen again to get a cloth to clean up the mess and Leon would certainly lose his temper now that the carpet had been marked. However, there was nothing for it but to go back in the kitchen and fetch a cloth; if I left the tea to soak, the stain wouldn't lift and then I would definitely get a beating.

On the other side of the scale, my mother was sitting there apologising about putting her cup on the carpet and I was just secretly thinking, *Please be quiet.*

I didn't want Leon to know what had happened if I could help it.

'It's no big deal, Mum. I'll get a cloth,' I said, pretending that this was not a problem. The awful thing was that it was a major problem, but I could not let her know that. How bizarre would it have looked if I had panicked because I was going to get a beating, due to the fact that my child had accidentally knocked over a cup of tea? My mother was the last person I wanted to know what was going on because, quite frankly, I wouldn't have been able to stomach her concern. She might have been in caring mother and grandmother mode, but she could just as easily turn into aggressive controlling mother.

It would just give her another excuse to try to split us up and make me go back to her, even though she had never wanted me when I had needed her. To me, she was just as controlling as Leon, except the water I had in the well for my mother had run dry years ago, whereas I wasn't quite at that point with Leon yet. I suppose it was because I still thought I was in love with him when, in fact, I had merely been conditioned.

Bracing myself, I went back into the kitchen. I tried to ignore Leon and ran the tap, rinsing the dishcloth out. As I turned around he was standing right in front of me, his eyes blazing with fury. He looked insane as he chanted to me, 'Get that fucking slag out of my house now.'

'Okay, okay,' I replied, brushing past him into the living room with the cloth in my hand. I just couldn't take any more of the pressure. Mum was still muttering about the stain; maybe she was a little aware of what Leon was like and was making a fuss for his benefit. She must have sensed he was in the house because I was feeling very uneasy and the panic was quite obviously emanating from me.

I was at the point where I simply couldn't cope with this situation any more. In front of my mother I had to behave as if this was just a normal friendly visit, well aware that in the next room my husband was behaving like a maniac. It was impossible to split myself in two – the carefree hostess and the terrified wife. I was so frightened, I couldn't even think straight. I reasoned that the only way I could make my mother leave the house without offending her would be to pretend I had to go out myself.

To be honest, I had to get out of the house anyway, if only to give Leon time to calm down. I was too frightened to be alone with him once she had gone. So I went over to the television and turned it up so that he would not hear my plans – I had no doubt he was listening. My mother looked at me and I said to her in a very matter-of-fact way, 'I have to go out now.'

There was no ease or pretence in my voice this time, I just couldn't act as if there was nothing going for on a second longer. My mother nodded at me with a knowing look and helped me get the children's shoes on. Then we stood up and walked out of the house with the television still blasting. I didn't even shut the front door for fear of him hearing it.

When we got outside, Mum asked me gently to go home with her. Of course, it was a very kind gesture, but I was sick of being a pawn in people's games, and I didn't want to confide in her about what was going on. I knew one day she would throw it all back in my face if I let her help me now.

I just wanted to be with someone who genuinely cared and didn't have any hidden agendas. Lying, I told my mother that I was going to the shop, willing her to get in her car and drive away from the house. Luckily, she didn't push things and left. Then I got into the car, strapping the children in as fast as humanly possible, as I was half expecting Leon to run down the drive and drag me back into the house. When we finally pulled away, I let out a sigh of relief that he hadn't managed to capture me. My emotions were running high – fear, relief and turmoil. I needed to see my grandmother.

Nan was always there to sit and listen to my problems. She never judged me because she had lived through years of terrible domestic violence too, except in those days the women really did have to put up with it. She had been the light in the dark of my unhappy childhood. She had fussed me and made me comfortable, always taking my part when Mum was angry with me. She regularly gave me tea, biscuits and comfort.

The more I talked to Nan, the angrier I started to feel with Leon. He had made me feel so frightened and pressured. Whenever Leon's family came to visit I always made them feel welcome. Yet my mother had turned up this once, and though admittedly with her usually came problems, to put me under that kind of pressure had been extremely cruel and unnecessary. Surely it shouldn't have been too hard for him to at least pass the time of day in a civilised manner with my mother? If only for my sake.

The more I thought about what had happened, the angrier I became because there truly was no justification for him to have put me through that. So, I decided to go home, stand my ground and let him know how bad he had made me feel. He would surely have to apologise, I stupidly thought.

By the time I arrived home, I was quite annoyed and ready for him. Marching up the drive with the kids in tow, I rang the bell. The door swung open and Leon stood there with a placid look on his face. The children gently trotted over the threshold of the front doorstep, but before I had a chance to say anything Leon grabbed me by my jumper and flung me up against the wall in the hallway. The children stood there terrified as he began punching me repeatedly in the stomach.

Horrified that our poor children were watching, I cursed myself for coming back and being so naive as to think that he would apologise. In the end, I collapsed on the floor and he dragged me into the living room. The children climbed up on the chair and huddled there, too frightened to move as he threw me on to the settee. I sat up trying to retain some dignity, but I simply couldn't stop crying, thinking about what the children had just witnessed. How foolish I had been to think that I could make this man apologise to me. He had certainly brought me down a peg or two.

He began to go on at me, saying that I was inconsiderate for inviting my mother in knowing that he had just got back from working away. It was no use arguing; I knew I was on dangerous territory as it was. The only way to try and bring some normality back into the household would be for me to apologise and take the blame for what had just happened.

What mattered now were the children and I needed to make Leon shut up and believe he was right so that he could at least behave calmly and normally, whatever that may be. The word 'sorry' left my lips sounding sincere enough for Leon to say that he accepted my apology.

The rest of the evening went quite well on the surface, but deep inside I was hurt by what he had done. Even worse, when I went to bed that evening and he wanted sex with me, I had to pretend that I had forgiven him. So I lay there as he had his way with me, yet inside I was recoiling in disgust at his touch.

After that day I started to suffer from panic attacks. I didn't know at the time what was happening to me, but sometimes when I was in a relaxed environment, like at Leon's sister's for example, a feeling of dread and panic would consume me. Anywhere I was that felt relaxed and safe would make me realise the drastic gap between the calm of being somewhere normal and the storm of life at home. I would start to hyperventilate. My heart would pound and I would fight for breath and get red in the face. If I was indoors, I would rush outside and try to gasp some air and calm down, but often I would end up crying. I couldn't understand what was happening.

There was no one to tell me why I was feeling like this because Leon and his family dominated my whole life, and all they cared about was him and themselves. As for my own family, I didn't confide in them about what was happening because usually by the time I did see them, Leon had managed to convince me that we were doing fine, and he was going to change for the better.

Lady of the Night

Leon had sent me to the local shop with the children for some chocolates. The moment we got back home and stepped inside the door, he called out to me, 'Hold on a second.'

I replied, trying to get the children's coats off and get them settled. 'Come on, hurry up. I got something to show you,' he then shouted urgently.

I thought it was strange that he sounded very upbeat. I felt quite relieved, thinking that at least he hadn't found some way to make out I had done something wrong. Walking into our newly fitted oak kitchen, I found Leon leaning over the worktop, analysing the bargain pages paper, which I knew had a personal section at the back with ads for dating and prostitutes. Looking very much like the cat with the cream he seemed in such a good mood. I was intrigued now to see what was making him behave this way.

'I've just come off the telephone to someone,' he began. The newspaper was spread out on the work surface, open on the back pages. Suddenly my world started to spin and I felt a knot in my stomach. I had a feeling I knew where this was going. Did I really want to hear any more?

'It's an escort,' he continued, 'and her name is Jamie and she is going to come around tonight for a threesome, but she wants to speak to you first to make sure you are certain you want to go through with it.'

Certain I want to go through with it! I thought, exasperated. Who was he trying to kid? He knew I didn't want to do this. It felt as if every inch of my body, every organ, had turned ice cold with panic. This could not be happening.

My anxiety was building up, but Leon just stood there oblivious, telling me his good news. He was so pleased with himself. The worst part of it was, there was no way out for me.

I had to stand there smiling and looking interested. If I so much as gave a hint of my real feelings of horror and disgust it would ruin his night, and he would turn into Mr Nasty again. The children would have to hear all the arguing and banging about too. Looking at his happy face, I couldn't believe how selfish he was. He knew that I

154

couldn't be straight with him, he knew that I was far from happy with the idea. There was no one for me to turn to, nowhere for me to go, not with the children in tow. He wouldn't let me walk out of the house; he would stop me, lock me in, then hit me for trying to leave. It was no good praying for a miracle – a miracle had never saved me before.

Leon was eager for me to play along with him and phone this prostitute back. There was a bottle of vodka on the worktop, so I asked him if I could have a glass. 'Of course you can. Dutch courage, ay?' he mocked, rubbing my back in his easy-going mode.

Yes, of course I can, I thought sarcastically, *because everything's going your way you bullying bastard. That's why you're all happy and letting me have a drink.*

'How much is she charging?' I asked, hoping it would be really expensive because I knew Leon was extremely tight with money.

'Only one hundred and sixty pounds for the hour,' he replied.

Only! Here I was having to get the children's clothes from charity shops and rely on his mother and his sister to give me their old clothes so I could wear something half decent, yet he wanted to spend that amount of money on a prostitute.

Knocking the vodka back, I was trying to think of a way to get out of this situation, but every avenue I went down came to a dead end. I couldn't pretend I was ill because he'd know I was putting it on. Leon had made up his mind that a prostitute was coming to our house tonight, and what Leon wanted, Leon got. It was hurting me so much because he was being so nice right at that moment. Why couldn't he be like this normally? It was such a pity I was going to have to go through with something that I really didn't want to just to keep him in this pleasant mood.

Taking the children up to bed, I couldn't believe what he was planning downstairs. Looking at their innocent faces, I so wanted for us to be a normal family and for this to be a normal night – but it wasn't.

Standing in my bedroom alone for a few minutes, my mind was racing, panic gripping me. I had to pull myself together, but my head was swimming a little from the drink. My only option was to do what he wanted. I reasoned with myself that maybe if I went through with it then that would be an end to it all, he would get the fantasy out of his system and we would never have to speak of it again. I also thought that if I did this for him, he would be so pleased with me that it might be the turning point in our relationship. He might stay as happy as he was that night forever.

I knew I had to do this and get through it somehow, and I thought that if I drank enough vodka, it might not seem so bad. There was no way I could go downstairs and reason with him, I just didn't have the strength to go through that. Leon had never considered my feelings and where I was concerned, he didn't have a conscience.

So I took my only option, to get as pissed as I could and go downstairs to face the horror. My drunken self rationalised it, and I told my frightened self that I would pretend I was acting a role in a film, and try not to let what was happening affect me. I'd just go through the motions. It was only going to be for an hour, I reassured myself. What's an hour out of your whole life? Then maybe my husband would be happy with me. That would mean so much to me.

I marched back down the stairs. I was no longer Stacey, the downtrodden housewife, I was Stacey, the hot, swinging, dream wife – Leon's dream woman. Except, if it had been me planning this with another man and him, he would have broken my neck – the irony.

Tipping some more vodka down my throat, I found that my new character was taking over and I was squashing the real Stacey somewhere so far back in my mind she didn't exist any longer. *Let's get the show on the road,* I thought, grabbing the telephone and dialling Jamie's number.

'Hello, this is Stacey,' I began. 'My husband called you about an hour ago and said you wanted to speak to me.'

'Yes, he told me that you were both interested in a threesome tonight,' she replied.

I still couldn't quite believe I was actually having this conversation. Leon was leaning on the worktop watching me eagerly, gently trailing his fingers lovingly down my back as I spoke. It angered me so much that he was prepared to let me continue this charade. Jamie and I agreed that she would come to our house at ten o'clock. She had to travel all the way from Nottingham.

Ten o'clock came and we heard a car pulling up. Leon got up and said, 'Oh, I feel really nervous now.' I suggested that we called the whole thing off, but he dismissed me with, 'We may as well see it through now.' I guess he wasn't that nervous then.

The doorbell rang and Leon sent me to answer the door. In she came, with a waft of cheap perfume behind her. 'Hello,' she greeted me, obviously waiting to be ushered through. As we walked into the living room, Leon, like the gentleman he was to strangers, offered her a seat. She sat back as I went to fetch her a drink. Gulping more vodka down in the kitchen, I took a deep breath to calm my nerves and carried a drink back in for her. She was perched on the sofa with her raven-black dyed hair – possibly to cover her grey roots! She thanked me for the drink. She pressed the cup to her lips, which were coated in bright red lipstick that didn't really compliment her slightly yellow teeth. She was cocooned in a fur coat to add to the provocative look, and was in her late forties. She was considerably older than Leon and me. Don't get me wrong, I wasn't putting the woman down; she was here for the money and fair play to her. Leon was in it to fulfil his selfish sexual appetite, and I was involved because I was frightened to death of my husband.

We then engaged in some polite chitchat about her journey. I was trying to keep the conversation rolling along, but I didn't want things to progress any further than this. Anyway, they were both on a mission, and the sex was going to have to take place. She came over to me and started rubbing my legs. I started giggling because there was nothing else to do. It was nerves, I suppose. My mind kept wandering to my children sleeping innocently upstairs and thinking how this was so wrong, but I had to try and keep my focus off them, otherwise I would get upset.

Fantasies took over, of me just freaking out and smashing the place up and really embarrassing him. Because he liked to play Mr Nice Guy and Mr Easy Going in front of people, I wanted to take advantage of that and expose him for the bully he really was. Unfortunately, there was no point. Jamie would just run off, and once she had gone, he would give me hell and beat me up.

Ten minutes after that we were all lying on the living room floor doing unspeakable acts. My children were upstairs in bed, and here I was having sex with my husband and a prostitute. I couldn't let myself absorb that mentally, because I would have just freaked out. How embarrassing would that have been? So I acted as if I was enjoying it, made all the right noises and focused on the fact that this whole sordid episode would be behind me soon, and I hoped my husband would forget the idea.

I wondered what the neighbours in our quiet little cul-de-sac were doing tonight. It ended with Leon getting on top of me to finish himself off. I knew as soon as he had come, it would all be over. So I groaned and pretended I was in ecstasy in order to excite him, so that he would come quicker. At last he did. Jamie, I suspected, was almost as eager as me to get it finished, get her money and go home.

We all got dressed, feeling rather awkward, and the money was exchanged. Jamie left saying what a wonderful time she had had – yeah, right! I went upstairs to bathe. I felt hugely relieved that it was all over. I wasn't going to focus on what had happened, I wanted to erase it from my memory and try and get on with my life. As far as I was concerned I had done everything he could ask of me now and I was looking forward to the reward of some peace and harmony in my home life.

The next morning, I got up as usual, tending to the children and the housework and when Leon finally got up, I made him a drink. Passing him his coffee, I asked him what he thought of the previous night, as he had not mentioned it since, expecting him to say something about the experience in terms of it being done and dealt with. Then, I hoped, he wouldn't ever bully me into going down that path again. He replied, 'It wasn't as good as I thought it would be.'

Typical. I'd put myself through all that, behaved as he had expected, and he still wasn't happy. I had thought that it would have got it out of his system, and he would just be happy with me from now on.

But instead of getting better, it got worse. Leon started insisting on doing it again. My stomach hit the floor when he suggested it. Sometimes I felt that I was put on the earth to endure total torment from him. In the end, I agreed to go through with it one last time if he promised that he would let it drop. This time we got babysitters and arranged to go over to Jamie's.

Leon and I got dressed up as if for a night out. The children were dropped at the babysitters and the house was nice and quiet as I sipped my vodka before we set off on the journey. I was thinking to myself how much of an effort he had made to get this night arranged for us; it made me so angry inside. Why couldn't he just take me for a drink or a nice meal instead, like most normal couples? But I knew it was easier just to bite my lip and go with the flow, if only for a bit of peace. Sitting in the car, all dressed up, I imagined that we were going to a restaurant and my husband loved making me feel special – if only.

When we arrived at Jamie's in Nottingham, it was on a rough council estate. I think Leon had been under the impression that she would live in a big house in a nice area because he looked a little worried. 'We can always go for a nice drink and a meal instead,' I said in jest, but deep down hoping he would agree. Of course, he still wanted to go ahead with it. As we got out of the car, I felt really paranoid, thinking that all her neighbours were probably watching us through the window and saying, 'Look at that couple going in there for a threesome.' I assured myself that even if they were watching, it really didn't matter. They couldn't hurt me, not like Leon.

Jamie made us feel really welcome, but I could sense her nerves as well. We sat in her living room among pictures of her children. Part of me wanted to explain to her that I wasn't the one who wanted this, but what did it matter? She was in it simply for the money. She moved over to Leon and began kissing him. He was oozing the body language of a shy teenager, all coy! Then he said he felt a bit nervous. Jamie was reassuring him, and things moved on, but I was starting to get more and more anxious.

As Leon started having sex with me, I felt so disgusted by him I just wanted him off me. I told him to go to Jamie and see things through with her. Jamie looked at me a little shocked. 'Are you sure?' she asked. She didn't want him any more than I did, but I couldn't switch off any more and I knew she had years of practice at switching off.

'Yes, I am sure,' I said, trying to sound as if it was a turn on for me. So I watched as my husband mounted her until he came. All I could think of when I watched him was how glad I was he wasn't on top of me any longer. Once it was all over, the money was exchanged and I wondered who had felt the most violated that night, Jamie   or   me.

Marriage Guidance

We had been going to marriage guidance for a few months. It was my idea and I was hoping that the counsellor would be able to help us. She was an outsider and unbiased, but the problem was I couldn't tell her straight what was really going on. Instead of being open and honest, Leon put on a false front. Just like my mother, he acted like a caring, well-balanced person, and his act was so convincing that I worried she had been completely fooled by him.

He was honest enough about his background growing up around violence, but he didn't tell her about his violence towards me. Of course, I couldn't say outright that he was being violent because I would have had a beating later for showing him up. However, I was hoping that the counsellor would be able to pick up on things and that, in time, the truth would come out, and she would be able to get Leon to see how damaging his behaviour was.

One day we were due for another session, but Leon couldn't make it as he was working away. My panic attacks had been getting worse. Living with Leon had become totally intolerable, and I just couldn't see a way out. We had got to the point where I couldn't go to the toilet, or to bed, without checking it was okay with him. If I did go out to visit my grandmother, he was on the phone demanding that I get back home because he needed me.

I was determined to go to the session on my own and ask the counsellor for help.

I thought that if I gave her some insight as to what had been really going on she would be able to find a way of bringing it out in the open during the session. Maybe she could talk Leon into being amicable enough to leave me and the children in the marital home so that at least we could salvage something from the damage that had already been done.

I immediately burst out crying when I got into the room with the counsellor. I felt relieved that there was a chance for me to get things sorted out between me and Leon, and I thought this was going to be the turning point. However, when she realised that Leon wasn't going to attend the session she said that she couldn't discuss anything with me as the sessions were supposed to be with both of us. I tried to explain that all the previous sessions had been a waste of time because Leon was acting like the hard-working, caring, sharing young family man and I needed her help to get the root of our problems exposed and dealt with. 'Please help me,' I begged her.

She put her hands over her ears, nodding her head, blocking my sobbing out, apologising that she really couldn't hear any more. As a marriage counsellor, she would be breaking the rules, and if I needed to raise issues, I had to raise them in the sessions with Leon.

This, of course, was a complete waste of time as I was totally petrified of him and there was no way he would admit to what had been happening in front of this lady. I knew I was getting nowhere with my pleas for help, so I stood up, still crying, and went to leave the room. She apologised and said it would have been more than her job was worth for her to continue the session alone with me. However, she did say that if there was any violence going on, I should leave with the children. But that was my issue. I couldn't leave; I had nowhere to take my children.

My expectations with counselling had been that a third party could get Leon to leave us or change. Sobbing my heart out as I walked up the street, I realised that there was only one person who could put a stop to the hell the children and I were living in, and that wasn't Leon or any counsellor. It was going to have to come from me. All the years of violence and abuse had taken their toll on me and I didn't feel I had the energy or strength needed to fight my way out of the situation. That's why I was so heartbroken, I knew I had no choice but to summon up the strength to get us out of the family home or get Leon to leave.

The months ticked by and I was constantly on edge. My mind was so focused on tending to the children, and, most importantly, not doing anything to upset Leon, that I was no longer a person – I had evolved into a humanoid robot. I was still emotional and crying an awful lot of the time, of course, but that was just the norm.

Very often, I would think about leaving my awful life. Bath time had become my haven away from it all. The bathroom had not been updated, so it had a very seventies look to it, with dreary brown and cream tiles and a cream bath. The floor was a brown and cream carpet. It was a an off-cut from the hall, stairs and landing carpet and not really suitable for a bathroom, but it was warm.

Switching on the taps and letting the hot water gush out, I often sat on the toilet seat crying, while waiting for the bath to fill up, conveniently in reach of the toilet roll to dry my eyes before I left the bathroom. Ironically, the bathroom was my place of peace, yet Leon could never bathe on his own, so he always made me sit and talk to him while he had a bath.

Every time I was in the bath and left to my own devices, I would fall into the same fantasy. Lying there in the bubbles, in the warmth and quiet, the tranquillity of the moment would magnify around me and I would long to be in a house with no Leon to disturb the peace.

The hardest thing about leaving Leon and our home was the transition between that life and the free life I craved. In the bath, I would close my eyes and pray that when I opened them, the transition would have taken place and I would be in my new home, in my own bathroom, with the children safely settled in bed, my life with Leon just a horrible memory.

It was my bath time that started a snowball effect and I began to plan. The fantasy of the new life I pondered might not have to be a fantasy. I became excited at the thought that one day I might be lying in the bath in my new Leon-free life, thinking, *Thank God.*

As for strength, well that is an important ingredient in the leaving process, because once you have been abused, had your confidence totally shredded and lost your identity, your abuser will have sucked out any courage you might have had. That's what the abuser feeds on, your strength – like a parasite feeding on your pride, dignity, self-belief and confidence. Because they have none, they thrive on feeding off yours.

Christmas Time

Around the time we were seeing the woman at the marriage guidance service, Leon had another one of his bright ideas; he suggested we get a family pet. Suggested is the wrong word. He said we needed a pet, and then one day arrived with a Rottweiler puppy, a large sturdy breed of dog that would not have been my preference given the choice.

He said it would be good for the children, and every family should have a family pet; however, I would have liked something with a less ferocious reputation. That said, he was a loveable dog, albeit a bit difficult to toilet train, and we named him Ben.

We could walk Ben for hours along the local canal and he would not do a poo, but the minute he got back home, he would poo in his kennel in the garage. I think his previous owners must have treated him badly as he was quite a handful. As I had known I would be, I was the one who ended up walking him and looking after him. As much as I loved that dog, he was another responsibility and I felt overburdened. I was also worried that the dog would pick up on the aggression emanating from Leon and it would become part of his nature. Ben was so powerful, I dreaded to think what could happen.

Of course, Leon would not listen to my concerns; when I voiced them, he dismissed me as being a killjoy. Ben had a massive amount of energy and was always bounding around. The fact that he was such a big, strong puppy didn't help because when he was allowed in the house, the furniture would go flying everywhere. It was amusing though, at times, to see Leon lose his temper with Ben for breaking something or other. He would chase him round the room for a good ten minutes before giving up – he could never catch that dog. I wished I could have been as fast on my feet. Having said that, if I had been a Rottweiler, I would have probably ripped my husband's balls off by this point in my life.

Time passed, Christmas was upon us, and the poor dog was still pooing in the garage. Christmas is a time of good will to all men, and families uniting together – or so it's supposed to be. Somehow, Christmas with Leon was the worst time of the year. Maybe it was because everyone seemed to be celebrating and there was excitement

163

in the air that amplified just how miserable I felt. Or was it because the abuse actually got worse during the Christmas season? Maybe it was because Christmas is supposed to be for the children, therefore trying to shield them from the badness that was going on around them was even harder.

It was December 1996 and I was feeling ill again. I was still having regular bouts of tonsillitis that really knocked me off my feet. I had a very sore throat, temperature, headache, the shivers, and felt extremely ill. All I wanted to do was sleep to get through it. Leon had no regard whatsoever for the fact that I was ill. He just got annoyed with me and went on at me more because I wasn't able to keep everything up to the high standards he expected. It was almost as if Leon regarded me as a robot, not a person with feelings.

I don't know how I struggled through. I just wanted to collapse but I was made to feel that I was being lazy and miserable, ruining everyone's Christmas. It was all about self-discipline in order to get through each day without giving Leon a reason to instigate an argument. I was trying my damned best to keep functioning.

How I managed to get all the Christmas presents and the food shopping done, I will never know. Everything was still left up to me, right down to cleaning the dog poo up. On Christmas Eve, I put the children to bed, then went back downstairs as expected. All I wanted to do was crawl into bed, but I knew there was no way I would be allowed to relax, at least not until Leon was asleep himself.

Leon was all happiness and light; he had spent the day popping out to see his family and friends, and basically lounging about, throwing orders at me. He sat back in the armchair, glancing round the room, which was looking very Christmassy. The tree stood in the corner, sparkling with lights and tinsel. Christmas cards were pinned up all over the walls, and the television in the background emitted all the signals of the season. All the kids' Christmas presents were in two big piles at each end of the room so that when they woke, they could go straight to their own gifts. Leon was sitting there happy, looking round at the perfect Christmas setting. It would have been a cosy scene had we been a loving family.

I resented the fact that not once had he lifted a finger to help me create this lovely Christmas scene. All I could see when I looked around me was hard work that had drained me to the very core, and he was now taking all the credit for it in his head. He had thrown out the orders and I had obeyed.

It was getting late and I was tired. The prospect of getting up early to start all over again was getting me down. Even though it was Christmas Day in the morning, there was more pressure to be happy when I just didn't feel it. Leon decided to set up the toy garage I had bought for Reece. This was the beginning of a nightmare. I knew that once Leon had started a job he would expect my full attention. Did he care that I had been busy all day long? When I mentioned going to bed, he made it quite clear that he expected me to help him piece the garage together. It wasn't a straightforward toy garage to set up; it had lots of little pieces and a ramp going up to a pretend car park.

As I expected, Leon started to get irritated with me because setting it up wasn't going as easily as the instructions suggested. Anxiety was welling up inside me, and I sat there hating this bloody stupid toy garage. Why didn't I just buy something that was practical? That you could take straight out of the box and just play with? Leon was shouting now, but because it was Christmas Eve, I didn't want the kids to be woken up by his nasty, aggressive rants, so I sat there pretending it was no big deal and I could set it up. It was nearly four in the morning and I couldn't believe I was still awake, trying to piece together the toy garage. It was okay for Leon to dictate that we wouldn't go to bed until the garage was erected correctly; no doubt he would have a lie-in, whereas I would have to be up at around six in the morning to prepare for the day ahead. When we finally went to bed, I had hardly any sleep before having to get up again.

When I woke, I felt so ill again; I just wanted to cry and go back to sleep, but I knew I had to be up for the children, so I struggled out of bed. I was dripping wet with sweat due to my temperature. My head was thumping; I was weak and aching all over. I prepared the children's breakfast and, amazingly, Leon came bounding down the stairs full of the joys of the season, but when he saw I was ill, he was annoyed again. He glared at me, 'What the fuck's up with you? You better pull yourself together – this is the kids' day!' As if I didn't realise it was the kids' day; was it not I who had been preparing for this day for months now? I truly wanted to feel well and make it the best day ever for them, but my body was too weak and drained of energy.

The children came bumping down the stairs on their little bums all excited, screeching to each other that Father Christmas had been to visit. Leon got the camcorder out and filmed them opening their presents, and I did all the other tasks like make the drinks and clear up the wrapping paper, but I was just craving my bed. Stuffing the discarded wrapping paper into black bin bags, I caught sight of Leon filming me. 'Look at that for a miserable bugger,' he mocked. Smiling sarcastically, I thought to myself what I would love to say for the benefit of the camera, but I decided that hearing the children's voices high pitched with excitement in the background was a special moment and it wasn't very often this was a happy home, so I wasn't going to spoil that.

Back in the kitchen, I could smell the turkey and vegetables cooking. I knew there was no way I could eat any as I felt so ill. Stirring the vegetables, I looked over at the kitchen door to the garage; it was open so that the dog could be a bit more involved with us. He would stand up in the garage, with his big black paws resting on the baby stairgate that we had put there to prevent him from getting into the kitchen but allowing him to still interact with us. The aroma of dog poo was wafting its way into the house, and Leon came striding into the kitchen to have a cigarette.

'Stacey, you better get in the garage and clean the dog shit up,' he ordered. At any other time I was quite prepared to do it because I was always on autopilot. However, because I felt so ill, I really couldn't summon up the stamina to do it. It was annoyed, and I couldn't help but blurt out that maybe he could do it for once because I was so ill.

Next thing I knew, he had grabbed my hair and swung me down. Yelping, I fell to the floor, all the time aware that it was Christmas Day and I didn't want the children to hear the commotion and get upset.

'Okay, okay,' I pleaded calmly to let him know that I was prepared to be compliant. Scrambling to my knees and heaving myself off the ground before the children came in and noticed, I tried to make my way to the garage door to clean up the poo. All I could hear in the background was Leon cursing me for ruining everybody's Christmas. Yet it was quite plainly him who was ruining Christmas again! I was glad to get in that garage in some ways so that I could let out the sobs knotted in my belly. Kneeling on the floor, the tears were gushing from my eyes, so much so that I couldn't see what I was doing, and the stench of dog poo was filling my nostrils, making me heave. I had let the dog out into the back garden so that I could clean up the mess, as he usually scrambled about excited and I didn't want him running in the poo and getting it in his paws, giving me more work to do. As Ben barked excitedly to come back in and play, I cursed Leon and the dog under my breath.

Leon was leaning over the stairgate, calling me a lazy bitch. It was the worst Christmas ever, and what with this and the prostitute, I knew I could not take any more.

Internally, I wanted to stand up and scream at him to shut the fuck up, tell him what a bullying bastard he was, and demand that he clean the dog shit up himself, as he had wanted the dog in the first place. That's what I wanted, but for the sake of Christmas and my kids, and knowing if I antagonised him in any way, he would totally ruin the rest of the kids' day, I contained all my anger, as usual.

Eventually, I managed to get myself upstairs and get the kids ready for the rest of the day. My face was bright red from crying, and my make-up wasn't really doing a good job of camouflaging my hot ruddy cheeks and bloodshot eyes. It was best I put on a brave face to keep the peace for the sake of the children, I concluded, but I had finally reached a turning point where I had decided that somehow, I was going to leave.

The relief of making that decision helped me to go downstairs and get through the rest of the day. It was heartbreaking when my father and his girlfriend turned up at the door, presents bundled in their arms, and full of the Christmas spirit. It was difficult to answer the door, knowing my father would take one look at my red face and realise something was wrong with me, and I so didn't want to upset his day. Instead, I put on my happy mask, and as for the Stacey who was screaming for help inside, well, I managed to push her somewhere deep down in my soul for the time being, because it wasn't appropriate for her to surface right then.

Dad's face dropped with concern when he saw the state I was in, but I led him with my body language and my tone into my game of pretending everything was alright. When he got me alone and asked what was wrong, I made some excuse about crying because I felt so ill. It was sad for Dad to see me, his daughter, every Christmas, distraught from crying, but brushing my problems under the carpet.

There truly hadn't been one happy Christmas in my life with Leon. My husband sat on the settee with his dressing gown on, cigarette in his hand, acting fake with his easy-going persona. I was beginning to detest him without the entanglement of my love for him; he had been determined to break me and he had succeeded. Thinking back, I must have been pretty resilient, really, for I should have detested him from the moment he first laid his hands on me in anger.

The Never-Ending Cycle

From that Christmas Day on, I became fixated on forcing myself to leave, and daily I would try to make headway with a plan. The wheels were in motion, albeit moving very slowly. As soon as I woke, I would go through it all in my head like an obsession, 'I have got to leave today, I have got to leave.' Every morning I woke up in the house I was frustrated with myself for still being there and not having put a plan into action to leave.

Leaving was easier said than done, especially with Leon working away some of the time, as that gave me time to relax and enjoy my home and kids. However, when he came back, the peace and relaxed atmosphere disappeared and I realised why it was so important for me to make a plan to go. But where would I go with the children? What would I do for money? How would I cope? There was pressure on me constantly, as I knew that unless I came up with a proper plan, I would be chanting to myself about leaving forever.

It wasn't my home that was the problem, it was the person I lived with who made it unbearable. I was stuck between a rock and a hard place – my home was everything to me, it was my security and comfort.

Devising a plan was like trying to finish a jigsaw puzzle with a piece missing. My only alternative option was trying to negotiate with Leon about him leaving. At least that way the children's lives wouldn't be disrupted. This seemed the best way forward.

So, one afternoon, when the children were at school, and Leon was in quite a good mood and, I foolishly concluded, more approachable, I summoned up the courage to try and talk to him. I thought that if he did get angry with me for suggesting it, at least the children wouldn't have to witness the consequences.

'Leon, we really need to talk,' I began.

He looked at me, gesturing that I should continue, and I knew I had to be upfront and honest, regardless of the fear I felt in opening up to him, just in case there was a small chance he would see sense and agree to leave.

'The truth is, I want us to split up because I can't take any more, and I don't think the arguing and upset is good for the children. I really wanted to ask you if you would mind leaving. I've thought about leaving myself, but it doesn't seem fair to take the children away from their home and their school.'

Of course, I should have guessed that this man was beyond reason, but I needed at least to try to sort things this way. He started yelling and shouting, saying, 'It's my fucking house and if anyone is going to leave, it should be fucking you!' Then he said that I wanted the house and not him, which I guess was true.

'So, you don't want to be with me any more, then?'

This was another trick question. I knew that whatever the answer might be, I was going to get a smack. With anxiety whirling in my stomach, a certain amount of rage was building, and I couldn't keep it in; it's the moment when your mouth gets busy before your brain has had a chance to examine what you're going to say! With sarcasm and animosity, I replied, 'No, Leon, of course I don't want to leave you; I am really happy living with you and being hit all the fucking time!'

That was it, he exploded – but at least I had said my piece. He lunged at me and began punching me in the stomach and pulling my hair, all the time being careful not to mark my face. Feeling so vulnerable, I just tried to curl up in a ball, crying and screaming. How the hell could Leon realistically expect me to backtrack on what I had said after he had reacted to my admission with the very actions that made me want to leave him in the first place?

Once he had calmed down, he began to rant about how I had had to spoil the day again and wind him up. He went on for about an hour, interrogating me to make sure I wasn't going to leave. The children were due back from school, and I didn't want them coming home to this atmosphere, so the only way to calm Leon down and make him believe I still wanted to stay was to go to bed with him. By the time I went to pick the children up, I was completely exhausted.

As usual, I started to cry as soon as I got out of the house and into the car, and, as usual, I walked through the school playground among the other mums with my face bright red from weeping. I didn't care about any of them staring, or what they must have thought of this strange woman who regularly came to collect her kids from school in a state. All I cared about were my babies, the innocents.

The mums were all huddled talking in the playground, and Anne, one of the mums I had made friends with, called me over to join them. Reluctantly, as I felt so dishevelled, I made my way over. Anne saw the red mark on my forehead hidden under my hairline, which had been exposed by the wind blowing.

One time, over a cup of tea at her house, I had opened up to her about some of my situation. Her husband Scott was a good father and husband; her life was similar to mine in so many ways, but so far off the scale in others. She had no understanding and I felt her judging me when she probed me about what was going on.

Nodding her head in sanctimonious despair, she said, 'Still there then? I thought you were going to leave?' Naively I had confided in her that I was going to leave, but I didn't elaborate how I intended to do it, as I myself did not know!

Feeling I had to justify myself, I told her I was sorting it out and I was going to leave. She folded her arms as the wind blew an empty crisp packet at her, and she rolled her eyes at me. She was sick of hearing me say I was going. She had asked me so many times, 'Why don't you just leave him?' assuming I must be happy to put up with what I was enduring. I felt such a failure.

Just at that point, the teacher came to open the doors and the bell went, the children poured into the playground, not nearly as tidy as they had been when they had been dropped off at school that morning.

For God's sake, Stacey, I thought, looking at their innocent little faces as they ran out of school and up to me, totally oblivious to the hell that we were living in. *If you can't do it for you, do it for them.* I squeezed them tightly and felt like crying some more. Guilt overwhelmed me for how much I had let them down by bringing them into this toxic environment.

Fear was the prime obstacle in my life: fear of Leon, fear of change, fear of the unknown, fear of letting go. Weeks went by and I kept thinking how I wouldn't be there much longer. However, I wasn't actively doing anything to move the situation along. Strange things began to happen around me. When I was in bed at night, I could hear somebody breathing heavily into my ear. It wasn't my breath, and when Leon was at home, it wasn't his either. I was becoming fearful of the dark and I could sense the presence of something evil around me. The only way I can describe it is that I was losing touch with normal life as I knew it, and being sucked into some paranormal world. One day, I was in the house alone and the feeling was so strong I knew I was being taken away to the unknown. Just as the feeling was about to overwhelm me, Leon came home from the gym and as soon as he got through the door I clung to him as if he was my anchor to life in the real world.

'Please hold me, please don't let me go,' I begged. I wanted to stay in touch with reality, but I felt that my physical form was disintegrating.

Leon looked at me amused as I clung onto his body. 'What are you talking about, Stacey?' he said, as if I had lost my mind. That was exactly what was happening to me, although I didn't know it at the time. I was losing touch with reality.

'I don't know, Leon, I feel as if I am going to die. I am going to leave this earth and I can't stop it happening. Hold me, please, don't let me go away,' I begged. Leon just pushed me aside and laughed, his face twisted with triumph because he had finally broken me. He was more than happy to let me go.

That same evening, I sat on the settee crying – that was all I seemed to do at that time in my life, as I felt so completely run down. Leon came in and, seeing me crying, he asked me what the matter was. He seemed to be being quite nice to me for a change, so I felt I had to be honest. 'I really can't take any more of this, Leon, it's got to end.'

Somehow, I sensed that he was not going to get aggressive, so I continued to let it all out. Leon in turn told me that he had been to visit his grandmother that day and she had apparently had a go at him and even called him a bastard.

I had paid his grandmother a visit a week or two beforehand, and because I was so depressed and run down, I had started to cry when she offered me a cup of tea. It wasn't that I wanted sympathy, it was just that I had got so low, tears had been flooding out of me involuntarily every day.

Nancy was very kind to me, and I couldn't help but tell her when she probed me about why I was so upset. In a way, I felt foolish opening the floodgates as much as I did that day, but her kindness had triggered something within me. When I left her house later that afternoon, I never gave it a second thought that anything would be said because no one ever said anything to Leon about his behaviour, especially not his own blood relatives.

However, Nancy had, and her words appeared to have had some effect on him because he put his arms round me and told me that he didn't realise how bad I felt. Then he said the unbelievable words I had longed to hear, 'Stacey, I think it's best if I move out!'

Those words were the best words I could ever have wished to hear. I hadn't got the strength within me to do it myself. To me, it meant that the children and I could stay in our home, and Leon had finally accepted that we simply couldn't go on the way we were any longer.

I knew Leon wouldn't like me to be happy about the fact that he was leaving, so I had to disguise my feelings of joy. I just looked at him and nodded sadly, as if it was something I didn't want but there was no other way for us. Then to my delight, he picked up the paper and started to look at the advertisements for flats to let. He was actually serious, and my mind was going into joyous overdrive – freedom was near. Happy energy was racing through me. I felt as if I needed to dance to expel it, but I just sat there.

It just so happened that a comedy called *The Young Ones* came on the television at that moment, starring the late Rik Mayall; the timing was perfect. It was so stupid you had to laugh at it and it was as if God had put it on the television so I could use it as a release for all the happiness I was feeling inside. As the programme played its mad, funny sketches, I was howling with laughter. It was genuinely funny, but the main reason for the laughter was all the relief and elation bursting out, because finally I had got Leon to accept he had to go and it meant the children and I wouldn't have our lives disrupted. Leon was studying the accommodation to let ads in the paper with a frown on his face; he didn't seem quite as enthusiastic as when he had been looking at his seedy magazines.

The next morning, Leon suggested we paint the hall, stairs and landing as it was looking a little dirty. Of course, I didn't mind that now he was planning to leave. Inside, I felt as if I was walking on air, so I could have happily painted the whole house from top to bottom inside and out. I had a new-found energy derived from hope.

We went out together and purchased some paint and spent the day decorating together while the kids were at school. I was quite tempted to ask him when he planned to leave but I didn't want him to pick up on how keen I was for him to go as I feared that would only make him stay longer. When we had finished painting, the hallway looked lovely. *At least that's one less job for me to tackle in the house,* I thought to myself.

The next afternoon, I went to the local shop to fetch something for lunch. I chose some ham, thinking we could have something heavier for dinner later when I fetched the children from school. When I got home, Leon seemed strangely quiet, and I guessed he was worrying about getting somewhere new to live. It was a shame, I supposed, but it would be easier for him to leave than me with two lively young children. Fixing our lunch – ham sandwiches and crisps – I carried the plates into the living room and passed Leon his, then I sat down beside him and began to eat.

Leon had a disgusted expression on his face as he bit into his sandwich.

'What's the matter?' I asked, but he ignored me and pulled the top layer of bread off the sandwich and began to inspect it. Then he pulled out the piece of ham and dangled it in front of him. My stomach began churning because I knew what was coming next. 'What the fucking hell is this?' he shouted, flinging the plate and all its contents at the wall.

The plate smashed into smithereens and food was scattered all over the place. Screaming, I got up to run out of the room, but he pulled me back by my hair and flung me on the floor. Then he grabbed my arms and demanded to know why I had bought that ham when I knew he didn't like it.

My mind went back over the little shopping trip I had so innocently taken a couple of hours before. How I had been careful to get the ham that looked the best, but of course not too pricey as Leon always kept me on a tight budget. Leon had completely got me in the mindset of analysing everything I did, seeking out faults, when the truth of the situation was that Leon would find anything to blow a fuse over, so I could never do the right thing anyway.

He viciously smacked me in the face, then as he stood back up he booted me in the side and said, 'Ere, look at ya... Tell you what, if you think I'm leaving this house now you have got another thing coming. If anyone's going to leave, it will be you. This is my fucking house. I am the one who goes to work to pay for it!'

I didn't say a word but just thought that it was the benefits system that had been paying the mortgage. He never had any intention of going, did he?

The Winds of Change

The next morning, I woke up in my nice, clean, warm bed, in my beautiful home. It was like Groundhog Day because my first thought of the day, again, was that I must make plans to leave. My only respite from the planning cycle in my head was when I was asleep, and, for a few fleeting moments in the mornings, I would be okay, until my conscious mind would remind me that I needed to make changes. That morning, I knew it was the day. There would be no more staying in this familiar comfort zone; I had to get the ball rolling. Leon was still asleep, so I slid myself out of bed so as not to disturb him and crept down the stairs.

It was February and still dark outside. Shivering, I hovered round in the kitchen for a little while, looking at the phone, psyching myself up to make the call. The call that was going to take me and my children away from our lovely home and into the wilderness of the unknown.

The words I had heard so many times were swimming around in my head planting seeds of doubt as I shuffled my hands about anxiously in the knife and fork drawer, feeling for the card I had hidden underneath the tray of cutlery a year earlier. Leon's words:

'You'll never manage without me.'

'You can't manage financially, that's why I have to control the money.'

'Nobody else would want you.'

'Don't think about leaving because if I find you, I'll kill you.'

'If you think about hitting me back, make sure you put me down for good because if I get back up your dead.'

It was true, how would I manage financially? I had no money of my own. How would I feed and clothe the children? Everything I did went wrong, so how could I expect to be able to take the children and start a life on our own? I had nothing to offer. I couldn't even work – I had no skills. Even if I got a job, who would have the children while I worked? How would the children feel about me taking them away from their dad, their home?

'Enough,' I said, snapping myself out of it, because I couldn't go on another day longer thinking that I would do it 'tomorrow', because the situation would just go on and on and drive me mad. I was going crazy anyway. I may as well go crazy and take a chance as go crazy staying here and getting nowhere.

It was the biggest challenge of my life and I had to overcome it. Functioning on empty, I had to draw strength from deep inside myself to do what I was about to do. Little did I know that this was teaching me resilience – and what a valuable quality that was to have.

Grasping the small card, the one I had picked up from the doctor's waiting room, I re-read the words on it. It read, in big, bold letters, 'Are you a victim of domestic violence?'

I could say I had suffered from every definition on that card of domestic violence. Mental abuse, physical abuse, controlling behaviour, to name a few.

The card was promoting Women's Aid, a charity that helped people who were victims of abuse by their partners. My heart was thudding as I picked up the phone, and I could almost hear it pounding in my ears. Nervously, I dialled the number and quite quickly a lady answered.

Fearful that Leon could be hiding around the corner listening, I told the lady to wait for a minute as I opened the kitchen door to have a quick peek around and check that the coast was clear. He was still in bed asleep, unaware that all our lives were about to change in a major way. The voice on the other end of the phone was comforting and encouraging, so I got straight to the point and told her that I was terrified of my husband and I could no longer stay with him.

She asked me questions such as did I have children? Did he work? Did I work? Trying to establish the situation I was in. She asked me to ring her back later that afternoon when it was safe and convenient for me to talk, aware that I was paranoid that Leon could be listening. She assured me that in the meantime she would sort something out.

My stomach was churning anxiously because I knew this was for real, she was going to find us somewhere to go. As much as I hated my life with Leon, the prospect of taking the children to a strange place was almost more daunting than staying at home where it was familiar. There is a saying 'better the devil you know than the devil you don't' but not in this case. Putting my faith in the woman I spoke to that day I ended the call and knew I had to persevere and leave the devil I knew.

All of a sudden, I heard him thump the floorboards three times – he wanted me to go up to him. Hearing that sound made me feel a little smug and I smiled to myself. It felt empowering realising that I knew something he didn't. This might be the last day I'd take his coffee and cigarettes up after the treble bang of the floorboards.

Acting normally, I took his drink up and he seemed in a nice mood; it made wonder if I had overreacted. He patted the bed, enticing me to come and sit beside him. He smelt lovely and familiar, and I felt terribly sad that it had come to this, but I knew I couldn't let one moment in time knock me off my stride. I had to keep moving forward, making progress towards a normal life.

He eventually surfaced and got ready to go out for the day. I had been on tenterhooks waiting for him to leave so that I could phone Women's Aid back.

I kept telling myself that there was no other option. Dad and Helen had an empty furnished bungalow attached to their house, but I didn't want to be a burden on them. It was a lot to expect of anyone that I should move in with them, let alone with two children. After all, the children were a handful, and I knew we would be noisy. So, living next door to Dad and his girlfriend was out of the question. I didn't need to be under any more pressure worrying about noise, and I didn't want to bring any trouble to his door with repercussions from Leon if he learned I had moved in next to Dad. No, it had to be somewhere Leon could not find us, it was the only way.

It had to be somewhere where I would get support for my children and for me; somewhere we would be comfortable. I needed to do this independently – to break free, cut the cord.

After I had taken the children to school, Leon finally went to his parents. He would probably be back late teatime to get ready for work that evening. When he had gone, I picked up the phone and spoke to the lady at Women's Aid.

'Now, Stacey,' she said, 'we have managed to find you a place that you and the children can stay in. It's a refuge in the midland's, but the staff there could do with you popping over today to sign the paperwork and let them know when you can officially get there with your belongings.'

This was all going too quickly. The thought of taking my belongings seemed so final, and somehow I felt as if I was being forced into leaving. Logic swept in; this was my choice, these people were trying to help me and, like it or not, there was no excuse for me to stay at home any longer. The determination to leave now wasn't so much because of Leon being violent, it was more due to my daily obsession with planning to leave. Now I had finally made the call and taken the first big step, I just needed to push myself that one step further.

So, acting bravely, assuring myself this was for the best, I took the address and wrote down the directions and told her to tell the refuge staff I would be there around one o'clock that afternoon. Putting the phone down my mind was in a whirl. Part of me was tempted just to get back into bed and pull the duvet over my head, go to sleep and pretend the conversation I had just had hadn't happened. After all, Women's Aid couldn't call me back or shout at me for messing them around.

'No, no, no, Stacey,' I reasoned to my anxious side, 'you have got to do this.' I knew I had to do it for my safety and sanity and the safety of my children.

I set out early to give myself plenty of time to find the place. Leon had phoned, checking up on me, but I lied and told him I was on my way out to take some library books back. I drove through the busy streets, the rain spotting on the windscreen; it was a cold and dull day. I eventually found the place; it was on a dead-end street with about five tall terraced houses. I could make out a slide looming over the fence in the back garden and hear the sound of children shouting.

Checking my paperwork to make sure I had the right house number, I got out of the car and looked over at the tall Victorian terraced property. It was so different from the new detached house I called home, and it looked – I hate to sound ungrateful – dowdy. The windows were dirty and untidy, with different curtains hanging in them that didn't match. They were far too long for the windows so lay crumpled on the bottom of the dusty sills. The front garden was besieged by a large bush that blocked most of the view into the downstairs windows.

Walking up the steps to the front door, I kept thinking to myself that I didn't belong here, that I should just turn around and go home, but still I kept on walking, as I knew that if I went home I would be on the planning to leave merry-go-round again. The front door was filthy, and reluctantly I grabbed the big brass knocker and rapped it loudly a couple of times. I half expected Lurch from the Addams family to put his head round the door and say, 'You rang?'

After much noise of bolts being pulled across, keys being turned and chains being taken off, a large lady with greying hair, ruddy cheeks and glasses answered the door.

'Can I help you?' she said, looking confused.

I thought I must have the wrong address, so I told her my name and that I'd been given this address.

'Oh!' she replied, looking rather annoyed. 'Didn't they tell you to come the back way because we don't use this front door?'

I apologised and offered to go around the back, but she brushed me off and insisted I came in that way seeing as she had spent ten minutes unlocking the door.

As I walked into the house, the smell of damp walls and soiled nappies engulfed me. In the tiled corridor, there were about ten coats hung on the banister stand; it was so overloaded a couple of coats had fallen on the floor and had the imprint of dirty trainers on them. The aroma of a casserole cooking in the kitchen wafted under my nostrils as I turned the corner behind the stout lady, moving through the hallways as she beckoned me to follow her to wherever she was leading me. Children's voices echoed in the background as they played in the rain in the back garden.

The poor children I thought, laughing and playing innocently, totally oblivious as to why they were in this big, strange house. The walls were all painted pale pink, covered in smudges and finger marks. The floors were covered in cheap lino that had long since seen its best days.

The lady led me into the office where we were met by Patricia, the manager, who was a far warmer soul, and she gave me the nicest welcome you could imagine. A woman in her fifties, she was attractive and well spoken, with a confident demeanour that immediately put me at my ease. She made me feel like a little girl, not in a controlling way, but more in the way of a nurse to a sick child, assuring the child that everything would be alright now after giving them the biggest spoonful of healing medicine. This was the first step to making a change in my life and I sensed Patricia realised that and would support me in any way she could.

'Take a seat, Stacey,' she said kindly, 'and tell me a little about yourself and what brings you here.'

Where to start? I supposed it was just best to be honest. So, I told her about how Leon was with me and that I needed to get away, especially for the sake of my children. Patricia listened intently but all the time I was talking to her the stench of the house was going up my nose. The situation was spilling from my lips, but in my head I was already having doubts that I could actually leave my home tonight and bring the children here. When I had finally finished telling her about my situation, she gave me some forms to fill in. The forms were requests for my details so that social security could start paying for my lodgings.

We arranged that I would go back there later on that evening when Leon had gone to work so that he wouldn't get suspicious. It would give me time to pack and sort things out. None of it felt real. I felt as if I was in somebody else's body living somebody else's life – that's probably why I wasn't crying at the thought of where I was going to be living.

My head was in a complete spin that day, but I knew I had to leave. Evening came and Leon finally left for work. The door shut and I watched him get in the car and disappear out of sight. I didn't feel sad or elated. There was no room for procrastination I was fully focused on leaving.

Reece was six, and Sophie was four, so they were at the age where they were aware of things to a degree but wouldn't really question what was going on.

It wasn't a matter of emptying the whole contents of the house because I knew there wasn't a lot of room where we were going, and I wasn't aware that the refuge would have collected our furniture and put it into storage until I was housed. However, that wouldn't have made any difference to me because I felt so guilty for leaving Leon that I didn't want to take a lot with me. I began packing the bare essentials into black bin bags. In went our clothes, our toiletries and the children's favourite toys. Even though it was supposed to be the bare minimum, I still ended up with six large bin bags.

Now to tell the children.

I explained to them that we were going away for a little while. Reece got a bit upset so I told him we were going on a little holiday to try to ease the situation; even so, I think he sensed the enormity of what was happening.

Even the dog, as daft as he was, seemed aware that we were saying a final farewell, and he had a sad expression on his face, his big paws balancing on the stairgate. Normally, his tail was happily wagging, but he was just staring and still. It wasn't really his fault that he was such a big responsibility. I felt guilty that I intended to leave the poor dog alone for twenty-four hours until Leon returned. Feeling bad, I held his face in my hands and gently smoothed back the fur on his brow as he looked at me. I swear he knew we were leaving. Normally, he would have been jumping around so much I would never have got so close to him.

'I'm so sorry, Ben, my darling, I wish I could have appreciated you,' I cried, and buried my face against his furry head, another innocent suffering in the crossfire of domestic violence. Of course, I left him plenty of food and drink, but unfortunately there wasn't anyone I felt I could get to check on him because I knew my priority had to be getting out of the house.

The bags were packed, and I had said goodbye to the dog. Picking up the handset I called a taxi. Everything seemed so urgent, pushing me reluctantly along the path of leaving my home.

Taking one last look around the house, I climbed the stairs and peered in at my children's lovely clean bedrooms with their character quilt covers. Looking at the picture on the wall in Reece's room of the hedgehog doing a spot of fishing on his canal boat, I thought that everything looked so innocent, but then nothing that had gone on in this home had been pure and innocent.

The sound of the taxi driver urgently blasting his horn outside to let us know he was here broke my train of wistful thoughts. He was in a rush to get on to his next job but I wanted to have these last few moments in my home. I took one desperately quick last look around, my heart heavy. Heat radiated out of me; my face felt red hot and I realised I was sweating. It wasn't hot outside – on the contrary, it was still winter – but I was burning up with anxious energy.

The children were excited, oblivious to the reality that we were leaving home and going to live in a hostel, leaving their dad behind. The driver hopped out of the cab to open the doors for us, the sound of the radio playing 'Please Don't Go' by KWS loudly in the background. How appropriate, I thought, as the words rang out 'Babe, I love you so, and I just want you to know, that I'm going to miss your love, the minute you walk out that door, please don't go.'

The driver looked at me struggling with the black bin bags and came running over to grab them off me; he must have wondered what was going on as I started to cry at his act of kindness. The words to the song resonated in my soul at the thought of Leon and how he would feel when he got home to the empty house, his wife and children gone, and the note I had left saying, 'I tried!'

Stepping into the taxi, I made sure the children's seatbelts were in place securely. Let's say goodbye to the house, Sophie suggested, smiling, as she sat up on her knees to look behind her out of the window. Reece followed suit and so did I. The taxi door shut loudly, and the car engine turned over. We started moving. 'Bye house' we all said and laughed, waving excitedly as if we were waving to a friend. The car pulled out of the street where we had lived, leaving behind like a blot on the landscape, the house we had shared with Leon.

Why did I always feel so sorry for Leon? Engulfed with guilt, I burst out crying for the umpteenth time, feeling I had given up on him. That's why I didn't feel too bad about leaving him with the house and car, it was the least I could do, a trade for the guilt. He was going to be devastated when he got back from work. He would know something was wrong when he rang the house phone on the way back and I didn't answer.

Pulling myself together, I had to stop my thoughts from going down this path as I was overcome with waves of sadness. I fought the urge to shout and tell the driver to turn back round. Reasoning with myself, mind over matter, I had got away from the house, and I was in the transition now to a new life.

The taxi turned the corner and the realisation hit me that I had left I had finally done it!

'What are you crying for, Mummy?' asked Reece innocently.

'Oh, Mummy's just happy,' I lied, wiping my eyes with the back of my coat sleeves. Reece held my hand and, amid all the fear of the unknown, I knew that we were going to be safer where we were going than at home, and that was all that mattered right then. Anything else I would deal with later.

Refuge Life

It was a freezing cold February evening when the children and I finally got to our new home. Patricia had instructed me that day that when I arrived that I was to let myself in through the back gate. It wasn't as easy as that though, as when I got there it was dark and the latch on the gate was very stiff. I was fiddling around in the dark trying to click the latch open, and the children were clinging to me. *God*, I thought frustrated, *if Leon were here now he'd have this open in two minutes.*

Straightaway, I tried to erase that comforting thought of Leon, realising how much I had relied on him. I had to be strong. At last, I managed to open the gate, and, with arms laden with black bin bags full of our belongings, we trotted down the path, through the little garden to the back door. The children were excited as they could make out the silhouette of the climbing frame and slides. Lights were on in the house, and I could hear the noises of the residents shouting at their children, as I reluctantly tapped on the door.

A solemn-looking lady, with short black hair and a face as pale as death, opened the door for us. Fortunately, she was very pleasant and helped us in with our stuff. She introduced herself as Max. As we walked through the kitchen, everyone was staring at us and I suddenly felt like the new girl at school. Not wanting to be deterred having come this far, I maintained an air of confidence, although inside I was terrified.

The other mums were all sitting round smoking and looked up and said hello one by one, after brief introductions. They all seemed pleasant enough. It was a relief when we moved on, as Max said she would show us to our room. The radiators were pouring out heat, which was at least some form of comfort on this cold evening. Climbing to the first floor of this big old Victorian house we reached room eight, our new home. Max shuffled with the keys and let us into our room, passing me my own key.

The dreary room contained a bunk bed, a single bed and one wardrobe. It, too, was painted in the same dirty pink as the rest of the house, and the beds were made up of mismatched old blankets – but fortunately they looked clean. The communal bathroom was just down the corridor. I didn't like the idea of sharing a bathroom with lots of strangers, and the bedroom didn't look too inviting either, but in comparison to where I had left, it was safe.

A few moments later there was a knock on the bedroom door and I opened it to a couple of the rough-looking mums from downstairs. 'Listen, when you've settled the kids, come down and have a drink with us if you like. Okay?'

Bless them for being so kind, it was very thoughtful of them, and at this specific time in my life when I felt truly vulnerable their offer of friendship was really comforting. That evening though, I stayed in the bedroom with my children. They needed me tonight more than ever; probably as much as I needed them. Trying to act at ease in front of the children, I began unpacking our things. We got our pyjamas on and got into our new beds. They argued over who would have the top bunk, but eventually the dispute was settled when Sophie won the place high up, and I agreed to share the bottom bunk with Reece as he didn't want to sleep alone.

Then the guilt started to set in for taking the children away from their lovely clean home and routine, but still I knew there was no other way. Reece said he wanted to go home, and even though I tried to cry as discreetly as I could, somehow the poor little mite must have sensed I was upset, as he said, 'It will be okay, Mum,' and gave me a gentle little hug.

Tormented memories of longing to see my own father as a child, and not being allowed to by my mother, amplified the guilt I was feeling for my children, who were obviously homesick and missing their dad. Cuddling Reece, I convinced him we were all going to be just fine and have a new home of our own soon.

The next morning, we woke about half-past eight and I got us all ready. The strangeness of being in this new environment consumed me, evoking anxiety in the pit of my stomach. As we brushed our teeth in the damp bathroom, my eyes wandered over the chipped tiles and mildew surrounding the bath. The plughole was full of gunge, so I watched the children keenly to ensure that they didn't let their brushes drop into the sink.

In the kitchen there were cups and overflowing ashtrays everywhere. The dirty crockery was piled up high in the sink. We went into the living room, which was filled with a selection of old chairs and settees. A big, old-fashioned television took pride of place in the corner of the room. It was still fairly early and no one else seemed to be up and about, so we made ourselves comfortable on the chairs. The clock didn't seem to move; time, it seemed, had come to a standstill, and each second that ticked by was a reminder of my loss of routine.

What was I to do here all day, other than be safe? There had been so much drama in my life and suddenly I was filled with quiet, dull space. This is how criminals must feel in prison I surmised, bored and empty. We weren't allowed visitors because the location of the refuge was supposed to be a secret for safeguarding reasons. After all, this was a hostel where the majority of women were fleeing violent and abusive partners.

It wasn't like having your own home where you had access to your creature comforts. The place was not very clean, and I longed for my own bath that only my family had lain in. The kitchen was shared and it was pointless cleaning it properly as people were in and out of it all the time, using the facilities.

The children were hungry and there was a packet of morning coffee biscuits on the side so I said they could have them, assuming the food was free for the housemates. Trotting into the kitchen I found some bread and made us all some toast and a cup of tea. Eventually, one of the girls came down and I recognised her from my younger days as she'd gone to school with Leon. Her name was Debbie, she had come to stay with her two children, and she was very skinny, to the point of looking ill.

'Have you seen the packet of morning coffee biscuits that were on the fireplace?' she asked. *Oh God*, I thought, *please don't let them have been her biscuits.*

'Yes, I'm sorry,' I replied sheepishly, 'the kids were hungry so I said they could have them. Were they yours?'

Debbie laughed and explained how things were ran there. We were all allocated our own cupboards for our own food, which we had to buy. Feeling embarrassed, I made a mental note that when I went shopping later that day, I would buy her a new packet of biscuits. 'Don't worry about it, Stacey,' she laughed, but I did.

At least that gave me something to do for that day, although I didn't relish the idea of going out in the freezing cold to walk into town and fetch shopping – especially having to start from scratch. It would have to be all the necessities: washing powder, teabags, condiments and so on. There was a lot of shopping to be done and I thought how much easier it was at home, having my car to go and fetch the shopping.

So, that freezing cold February afternoon, I walked into town with the children. It was such a dark dismal day, the roads and town looked grey, and then to top it off it started to pour with cold, hard, freezing rain. We hurried into town as the icy drops pelted down on us. It was so depressing. We went into the cheap supermarket, and I tried to keep my shopping as light as possible. I hardly had any money, and I was going to have to carry it all back on my own.

Walking back, my fingers were being strangled by the handles of the heavy carrier bags and the cold rain was hitting my face. The children were loitering behind me and I kept telling them to hurry. Just when I thought things couldn't get any worse, Reece yelled, 'Urgh, Mum!' Turning around, I saw he had just walked through a great big lump of dog mess. It was squashed into his shoes and had gone right up his trouser leg.

Feeling totally fed up and defeated, I almost cried, but I knew I had to portray a positive persona for the sake of the children. Taking him by the hand I led him to a little patch of grass behind some garages. Reece wiped the bulk of it off and then we ran back to the refuge to finish cleaning him up. Getting in through the door, I pulled Reece's shoes off and tugged his trousers off. Making Reece wait in the entrance I had to go into the kitchen where the other mums were cooking and ask if anyone had an old carrier bag spare. One of the mums passed me one and I put Reece's trousers in and rushed upstairs to our room. Throwing the bag in the corner I rushed back down to the kids and the shopping. The kids and I very quickly got washed and changed, then I put the shopping away. It was day one and I was desperately missing home already.

Lying on the bed later that day, I wondered how I was going to get through each day in this strange environment, but I knew I had to persevere. The peace of mind I had sought by coming to the refuge was overridden by missing my familiar home.

Fortunately, before too long, the refuge staff kindly arranged for the children to attend a local school. It was an enormous relief for me because I knew the children would have a bit of normality in their daily routine, and it would give me time to get the rest I needed.

When the children were at school, I could relax and let go of all the tears. It was hard trying to maintain a bright and breezy manner in front of the children all the time. My only relief was sleep and I was so tired I would sleep for the whole day when they were at school and still sleep easily at night.

It was during these rest times in the day that strange things started to happen to me. A mystical, soothing habit was forming. It was the only time in my life I had ever experienced anything like this. I desperately craved the peace of sleep and shutting away from the world. It was like a drug to me, something I needed to do. Once I had dropped the children off, I would rush back to the refuge, climb the stairs, strip off and get into my bed, pulling the bedding around myself to keep warm.

Nestling into my quilt with no one there but me was complete and utter bliss. Within minutes, I could feel myself drifting deeper and deeper into a sleep-like state that was like nothing I'd ever felt before. One day, within what seemed like an hour, suddenly I woke feeling very conscious of where I was. I felt very cognizant of being present in my body; however, I was paralysed. My eyes were shut tight, trapped in my body where I could not move a muscle.

It was scary because I was mentally awake and completely aware of my surroundings. In what seemed like seconds, I started to see what was physically around me, even though my eyes were shut. I could see the ceiling above me and make out the colour of the duvet through my peripheral vision.

In a lame attempt to get upright (as I was completely aware I was in a sleep state), I tried to sit myself up, but my body felt like a lead weight. Feeling completely trapped in my own shell of my body I tried to scream, hoping that someone could hear me and come in and shake me awake, but my voice box couldn't even manage a groan. The effort was immense, but nothing could take me out of this trance-like state. Desperately I tried to move but I was completely frozen.

Suddenly I managed to move, shaking myself free from the overpowering feeling of the confinement of my human body. It was as if my soul had been disconnected from my body. My human body was a mere shell, and my conscious soul knew it was free to explore. Intrigued, I sat up, realising how light I felt. *What the hell is happening here?* I thought, bewildered. Then an overwhelming feeling dragged me back inside my body and the overpowering urge to sleep took over. It happened repeatedly, as if my soul was trying to break free of me, the person.

Somehow, when I sensed it had been four or five hours that I had been in bed, I tried to get back into my body to wake myself up, as I knew it would soon be time to collect the children from school, but it seemed impossible to burst through the paralysis, as much as I tried to move. I managed to wake up about ten minutes before I was due to pick the children up from school.

Walking to the school to collect the children, I was astonished at what had taken place that afternoon, realising I had been in bed for over five hours. It felt sort of euphoric knowing I had visited another dimension. It was quite frightening too, but I had liked the idea I had entered another realm where nobody could get to me! It felt like a superpower.

The next day, I took the children to their new school again. Guilt stung me as I watched them line up in the playground in their little duffle jackets. Each line of children contained about twenty-five to thirty kids, and my two children didn't know any of them. I felt so bad for them as they must have been anxious being the new boy and girl. The bell rang and they reluctantly trotted into the school in single file, holding their little satchels.

At least once I got back to the refuge I could get straight in bed and go to sleep, not feeling anything until it was time to collect them. Getting straight into bed at 9.10 a.m., I set the alarm for 2:50 p.m., hoping this would be long enough for me to rest as I knew I could easily sleep all day.

Not too long into my sleep I woke again feeling paralysed. This time I tried not to be so alarmed so that I could try and experiment with what was happening to me. I fought to sit up many times, but I was restrained by my own body. Then one time I broke through it and the feeling of being on another plane intoxicated me. It was strange feeling as I was light as a feather.

I was aware that my movements were no longer restricted by the complexities of my human body which I had detached from. Suddenly, I was sitting up and I could see all round the room. Then, strangely within a split second on I was lying back down, back in my body, feeling paralysed again.

In vain I tried to shake myself awake but it seemed impossible to move, then my eyes sharply opened, and I breathed a sigh of relief. I had woken up back in the world as a human! It had been an absolutely amazing feeling. I had looked round my bedroom and saw every little detail, even the time on the clock had been in synch with the time now. It was a few minutes along now. This convinced me that I hadn't been dreaming. I felt excited. If I could come out of my body, just how far could I travel?

When I fetched the children from school, I took them to the library so they could read some books and I could do some research, as I was curious to find out more. Now I was totally convinced of the concept of the body and the soul connection, so I searched for books and discovered the theory of astral travelling (out-of-body experiences) and spirituality. I felt I was going on a journey, and I needed to arm myself with as much knowledge as possible along the way.

From my research, I learnt that we are spirits and our bodies are just shells. Furthermore, I learnt that by leaving the body we could travel further then just our immediate vicinity, if we had the courage. This was something I desperately intended to do, to see how far I could go.

The next day I took the children to school as usual and rushed straight back to go to sleep. I couldn't wait to experiment and see what happened. Once again, it wasn't long before I was aware I was in a paralysed state. This time I was calm and endeavoured to sit myself up. Not only did I sit myself up but before long I felt myself flying round the bedroom, one minute it seemed at the speed of light, the next manoeuvring very slowly.

Gliding freely, my vision was abruptly inhibited by a white glare which covered the whole of my eyes. What was happening? As I slowly reversed, I realised I had actually flown up to the white chest of drawers that was in the corner of my bedroom, and I had been so close to it that all I could see was the whiteness from the front of the chest. It felt as if I were looking through my eyes and my eyes were within a millimetre of the cupboard.

Then within what felt like a second in time I found myself back on the bed and in my body. Excited at what I had experienced, I thought that was enough for today and tried to shake myself awake. I lay on the bed again, struggling to wake myself up. It was beginning to frighten me as it was stifling trying to move and not being able to. It worried me that I would stay this way forever, trapped in another dimension in a soulless body, never to be with my children again. Finally, my eyes opened, and I lay there, bewildered but fascinated by the whole experience.

The strange thing was that the out-of-body experiences never happened to me at night. They only ever seemed to happen in the afternoons when I slept as the children were at school. It was becoming a habit, and an out-of-control one at that. One afternoon as I slept, I woke in my out-of-body state and tried to get through the bedroom door because I wanted to go further than just my bedroom and see people, but I couldn't work out how to do it.

Standing by the door, I could almost feel the force of the invisible elastic that was still connecting me to my body that lay on the bed a few feet away. Then I heard footsteps coming up the stairs outside the bedroom door. The house was three stories high but there was only me and the children, and another girl, Dawn, who shared the house. The whole refuge complex was actually four houses next door to each other.

Dawn was always out during the day so it couldn't have been her. I could hear keys jangling and I realised it must have been one of the office staff. I wanted to see who was there in their physical form, and what they were wearing so I could prove to myself that I was not dreaming and confirm that I was indeed leaving my body.

If I could just see their clothes and make a mental note of them, then when I woke, I could go to the office and check if that was what the person I could hear was actually wearing that day. In this otherworldly state, I tried with my entire might to shout to them, but no sound would leave my lips. I could hear the person go up the next flight of stairs. Excitedly, I struggled to try and make them hear me but to no avail.

Eventually, the key jangler left the house and I struggled to wake myself up, keen to go to the staff quarters to see if anyone had been in the house. Quickly, I got myself dressed and ran round to the house next door where the office was. The staff were all sitting talking and I rushed into the room asking them excitedly if one of them had been into my house.

They all looked at each other a little bewildered as if to say what's she talking about? Tracey, one of the volunteers who was a bit of a hippy, sitting with a cotton shawl wrapped round her shoulder and a matching cotton head band around her long red hair, confirmed that she had been in the house to check some of the fire exits. 'Did you have some keys?' I asked excitedly. 'Yes, I did. Why?' She replied.

Then I began to tell them that I had been coming out of my body while asleep and I could prove it. I had heard Tracey come into the house. Surely this would confirm that I was not dreaming, but I was actually just an energy floating around the room. They didn't really comment, in fact they made me feel uncomfortable as they looked at each other as if I was being a bit strange, but I knew what had happened to me. This validated to me that we are all spirits in a physical realm.

A month into our stay, it was another boring weekend and I felt fed up. I wanted to sleep but I couldn't as I needed to keep the children occupied.

It was dismal and raining again outside. The refuge was located on a busy street that led into town. The windows were thin, and it was noisy outside. The traffic swept passed quickly and I could hear the sound of the tyres rolling along the wet roads. Looking out of the window, I watched the cars speeding past. My heart ached with the emptiness of missing the nice side of my husband. It was confusing. I was in a refuge fleeing my violent and controlling husband, yet I was missing him. I was missing home and missing the familiar routine of my old life. My life had gone from utter madness and drama to a complete anti-climax.

There was a public telephone in the corridor, and I wanted to hear a familiar voice. Despite creating trouble for me at times, Diane had been the nearest thing to a mother I had had over the years, and I felt guilty I had not told her of my intentions. So, I decided to call her and let her know her grandchildren were safe and well. I wondered how Leon was and hoped that the dog had been okay after we left. She was so pleased to hear from me, and her voice was a comfort. She told me how ill Leon was, and how he was missing us. She said he had learned his lesson and couldn't understand why now I couldn't go back. Poor Diane, she was worried about her son and her grandchildren.

'Please, at least let me know where you and children are staying,' she begged. 'I won't tell Leon, I promise, but at least if we know where you are, if anything happens, we can be there.' She sounded so sincere, and they were her grandchildren after all. So I gave her the address we were staying at, in confidence, and she promised me faithfully she would not betray my trust. After all, she knew the implications should she break her promise.

The next day, the children and I were walking back from the shops. They were running along merrily ahead of me, despite the rain and the dullness of the uneventful day looming ahead of us. Oblivious to the car that had pulled up behind me, I was shouting at the children to be careful as they were running so fast, I feared they would trip over.

'Stacey!' A hand gripped my shoulder, turning me round. I came face-to-face with Leon. He fell to his knees, sobbing uncontrollably. He had difficulty getting his words out between sobs.

'Stacey, please, please, come back home. This has been the worst time of my life; I miss you and the kids so much! I'm going to get help with my anger, I cannot go on without you.'

Looking up, he shouted to the children, 'Reece, Sophie!' Holding his arms out to them, he looked a broken man, so happy to see his children. 'Come to Daddy!'

The children stopped what they were doing and, with a look of joy on their little faces, as fast as their legs could carry them they ran into the waiting arms of their daddy. They had missed him so much, it was clear to see, and he had missed them. I felt responsible for the loss that they had experienced. The memories of what had driven me to leave him had been drowned out by this scene of loss and love. We were a family – we needed to be together, and if Leon was going to get help, then I had to give our family this chance.

Just hearing his desperate pleas and the thought of my nice comfortable home was too much temptation. 'Look Stacey,' he went on, 'I have a little bit of money put away. If you could just come home and give things another chance, we can book a nice holiday for us all abroad.' We had never been out of the country on holiday.

Images of hot sandy beaches, the sun shining, us all together as a happy family, were a far cry from the dismal situation I was in at the moment. Desperate for some normality and fooling myself again that this had been the shock Leon had needed, I reasoned to myself that surely, now I had proven I could leave, he would realise that I wasn't prepared to put up with the violence and abuse any longer. The idea of us all going away on holiday was just too appealing for me. Convincing myself that I had made my point, I agreed to go back home.

The Epiphany

So, I returned home having lost over a stone in weight, due to anxiety suppressing my appetite, and sleeping every hour that the children were not in my presence. With the additional strain of trying to cope with two energetic children in an environment devoid of the comforts and facilities that my home contained. The stress of not knowing where we were going to end up living, the years of violence and manipulation of living with a tyrant had taken their toll.

This time, as soon as I walked through the door of my home, it did not feel as comforting as it had done the first time I went back after leaving, all those years ago when Reece was a baby. However, I was home and that's where I felt I needed to be at this point.

Taking it all in, as I looked round, I couldn't believe how much the house had deteriorated. The bath had a big black ring of scum; the toilet water was murky from not having any bleach. He had sold the dog, his precious pet that he couldn't bear to get rid of when I had to look after it, yet a few weeks of responsibility for him had been too much and he had sold him to his friend. It was some comfort knowing he had gone to a good home, at least. The phone had been cut off, and the bills were in the red. It was amazing to me to see how much I had actually been doing to keep him in the lifestyle he had been accustomed to. And it was amazing that he had repeatedly told me I would never cope without him.

All that fuss over housework, all the arguments that had derived from kids' finger marks on the windows, yet, left to his own devices, he had been too lazy to keep clean and organised himself. It's so easy when you're cracking the whip! It gave me new-found confidence, as I realised that I wasn't so hopeless after all. When I'd been here, everything had been taken care of. All this time away from Leon had given my mind a chance to find itself, and I was seeing things for what they were, rather than what I'd been told they were. It was a life changing moment when I realised I actually could cope quite well on my own.

The children were very happy to be back, and Leon, as usual when reconciling, was making an effort to make me feel loved again. We sat at the table with a cup of tea, and he began to open up to me about how he had missed us. Gently cupping my face in his big hands, he promised me sincerely he was going to be a different man. He would never hurt me and drive me and the children away again. He looked into my eyes with so much love and intensity, I knew he meant it.

The moment was interrupted by a knock on the door. Leon quickly stood up as if he had been expecting someone and walked into the hall to get the door. It was Les and Diane. I heard their loud cheery voices and shuffled uncomfortably in my chair as it dawned on me that Diane must have been the one to tell Leon the address of where we had been staying. The sound of their happy voices annoyed me. I almost felt that I had been lulled into a false sense of security. I had walked right into their hands, and I was back to square one, playing happy families.

They came in and sat themselves down, asking how we were. They were full of excitable energy that things were back to normal. I was home and their son was happy. Leon went and made them drinks and they lit their cigarettes. 'It all worked out well in the end then?' said Les, breaking the silence. Having no idea what he meant I shrugged and screwed my face up, eyes looking to the side in confusion. 'Sorry,' I said. 'I am not sure what you mean?'

'Leon finding you,' Les went on. 'Diane had just come off the phone to you; you know, when you called her from the refuge?' he said looking at Diane for some support. Diane was nodding in agreement. 'Yes' she said, taking over where Les had left off. 'I had just written your address down on a slip of paper when you gave it to me, and Leon turned up at our house. I'd gone to answer the door to him and forgot about the paper with the address on which I had left on top of the microwave. Leon came in and saw it and worked out it was where you were staying. I wanted to explain this to you because I didn't want you to think that I had told him where you were.'

At that point, Leon came in with the tray of coffees and began handing everyone their cups. As they continued their conversation, the focus was clearly 'poor' Leon. Trying to be courteous, I sat for some time attempting to look nonchalant about the whole situation before making my excuses to go upstairs and unpack the clothes that we'd bought home from the refuge. It was perplexing to think that a few hours ago the children and I had been in a safe house because of

Leon's behaviour, and now we were home I got the impression that Leon and his family saw him as the victim.

The children and I had lost everything and had our worlds turned upside down. If anyone had suffered, I thought bitterly to myself, then surely it was me and the children? No matter how difficult things were, I always tried to act responsibly even though it had been tremendously hard at home and at the refuge. Putting the clothes away, bitter tears stung my eyes for me and my poor little children.

Leon hadn't lost his home, he had been leading the high life, going out drinking in bars, and sleeping the drink off at his leisure whenever he felt like it, yet once again he was the one getting the sympathy. The resentment I felt for him, and his biased parents, was clawing at my very soul. Yet I said nothing because things hadn't really changed, I was still suppressed. Frustrated at myself for leaving the refuge, the cycle began again, like a television stuck on repeat, my mind screaming I had to get out. But what to? Back to the dull existence of life in the refuge?

Predictably, the old way of life slowly resumed. It was Sophie's fifth birthday, and I had spent the last few months thinking about leaving again. I didn't want Sophie to spend her birthday in the refuge, so I decided to stay at home until her birthday was over. We had a party for her and only Leon's family were invited. I just faded into the background, making the tea and being the hostess.

My heart sank for my darling little girl, blowing out the candles on her cake and enjoying her party. If only underneath the surface, home life was as normal as it seemed today and the children and I didn't have to leave again, I thought sadly.

I knew I would leave again if a line was crossed, but just in case it was never crossed again, I tried my best to slot back into my old life. Leon gradually became moody again, and I knew I had to leave while I had any strength left. Things were spiralling and I feared his behaviour would be worse than ever now as I had practically given him the green light by going back to him. One morning, some time after Sophie's party, I was downstairs sorting the kids' breakfasts out and I heard Leon stamp on the floor with his foot in his usual demanding manner.

The previous night, he had shoved me out of bed for not wanting sex with him. As I lay on the floor he leapt up and stood over me, then he kicked me in the stomach and arms as I curled myself into the foetal position in a bid to protect myself. Lurching towards me he grabbed my hair, pulling me into a sitting position. My hair was sticking to my face in knots from the combination of the way he had pulled it and the tears I'd shed. He then grabbed both my ears and smacked my head on the wall behind me.

'You frigid bitch,' he screamed into my face. My heart thumped nineteen to the dozen and I was absolutely terrified. Finally, when the attack was over, he let me get into bed. Given a choice, I would have gone and got into bed with one of the kids, but I knew that would just instigate more trouble for me.

Lying there in the dark next to him, I was fuelled with resentment.

'I suppose you're going to leave me again now,' he said bitterly. I said nothing.

It wasn't long before I heard him snoring as he had nodded off to sleep. How could he be so contented after what he had just done?

The next morning when Leon was demanding his coffee, I murmured angrily under my breath, 'Fuck off, and get your own fucking coffee.' As I took his coffee into the bedroom, he was red eyed and seething with temper, going on about how I had rejected him the night before. Fortunately, his yelling didn't go on for too long, and I managed to get out of the bedroom and leave him to drink his coffee.

Back in the kitchen, I picked up the landline phone. It was locked. Leon had put a lock on it so that it could only be opened using a pin number. He wasn't that clever though, because when I tried the obvious choice for the pin – his date of birth – the phone came on. Urgently, I dialled the number at the refuge I had been staying in before I had gone back to him. God must have been watching over me because Patricia answered the phone as soon as it rang. She listened intently. She did not judge me and by some stroke of luck she had just been on the phone to the staff at a different refuge discussing a vacancy they had, and as she had hung up, my call had come through immediately. She quickly provided me with the address. As I put the phone down to her, I knew she would be on the phone to them arranging for the arrival of me and my children. I then called the domestic violence unit at the police station as it wasn't really an emergency as such – well to the emergency services anyway.

'Please can you send a police officer round to my house now? I need to leave my husband and I know he won't let me just walk out. I need to get out now.'

Their response was, 'Has he hit you?'

'No, he hasn't, well not yet anyway,' I whispered.

'Well,' replied the officer on the other end of the line 'if no offence has been committed, I am afraid that we don't have any rights to come round.'

Normally, I would have let them brush me off, but I was determined to leave the house and soon, because I knew he was going to lose his temper again.

'You don't understand,' I pushed, 'if you don't send an officer round he is going to hit me. He is upstairs now getting all wound up and I have children here. I need to get out now.'

At that moment, Leon was shouting at me, so I had to put the phone down and go upstairs. As soon as I walked into the bedroom he sprang out of the bed and pushed his face into mine, pinning my head to the wall with his. I can't even recall what he was angry about, but he always found something that I had done wrong to have a go at me.

Although he was spitting venom into my face and winding himself up for the next phase of the attack, I wasn't feeling my usual petrified self. I was calm because I knew that at any minute the police would turn up, and even if they were a little late and he had hit me, then that would be even better because nothing at that moment in time would have given me greater pleasure than to press charges on him.

The yelling was interrupted by a perfectly timed loud knock on the door. Leon looked like a bewildered rabbit caught in the headlights. 'Who's that?' he asked, his facial expression altering from twisted to wide eyed and scared.

It amazed me how he could turn his temper off for a knock on the door, yet he couldn't turn it off to stop himself hitting me!

Cool as a cucumber, I released myself from his hard grasp and made my way down the stairs. Opening the door, two police officers stood there, and I yelled up the stairs triumphantly, 'Oh, Leon, it's the police.'

Like a skulking little mouse, he peered round the landing wall to see what they wanted. 'We've had a complaint,' they said.

Just to make sure that Leon heard it, and while I was in a position to get away with saying what I wanted to say for a change, I shouted, obviously for the benefit of Leon's ears, 'Yes, officers, do come in, the complaint was from me. My husband was just about to beat me up again, and I need to get out.'

Now, from the police's point of view, this probably looked like an average domestic where I, the wife, was being a right bitch to my poor, unsuspecting husband.

Leon fell straight into the innocent husband role and came down the stairs in his dressing gown. 'Stacey, why are you doing this to me? I haven't hit her, officers, we were just having a little argument and she's blowing it all out of proportion.'

I called a taxi in front of Leon as the police looked on, making it blatantly obvious that they were disgusted with me.

Leon sat crying on the chair. 'Come on, kids, give Daddy a hug.'

He wouldn't have been bothered about hugging the kids if the police hadn't turned up; he wouldn't have cared about them hearing him beat me up, either. Leon could have won an Oscar for playing the part of the heartbroken husband.

The taxi pulled up and I began to load our stuff, which I had secretly packed, into it. This time I was a little more organised because I knew what I was doing. I loaded the portable television from the kids' room, but Leon came and took it back. The officers looked on without saying a word. 'Look, he's got all the furniture. Please can I at least take a television for the children?'

They had no intention of helping me, the cunning wife, with my heartless plan. One of them said, 'Sorry, but we can't get involved.' I suppose they got fed up with being involved with domestics. Fine, I thought, because there was one thing I knew about myself now, and that was that I could work my way up, even from having nothing. To have got through what I had gone through, and still plan to leave again, took a lot of strength, so he could keep the television.

The children were upset because Leon was making out that I was the bad mum taking them away, but I had to remind myself that this hurt now was better for them than what they would have witnessed had I stayed. It angered me that Leon could put on such a display of heartbreak in front of the children; it was only making things worse for them.

Finally, we got into the taxi and drove away. As the taxi rounded the corner on our lovely little cul-de-sac I felt that this would be the last time I would ever come down this street again. The relief to be driving away safely was indescribable. If I hadn't acted so quickly, I would have been on the floor now praying for a miracle to stop him getting angry, as well as praying for my two innocent children. Yet here we were, safe and on our way to another refuge.

We arrived at the new refuge in Worcester. It was a big, fine house on a main road, a much cleaner place than the one we had stayed in before. The back garden was lovely; it had a tarmacked play area with swings and slides where the children could play, and a wooden summer house full of toys and puzzles to keep the children occupied.

It took me some time to let my guard down. I'm not sure if it was just me naturally or if it was because of all the trauma, but I was a complete introvert. However, the women were really friendly, and the children were happy to socialise. As they made friends with the other children there, I naturally struck up conversation with some of the other mums and bit by bit got to know them, which made me feel a touch more comfortable. We all had stories to tell, and we bonded over our experiences.

The house was on a very nice, private housing estate. The local school was lovely, and I was fortunate enough to get the children in there pretty much straightaway. The walk to school meant crossing lots of busy roads. At this stage of my life everything felt unreal, and I remember studying people driving past me and wondering how they were just carrying on with their lives as if everything was normal. My weight had plummeted too – I could not eat and my anxiety completely killed off my appetite.

The lady who ran the refuge was called Linda and was extremely regimented, like a sergeant major. She was a big, stout woman with short greying hair, glasses and a hard face. Her rules meant the house was clean, tidy and comfortable.

She summoned me into her office when I first arrived there. She loved a cigarette and sat back in her chair like a psychologist, listening to me intently. Taking long drags of her cigarette, she questioned me about my relationship with Leon. She gave me some good advice – the same advice my father had given me to me after seeing me crying again on a Christmas day. He suggested to me that, should I find the strength to leave Leon I should break contact with him as he knew exactly how to talk me round.

Now Linda was telling me the same thing so it was clearly advice I should consider adhering to if two people were suggesting it. She told me that I must promise myself to give it at least a couple of months and, no matter how hard it got, or how homesick I felt, I was not to contact Leon because that's where the problem was. She said I needed to get strong and get my head right.

I took heed of this advice and even though there were some days when I desperately wanted to speak to him, regardless of what he had done, my resolve grew stronger. My sleep state was still very strange, and I still felt I was having out-of-body experiences. Overall, though, the less I spoke to Leon, the clearer my head felt.

Linda also suggested that should I ever weaken and go back and find myself in a situation I couldn't get out of, I should 'become an actress': act as if I wanted to be there, do and say whatever I needed to until I could get away safely. And that's what exactly happened. One weekend, a couple of months into my time staying at the refuge, I weakened and foolishly contacted Leon. He managed to talk me into meeting him. What harm could it do, I kidded myself, he sounded broken. Inevitably, I went to see him, but once inside my old family home it felt wrong, my anxiety kicked in and I knew I had made a terrible mistake. Fortunately for me, he did not realise this.

He said all the right things, but I had heard them so many times before. My head was already trying to work out how the hell I was going to get out of this. No one knew I was there. That evening I became as, Linda had advised, 'an actress', playing my role so well to make him think I was under his spell again. To execute my plan to get away, I convinced him that I was taken in by his loving promises and was going to come home for good.

If I had not focused on the task and thrown myself into the role, I would have buckled, which would have led to me panicking and then to me probably being held captive. He trusted me when I told him I needed to go back to the hostel to collect our things and tie up loose ends. I felt a fake, and a manipulator, but I had to protect myself. He allowed me to go back to the refuge in a taxi with a promise that I would be packing up and coming home within a few days.

The next day, I woke feeling both dreadful and grateful at the same time: dreadful that I had stirred up a situation that was best left dead; grateful that I had played my role and I was safe in the four walls of my refuge bedroom and he could not get to me. Then there was the guilt, thinking of him waiting for me to get in touch. He was desperate to have me home and I felt I had played a cruel trick.

Eventually, I made my way downstairs to start the breakfast for the children. Walking into the kitchen, I bumped into another housemate, Jade. She had been in the refuge for a few weeks, a single mum to a seven-year-old daughter, and had been through a very similar experience to me. She understood that even after everything Leon had done, I still felt pity for him and for the fact that I had left him. She did not judge me when I confided in her about my bad decision to go home, and reassured me that all was not lost as I was here now and safe.

Under the stairs there was a phone booth for our use should we wish to contact our family or call the staff in an emergency. With so much on my mind, I opened the door to the booth intending to call Leon's sister but, without realising, I dialled Leon's number. Unaware of this, the number was ringing out, and to my horror I heard Leon answer saying, 'Hello.' For a split second, I wondered how it was Leon's voice, then I realised I had dialled his number in error.

Not wanting to put the phone down on him because his voice had such an effect on me, I listened to him desperately asking, 'Stacey, Stacey, is that you?' At that moment, my friend Jade came past and saw my face. She mouthed silently, 'What?' and shrugged her shoulders in confusion – she must have seen that the colour had drained from my face.

Leon was still on the line and I peeked my head round the door to Jade, covering the mouthpiece of the phone so Leon could not hear me talking to someone else. 'Jade, I've made a mistake. I meant to call a friend and I've called Leon instead.' Jades's jaw dropped open in an exaggerated look of shock. 'Well, put the phone down then,' she whispered back to me.

The thought of putting the phone down on him seemed really cruel after hearing his gentle voice. All thoughts of his demonic side completely left my head. Not having time to think about what I was doing, and with panic hindering my logic, I made a hasty decision to ask Jade to speak to him. I knew she wasn't emotionally attached, and I knew if I spoke to him that, just as the snake hypnotises

Mowgli in the Jungle Book story, I would be convinced to come home.

'Please apologise to him, Jade, for me, and tell him I called him in error. I didn't mean to rub salt in the wounds, but I'm not coming home.'

After a couple of seconds of whispering, Jade took the phone off me, squeezing her plump little body into the booth as I moved out. In her light green T-shirt and baggy grey sweatpants, she swished her auburn fringe out of her brown eyes and looked at me seriously, taking a deep breath before placing the receiver to her ear.

Jade must have been really nervous and instead of speaking, she laughed out loud for a second, then said to me, and into the mouthpiece, 'Oh fuck.' Then she put the phone down, giggling.

'Jade,' I hissed, a little bit annoyed. Although I knew she was just nervous and couldn't help it, it had made the situation worse. Now it looked as if I was trying to mock him while he was in pain. The call was going to devastate him.

We retreated back to the living room to chill out, and although I felt sad for Leon, I felt a sense of relief too that I had not spoken to him. I would definitely be in a much worse position now if I had. There was no way now I could contemplate contacting him again to apologise for the call because it really would be playing with his emotions.

As much of a monster as he was, inside he was a little boy affected by what he had witnessed as a child, and I didn't want to hurt him. He was his own worst enemy and I pitied him for that. More than anything, I still wanted to be with him – a least his nice side – but I knew the ugly side would keep rearing its head. My softer self didn't want to leave things like this. I felt I owed him a proper explanation, but I knew I had to be cruel to be kind for both of us and keep well away.

Later that day, Heather, another one of the abused women in the hostel, asked me if I'd take a walk down to the shop with her. The children were all in bed and Jade said she'd listen out for them, so I decided to go.

It was evening and the sun was cooling down; I was wearing a light sarong skirt and vest to cope with the heat. Talking away as we walked across the busy roads, oblivious to anyone else, we headed for the shops. The sound of wheels screeching on the opposite side of the road stopped us in our tracks. My heart went into my mouth as, before I had a chance to register what was happening, Leon came bounding towards me from his car.

He looked angry, and the fact that I was with Heather was no deterrent to him. Heather saw my face and looked at him in shock, but before we had time to run, he grabbed hold of my arm and tried to pull me across the road to the car, which was parked erratically in the middle of the street with the driver's door not quite shut.

Heather was screaming at him to stop; she was obviously very frightened. Oblivious to the traffic having to stop for us as he pulled me over the road, I desperately tried to drop myself to the ground so that he would have to drag me to get me to the car. Somewhere in the panic, I was hoping that the police or someone would at least stop their car and intervene. It was all going too fast, and I knew that if he got me in that car with him, in the mood he was in he would kill me. He did not care who could see.

When he realised he couldn't make it over the road with me, he dragged me along the ground to the bus shelter. Once inside, he pulled me up by my clothes and pushed me up against the wall. All the time I was begging, 'Please don't hit me, please don't hurt me.'

His eyes were almost popping out of his head in anger, and he spoke with so much hatred he was almost spitting venom. 'Think it was funny, did you? Ay? Having a good laugh at me, getting your mate to phone me. Did it amuse you? Because I heard you both having a good laugh about me!' he seethed, angrily nodding his head, one of his habitual gestures when he was mad, threatening as if to say 'you've had it'.

'You're fucking with my head. My head's fucked, Stacey. I was coping okay till you made contact and made me believe you were coming home. You led me on, you got my hopes up. You had no intention of coming back, did you? You just fucked me over and laughed at me while you did it.'

As he was shouting at me, I went into a dream, studying his angry face. He had had his nose pierced. For a brief moment I wondered why he had done that as it made him look untidy, and he was always so well presented. Snapping out of my daydream as he continued, I tried desperately to redeem myself.

'No, no,' I insisted, wondering how the hell was I going to get him to calm down. 'You don't understand, I felt terrible for having to do what I did but…'

Next thing I knew, stars were floating in my eyes as bang, bang, he punched me around the face and head, specifically aiming for my temples. I vaguely remembered him telling me once that there was a sensitive area where you could punch someone near the temples and kill them. Each punch caused a flash of light as I dropped to the ground. For a few moments, I was totally out of it on the cold, dirty bus stop floor, then I came round to Heather pulling me up.

She was in floods of tears. 'Come on, man,' she was saying, trying to drag me to my feet. Somehow, she managed to pull my left arm around her neck for support, and I leant on her as we came out of the bus stop. Leon was rushing back to his car, looking over his shoulder and shouting, 'Get her to the hospital.' The car door slammed, and he was gone like a bat out of hell.

Leaning on Heather, I could feel her panting for breath as she tried to get me back to the hostel. All I could think of were the consequences of Leon beating me up. Now the manager of the hostel would find out what instigated this, and worse still she would think that I had put everyone at risk by letting Leon know where the refuge was. She would probably move me to a new place now he knew my whereabouts.

Heather pulled me through the front door, and I collapsed on the settee. This was my own fault, I thought, embarrassed. All the refuge staff would think I was an idiot. I felt so ashamed. Linda, the refuge manager, came into the room and when she saw my face she knelt by my side and began saying prayers for me. She was a born-again Christian and was on a mission to get me converted. Jade, oblivious to what had gone on, came into the room singing Pulp's 'Common People', but she stopped in her tracks, 'Oh my God, what's happened?' She said, her mouth open wide in shock. Then she started to laugh with nerves.

The police were called, and they took a statement from me and advised me to go to hospital to get my injuries checked out. My temple had seemed to take the brunt of it, I had a black eye, and my head was cut open. Luckily, nothing was broken, but my skull needed to be glued where it had been split open from the punch. It was humiliating having to tell everyone the truth, that I had gone back to him, and that is what had started the trail of events. It was revealed later that Leon had called the taxi firm after I had left him that night and they had disclosed to him where they had dropped me off. That's how he knew where I was.

I lay on the couch feeling thoroughly defeated. Why did life have to be so hard? Living here was like being in prison, so boring and with no certainty of the future. I'd lost my sense of belonging anywhere. I felt like chucking the towel in, but I had to go on for the children's sake.

I had managed to stay away for months, on and off, surely my life should be shaping up and getting better by now. All the stress and heartache was relentless. I started this, it was me who caused the chaos. There was all this to cope with, as well as trying to be a responsible mother. There seemed to be no release. A big black cloud of depression hung over me. Leon had had self-imposed boundaries regarding his treatment of me, but now he had gone beyond even those.

The morning after the assault at the bus stop, my trance-like state was broken by the sound of Linda urgently knocking my bedroom door. 'Stacey, Stacey.' Bolting upright and back to my senses, I told her to come in. I wondered anxiously what it could be that was so urgent. Linda looked at me sternly and began to tell me how she had just come off the phone from the Social Security fraud office. There had been an allegation of benefit fraud and they were coming to see me that afternoon.

There was more trouble to come for me and I panicked. Linda must have seen the horrified expression on my face and she probed me for information as to what it was about. How on earth could I tell her that I had been claiming as a single parent under duress? Surely no one would believe me or understand?

I told Linda how Leon and I lived under the safety net of social security benefits and how I didn't declare that he was living with me. I explained how Leon had threatened me into claiming as a single parent so that we could get the mortgage paid, even though he was actually living with me and working. It had been something I was dead set against, but out of fear and to keep the peace for the children I had no choice but to go along with it. Linda advised me to tell the truth, but she couldn't guarantee that I wouldn't get into serious trouble for it.

Later that day, two burly looking women turned up in suits with briefcases, showing me their identity passes. They looked me up and down, making me feel quite intimidated. Then they told me that my husband Leon had made an allegation of fraud against me. Having lost his job, he had put in a claim for benefits as the only resident of the marital home. When they had asked about the mortgage being paid already, he had told them that he had always lived there and that he had no idea I had been claiming income support. He knew this could mean a prison sentence for me. He also knew that he had forced me to live this way, yet again he was out to save his own skin regardless of the repercussions for me.

'So,' they asked sternly, 'was Leon living with you or not?'

With nothing more to fear, telling the truth was a relief and what would be would be. Every cloud has a silver lining and the fact that I was sitting there, with my face black and blue from the beating that Leon had given me, helped to confirm the life I had been living. They told me that under the circumstances they could see that I was telling the truth and for that reason they wouldn't be taking any further action. I felt so relieved that I wasn't going to get into any more trouble.

I had hit an all-time low since the attack. Everything was a battle, and I could not cope with it. Feeling extremely low, Leon's words kept going round and round in my head. Remembering the demented look on his face, as if he was cracking up, I wondered if this was my fault. I thought back to the night I had gone home before he had turned up here, and I remembered his happy face, how he had trusted me to leave and come back, and how I had tricked him, betrayed him. No wonder he was angry.

Having had enough of the struggle, I got up to make myself a cup of tea, the only thing I could stomach these days. As I walked into the kitchen past the girls, no one spoke to me. It all felt so alien, it wasn't my home. Swilling a cup and clicking the kettle on, I had Leon's words going round and round in my head. Him missing me, me meaning so much to him and that's why he had got into the state he had been in. Walking out of the kitchen, I turned and headed up the stairs. My head was a complete mess, I couldn't see the wood for the trees. Packing our stuff, defeated, I called a taxi and we went home, back to Leon. Two weeks later predictably we ended up in another refuge again.

I was on the domestic violence merry go round, when when your defences are down, he wears you down and he breaks you, leaving you at your most vulnerable, aching for someone to take you in their arms and wash away all the mental anguish, and soothe away the bruises. That person who rescues you from the pain is the very person who created the awful existence in the first place.

Only there's a problem. The victim of the abuse is not thinking clearly after all she has endured, and of course the invitation of warm and tender arms, the sound of loving promises, the idea that maybe this time he has learnt his lesson, this time will be different and he will cherish you, are like water to a wilting flower that's been parched in a desert of hot sand.

The children and I would feel homesick and I confused that with missing Leon. Days of anxiety would build up inside me, as I craved security and familiarity. So, I would phone him, and Leon would say he had changed. He was very persuasive, so much so that I would relent. He would tempt me with promises of a new start and tell me how much he missed the children, and how the children needed a father. True the children did miss him, and I missed him – it must have been Stockholm syndrome. After all, he was all I had known in my adult life and we had grown up together.

We – the children and I – went back a few times and each time we got the same result. The same events would play out. Leon would behave himself for a short while but, like the proverbial leopard with the spots, he soon defaulted to character. My hopeful and wishful thinking was clearly displayed to Leon as weakness, as I yo-yoed between leaving him and going back to him again. This inevitably led him to believe that I was his puppet, and he could pull my strings. He began to believe that he was invincible, so over time, when I did go back, he became aggressive more quickly.

Losses and Gains

It's difficult for anyone who has not been in the situation to comprehend why a woman keeps going back time after time to a man who is abusive to her. It is a vicious cycle. It starts with the grief cycle when you initially make the break. From my perspective, I was leaving the person I loved, the person I was closest too, and the person I had children with.

I frequently went through a denial stage, thinking it wasn't that bad. This was especially prominent on the few occasions when things were going well between us. The more time that went by, the more normal the situation seemed.

Then the anger stage would come, knowing that the way he treated me wasn't fair and I deserved better. Because my husband was abusive, I was unable to express my anger towards him. When, for instance, he shouted at me in front of the children, usually over something trivial, and caused us all to feel anxious, my internal response to this was pure frustration and anger. He had caused an unnecessary commotion and was upsetting us all, but I had to hold in these strong emotions. This left me suffering with stress and health issues, which explained my recurring tonsillitis.

Then there was the bargaining stage. Maybe if I tried harder, maybe if we moved house, had a fresh start, maybe if I was different, things would change? How could I change my behaviour to improve the situation?

Then came the depression stage, where I didn't feel strong enough to cope. I felt weak and my home life was affecting everything around me. Even trips to pick the children up from school were impacted, when I would release the pain kept inside me and cry in the car on the journey there, often standing at the school gates with a red, tear-stained face. I would feel shame, humiliation, hopelessness, and as if I was stuck and nothing would ever change. I was trapped, and frustrated with myself at not having enough strength to leave but knowing I should.

Then acceptance comes, when you know the relationship is over. This was the stage I so desperately wanted to get to but somehow it was so hard to make it through the other stages first that it would seem impossible to get to the point where I accepted that breaking up would be for the best.

Then there is the hope stage, where you tell yourself that you can do it, and you leave for good and eventually recover from the relationship. You accept things are never going to get better in your relationship, you conclude it's sad, but you had to end it and you are happier alone.

It's difficult to arrive at the point where you are ready to leave a relationship that you have emotionally invested in. This was a relationship I had chosen to go into myself, and at the start we had been happy. We cared about each other and shared the same hopes and dreams. My whole life was based around Leon, and I didn't know any other way. I wanted the abuse to stop but I didn't know how to leave the relationship.

It is said that a woman will leave her abusive partner several times before she makes the final break.

It was difficult to leave the relationship both practically and emotionally. I was in a domestic violence trap, worrying about the consequences of leaving. With so much to lose, it was hard to think of how much I would gain.

I still loved Leon, I just hadn't seen the subtle drip-feed of incidents that were developing over the time we were together. We had some good times, some good memories. My self-esteem had been shattered as I was frequently told that I would never manage on my own. Then I had to think of my children losing their dad. At that point, I did not realise the seriousness of the damage it was doing to them, and I felt guilty thinking about how much the kids would miss Leon and being part of a family unit.

Then if we moved, would I be able to see my family and where would we end up? Would we get a house? In terms of friends, I didn't have many to worry about as Leon had made it difficult for me to maintain friendships, or my friends had despaired of me, seeing how controlled I was, and we had lost contact.

I also had to think of the impact it would have on the children to leave their schools as I knew I would have to move out of the area. It would not be feasible to live near Leon, as he would not leave me alone.

My home was my comfort zone, it was our place of security and comfort – not when Leon was having one of his episodes but certainly when he was working away. It was blissful there then, and the uncertainty of where we would end up if we left was frightening. Leon took charge of the money, he was the earner, and considering I didn't work, I worried how I would manage financially.

It's difficult to imagine the pressure I was under, having to call a charity to arrange to leave my home within days, not knowing where we were going to live, and not being able to take many of our possessions. It was overwhelming to have to put a plan in place, then get through the obstacles ahead. God knows I did not have the strength when I was fighting a battle every day and that had taken its toll. It seemed as if there was a lot to lose and I wasn't thinking of the gains, as I could only foresee the barriers of leaving ahead of me.

Yet there was so much to gain. A fresh start away from all the upset and drama. The prospect of improved physical and mental health which was possible considering the stress I was living under constantly walking on eggshells.

In time, there would be the opportunity to make new friends (which I couldn't do now) and be reconnected with my family. My confidence and self-esteem would improve if I was away from the constant negative commentary and criticism.

The benefits of leaving were not immediate and would take time and effort. There were lots of immediate losses to consider in comparison to the gains, which would take time and hard work, and what scared me most of all was dealing with the fear of the unknown as to where the children and I would end up living.

Even if I left, I would still have to deal with Leon for child contact and I honestly could not see him just picking the kids up, putting them in his car and driving off to enjoy his fatherly duties. If I left, how would we get to a stage where we could be civil for the children, when I was dealing with someone who had no boundaries?

After he had beaten me so bad this time, the biggest question, and the one that didn't make any sense at all, was how could I let the memories of my lovely home take precedence in my head over the bad times? It was as if I completely wiped out what he was capable of, once I'd left, and I was homesick and I spoke to him when he was being nice on the phone. By the time I was reminded, it was too late, as it was usually when I was standing in front of him as he was getting angry. How could I forget the fear he instilled in me? Yes, I might have been bored in the refuge, but at least I was safe and calm.

And when faced with the aggression of my husband, I prayed to be magically transported to safety.

I decided that the most helpful thing I could do for myself would be to write down on paper what he had done to me again this time, and how petrified I had felt. These notes had to be clear and concise about the fact that, as well as me being beaten, the children were in the next room being exposed to this horrible, unhealthy atmosphere.

So, while it was fresh in my mind, I wrote myself a letter. The letter was to be my tool to prevent me being tempted to get involved with Leon ever again. He was manipulative to the point where he could make me lose focus of the terrible things he was capable of. I needed a reminder when I was feeling weak and missing him. When the letter was completed, I tucked it safely away. I would use this when I left him, to read whenever I was tempted to contact him.

A Letter to Myself

The weather was getting a lot colder but, luckily for us, the heating in the refuge was blasting. The place itself was worse than the one before – this one was small and dismal. It was getting close to Christmas, and I had previously managed to save about ninety pounds for the kids' Christmas presents. When I looked in my case in the little side compartment where I had hidden the money, I was appalled to discover it had gone. Leon had stolen my money, not just any old money, but the money meant to try and give his kids a decent Christmas.

My blood almost boiled with anger recalling the sacrifices I had made to save every penny. How I had walked with shopping instead of getting taxis, scrimped and saved at every opportunity so that I could put ten pounds a week away for the kids' presents. Leon had probably been out at the weekends, spending the money enjoying himself. I was quite tempted to phone him and ask him to have the decency to pass the money on to my mother for me. But I knew that he would only deny taking the money, and he would use the opportunity to try to talk me into coming home.

Christmas was dreary and depressing, but I kept reminding myself how much worse it would be if I were back at home with Leon. Memories of Christmases past with him came to mind and how they had all been ruined, so I had to be grateful for small mercies. Mum had invited us to hers for Christmas, but I was trying to keep her at arm's length too. Enough was going on in my life at the moment without adding more problems to it.

Luckily, the children did quite well for presents because the refuge had lots of toys donated by a local charity and it really made the difference to what would have been a miserable Christmas Day. I was so grateful. To see their little faces light up was a saving grace, even though they weren't at home where, in an ideal world, they should have been.

Again, the children and I shared a room with a set of bunk beds and a single bed. As before, for the first few nights I slept in the bunk bed with the children because they needed the comfort as much as me. At night, you could hear the other mums shouting at their kids, and the miserable hollering and crying of children who just wouldn't settle down.

The last time I went back to Leon I could not understand how I had put myself and the children in such a vulnerable position yet again. Despairing, I knew I couldn't trust myself not to go back to him again. He could easily put me under his spell. I didn't belong in a hostel, and I didn't belong in what was once my home, so it was no surprise I kept to-ing and fro-ing. All I wanted was a sense of security in my own environment for me and the children.

I was glad I had my tool – the letter I had written to myself before I left, something that would stop me putting myself and the children through this torture. Too mixed up with emotion and not even knowing who I was any more, I had struggled to see the wood for the trees, but it wasn't until I went back to the refuge this time that I knew for sure that there was no going back. Especially now I had my reminder in black and white. My pen had become my sword.

The letter I had written to myself after his last attack was to the future Stacey who inevitably would be contemplating going home again. It was a reminder from the Stacey who had just escaped from Leon and had it all fresh in her head and who had the wisdom and foresight to put it in writing. The language in it was hardly restrained, but I had to be tough on future Stacey.

It genuinely came from the heart and was somewhat erratic as I had scribbled it quickly. It was intended for me to save me, and as I read it, I felt the refuge really was my haven, which saved me from any further manipulation. The letter is scrambled, but it's where my head was at during that time.

Well, once again you have fucked things up. You had the craving to see him building up inside you, and you once again threw caution to the wind and gave in to temptation. Because of it you've ended up being beaten, having the fear of God, or rather Satan, put into you, lost over £90 in money (Leon robbed all the money you had in your purse, money saved for Christmas), had your privacy totally violated (Leon went through your diary while you were asleep and didn't take to you noting your feelings truthfully), neglected the kids (when Leon started an argument it would last for hours and you always tried to put the telly on for the children and go in another room so that they wouldn't hear the row) and ended up in yet another refuge, in another area. Because of this, every time your kids have to start all over again in a new school.

Stacey, you must read this when you get disillusioned by the situation, when time in the refuge is really boring, and a horrible way to live, and self-pity, insecurity, loneliness and desperation make you get back in touch with Leon.

Do not ever give Leon another chance again. He is completely mental, really off his head. All he cares about are his own needs, not yours and not the children's.

As soon as you went to bed, which he was being funny about because he likes you to go to bed when he goes up, he searched right through your things, he read your diary and woke you up at 2 a.m. to get aggressive and interrogate you about it.

In fact, once you walk back into that house that was once your home, boy does it hit you how it's not your home any more, and what a mistake you have made walking through the door, and how you've fucked things up.

This is because he is mental, which you keep forgetting when he turns on the tears and pleads for you to come home. You should not forget because all you do when you get back in that house with him is become paralysed with fear and go right into your shell trying to figure out how you are going to get out again. Let's face it, he has wised up to the situation now with you going home, then leaving, and if you ever go back in the future, you may not be fortunate enough to escape a last time, as he will watch you like a hawk to prevent it happening ever again.

Once you are in his company, you totally neglect your kids; not purposely, but Leon just sucks all your attention. All they do from the time you go back into that house is sit with a video on. They would sit there while Leon took you into the kitchen and went on and on about fuck knows what, and it wrenches your heart thinking that you have brought these two back into your mess. Poor, poor kids. Don't go back Stacey, because he is so selfish, he doesn't give a stuff about them.

Your neck, shoulders, and legs ache terribly. Remember that and remember it is because of the way he held you against the wall by the neck one time when you tried to leave. Remember how he pulled you by the hair, or when he threw you on the floor and stamped on you with that look of hatred on his face.

Remember when he got that knife and he was so close to stabbing you? He had such an insane look on his face, he kept jabbing you with the knife, not enough to penetrate the skin, but you know that he was thinking of how good it would feel to drive it into you. You could almost read his mind, 'Plea of insanity, sir.' Stacey, remember the fear and how much you wished there had been a Tardis there to whip you back to the safety of the refuge. At times like that, the refuge is heaven on earth.

Don't go back Stacey.

My best wishes,

Past Stacey. The one who didn't have me to tell her not to go back.

The letter is a dirty-brown colour now, discoloured from being kept in the drawer under my bed for years after I left him that final time. That letter served its purpose and has worked well over the years as I read it whenever I felt weak or homesick or missed the nice side of Leon. It gave me the strength not to get drawn back in by his tears, promises of how he was going to change, and my wishful thinking. As the days turned into weeks, and the weeks into months, and the months into years, I grew stronger, and everything became clearer.

It wasn't just the abuse that kept me trapped in my miserable life, although perhaps for the first years of marriage it was. It's a miracle I ever recognised what was going on and broke free. He was a master of his game, brainwashing and manipulating and controlling, whereas I, on the other end of the spectrum, was naive, vulnerable and just too damn trusting.

Growing up with a narcissistic parent set a precedent for the next part of my life, to go on and marry a narcissist. The strong personality of the narcissist kept me psychologically and physically imprisoned in my married life.

Home Sweet Home

Of course, it wasn't all smooth sailing after I left Leon. It took me a long time to get myself straight. I was damaged and didn't know who I was. Like a ship drifting aimlessly at sea, lost and not knowing where I was heading or what to do with myself, I was a prime target for dark souls on the lookout for easy prey. Dark days followed, trying to keep myself afloat with two children hanging on to me who were just as confused as me – they had to start a new school, and had lost their home and, more importantly, their father. My youthful life choices had implications I never envisaged.

Fortunately, when I left Leon, I was lucky enough to be able to break ties with his parents. All the interest they had in their grandchildren disappeared once I left their son. From that point on, the children didn't even receive so much as a birthday card.

The local council eventually rehoused us in the area I had hoped for. We were very blessed to be offered a three-bedroomed house, with a garden. I was also very fortunate to have a little financial support from my father. As I had to start again from scratch getting furniture for my new home, Dad bought me a cooker and beds for the children. He also gave me money to see me through occasionally, as struggling on benefits money was very tight.

The fridge was not as well stocked as it had been in my marriage, but I made sure we didn't go without. I didn't shop at the local shops as they were a little more expensive than the budget supermarkets in town. Every penny counted, so the children and I would walk into town to fetch the shopping most days of the week. It was a good hour's walk there and back, but worth it because my money seemed to stretch further.

Winter came and the buses were unreliable. We had been on a food shop, and it had got dark and by teatime there was a strong blizzard blowing. The snow came down so heavily, everywhere was white; it sat on the pavements about six inches high, and covered the shop window ledges. The sky was full of it and our hands were freezing.

We waited and waited for a bus to take us home, but it never came. The children were so cold that they began crying. I pondered on the benefits of being married to Leon as I always had a car to get the shopping. How I missed having a car! On one occasion, shortly after we had been rehoused, we were walking back from the town. A car drew up alongside us as I was tottering almost forward down the hill, struggling with the weight of the shopping bags. We still had about a mile left of the journey to go. Catching sight of the car I realised it was Leon. His electric window went down, 'Do you want a lift?' he said chirpily. I could see the satisfied expression on his face as he sat in the comfort of his car.

Feeling like Adam being tempted with the apple – except in this case I was being tempted to take the weight off my feet – I thought about his offer for a few seconds. I could almost feel the relief in my fingers as I imagined putting the bags in the boot of his car, and the children climbing into the back seat to be taken home in the comfort of a car.

'Can we, Mum?' the kids said in chorus. The dream was dashed as common sense prevailed as I knew if I got in the car with him there would be a high price to pay. He would think I owed him, and God knows what he would conjure up, so I declined. Seeing the children's faces I reassured them, 'No kids, we have not got far to go now.'

Leon smirked, 'Oh well, don't say I didn't offer'. He laughed at me for being so stubborn. Putting his foot to the accelerator he roared off into the distance. Watching the car go down the hill I wondered if I had done the right thing. I would have been home in five minutes flat!

It was a tough time, and I still missed Leon and the old life, but only the nice parts, which I knew were very few and far between, but still so much nicer than this new way of living. It was silly really, for I know if I had been back in the marital home with all the drama and upset, I'd have swapped places with the me struggling with shopping in a heartbeat. I just forgot sometimes.

Eventually, the marital home sold. The house that could have offered us so much as a family if only we had been happy there. Leon got offered a council flat in an undesirable area and accepted it. It saddened me to think of the loss we had all suffered and how different things could have been for all of us.

Leon was his own worst enemy. He had lost his children, his wife and his home, all because of his self-destructive behaviour. It saddened me for both of us, because he had lost so much too, and I don't believe for a minute that when he said he was going to change those times when he was desperate to have me home after I had left, that he did not mean it. I'm sure he did mean it with all his heart but for some reason he could not reign in the demon that took him over at times. Childhood is such a precious time, and the environment he had grown up in had badly affected him. Things were so final now, that we no longer lived under the same roof, where I had to put up with his treatment. It had taken so much effort and strength to get here I was never going back, and he knew it too. It filled me with sorrow to see where we had both ended up living. He had seemed to be hanging about quite a lot, like a lost soul. After everything that had happened, I still thought at this point that I loved him, and I still felt responsible for his pain. Still deluded, I hoped we could move on in a decent manner for the sake of the children, so I called him.

It was obvious when I spoke to Leon on the phone that he was suffering the loss of life as we knew it. He asked me what he could have done to win me back properly. It was so clear to me and so simple, but it wouldn't have entered his head. If he had put the children before himself, left us safely in our marital home, so that the children didn't have the upheaval of leaving their home and school where they were settled, that would have been a good start.

If he had moved out and got himself somewhere to live, sorted himself out and got help reconditioning his mind, then maybe there would have been a chance. If his natural instincts as a father were to make his children and their wellbeing his priority above everything, having enough self-control to stop subjecting his children to scenes of aggression and violence, then he could have won me back. I told him I would not have left in the first place had he commanded such self-discipline. He agreed I was right and that's how he should have been, but his regret was wasted on me as I felt he was saying this because he knew it was what I wanted him to feel.

The children and I had nothing from the marital home. Leon took all the furniture for his flat. He asked me if there was anything we needed. I told him the children needed a television. He said he wanted to make things up to the children. 'I'll bring the television down for the kids, it's the least I can do. I just need to do something as I understand I have been selfish,' he said sincerely.

Within ten minutes he was at the house with the television in his arms, and he installed it for me too. He looked at me as he was about to leave. He looked so sad and run down. He held me, and there was no doubt I still loved him, but if felt so wrong my insides were churning with unease.

However, in another way it felt so right as only he knew the pain I was feeling, the loss of the love we had felt for each other from the innocent children we were, to the toxic adults we became in our relationship.

I had loved him with every inch of me. My body was burning for him, and his for me. He pulled me to him, he kissed me with his soft familiar lips. I felt his big strong body pushed against me, and I was overcome with desire. His heavy breathing told me he was too. Tears fell. I knew we shouldn't, but it just made me want him more than ever. It was so nice to feel love, the comfort of each other. There was no room for consequences. Sense went out of the window as we went up to bed.

Once we were in bed and we were united, the urgency to have him close to me was now replaced with sheer panic and regret. Things should have never got this far. Where was my self-control now? Of course, I didn't tell him to stop because I didn't think I could. I let things take their course. When he left, I told him with trepidation it was a mistake, a one off, that I still loved him, but we could not be together.

I know I was giving him mixed messages, and I should have been stronger, but at the start of this episode I got carried away, and by the end of it I had come to my senses. He seemed happy when he left. I hoped he understood that this was the last time, and thanked God I was in my own home in my own four walls alone with the children. When he went without pressuring me to stay longer, I foolishly believed he had accepted we had had a moment of weakness, but that our road together had come to an end.

The next morning when I woke, I felt sad that we could not be a normal happy couple and enjoy the comfort of love and all the security that brings. It had been such a struggle to get my own place to get to this point, there was no way I was going to be weak again. Walking the children to school I dropped them off with a kiss and a hug. Once I got home the phone rang. I knew who it was. I knew what he wanted. I knew I had to be firm.

When I spoke to Leon, he was pushing to see me, but told me he respected my wishes if I did not want to see him. Something of what I had said to him yesterday had sunk in. I told him, 'I am glad you understand Leon, but what happened yesterday cannot happen again.' The phone went dead. There was no argument, just the tone of the line that he had disconnected. This left me in no doubt that he was annoyed, but at least I wasn't there to feel his wrath.

Walking into the kitchen, I opened the cupboard door under the sink and grabbed the duster and polish. Flicking the television on I put the music channel on. As the music played, I wiped the duster over the cabinet as I wiggled my body joyfully to the great songs that were pumping out one after the other. There was no aftermath from yesterday, no consequences. Finally, I had my own space and peace I felt free.

Some time went by before I opened the back door to put some rubbish in the bin outside. As I turned the key ready to go outside, I felt the weight of the door push into me, as Leon forced his way into the house. 'You fucking tricked me, you bitch!' he said, shoving me as hard as he could. I tried to keep my balance as I fell backwards onto the chair in the living room. He grabbed my hair and put his face into mine, entwining my hair in his fingers, so far from the loving man he had been yesterday. His face pressed into mine, and he shouted in my face that I had tricked him into giving me the television yesterday.

Letting me go he stood up, out of breath with temper, and placed himself dominantly in front of the television cabinet. Hands on his hips, he took a deep breath in and pulled his knee up into his chest and then forced his foot furiously into the television.

To my relief, the neighbours started banging on the wall. That had never happened before, and they were letting him know they could hear him. He hadn't smashed the television screen on his first attempt, so he gave it one more almighty kick as it smashed onto the floor. Satisfied with the job well done, he didn't hang about. He knew that the chances were that the police were on the way. That was the last time I was ever involved with Leon. The penny finally dropped. If I gave him an inch, he would take a mile.

Relief flooded through me that I wasn't in the marital home, the detached house that held all the noises inside, away from the ears of our neighbours. Then I sat back and analysed my situation. Was the chaos ever going to end? Why was life so hard? Was it too much to just want a bit of normality? The situation overwhelmed me as I looked at the smashed television, now in pieces on the floor. Sighing with despair I began picking the pieces up. There was so much for me to do. I had a whole house yet to furnish. I had been given a grant by the council to furnish the place, but it only stretched to cover the cost of carpets. Now I was sat with the television smashed, no car and no money. Leon didn't pay any child support for the children, and they needed all the usual stuff that children need other than the basics of food and clothes. It felt as if God was punishing me.

My father had given me the best advice and if I had listened to him none of this would have happened. He told me I was out of my depth, and that there should be no negotiating, no debating, and contact with Leon in all forms should be cut dead. If only I had taken his advice, instead of fooling myself that I could reason with Leon, for there was no let-up. He seemed to prosper. He had the car, the furniture and no responsibilities. How was I ever going to get on my feet financially? It was like divine intervention when Leon's sister phoned me later that week and said she had got some work as a kissogram, and it was good money. It was enough for me to be able to pay my sister to take care of the children when I went out.

Where had being good and decent got me, I thought to myself rebelliously? So, I ended up getting myself a little job doing kissograms with Mandy. Of course, the job wasn't right for me, but I forced myself to do it thinking of the money, and it was a sure-fire way for me to be able to save quickly for a car. I had been disrespected enough and suffered for it, so I might as well be disrespected and earn some good money for it.

Of course, I was still very low on self-esteem deep inside, so I used to down a few vodkas before I surprised an unsuspecting birthday boy at his party. The neat vodka, drunk from a disguised lemonade bottle shortly before I started my 'spot', as it was known in the trade, helped me to do the job. Head swimming with booze, I would walk into the crowd of men and take my clothes off for money. Not knowing who I was any more, I found solace for a while in losing myself in drink or recreational drugs on the very rare occasions when Leon had the children overnight.

The children had been affected by the life we had left behind, especially my son. He was seven when we had left, so those first few years, the vital formative years of his life, he had his father for his male role model, and sadly it affected him. Reece's behaviour started to reflect his father's and with his dad drip feeding him in the background, turning him against me, he became awkward and out of control. He had no respect for me whatsoever and would not take kindly to the word 'no'. Everything became a battle. If he wanted something and I said no, the pressure was on until I relented and said yes.

One occasion, Reece had been very naughty. The one person I knew Reece respected was Leon, so buckling under the pressure, I hoped Leon could have a word with him about the way he was behaving. When I dialled Leon's number, he answered fairly quickly and I blurted out that I was at my wits end with Reece and I hoped that as his father he would speak to Reece and get him to behave.

Reece looked at me in disbelief that I had called his dad, and all the drama that was taking place immediately fizzled out. 'Put him on the phone,' Leon commanded. Reece reluctantly took the handset from me, imploring me with his eyes now brimming with tears to stop this situation progressing. Leon was my only hope of getting through to Reece in a bid to get a grip of his increasingly erratic behaviour that was going to lead him into trouble if we didn't nip it in the bud now.

Reece knew he had no choice but to speak to his dad. If it was me, on the other hand, he would have just blatantly run away from the situation. Watching Reece now on the phone to his father, he looked like a terrified little boy, not the gangster child who five minutes previously had been mouthing off to me. Catching the first part of the conversation, before Reece pressed the phone to his ear stifling the volume, I heard Leon ask him gently what he was crying for. Reece sniffled and responded, 'Yes Dad, yes Dad,' nodding in response to whatever his father was saying, then at Leon's command, he passed the phone back to me.

Grabbing the handset back, I placed it to my ear. 'Right,' Leon said, 'I've just told my son that as I hardly see him, there is no way I am going to be telling him off. What would he think of me if the few times he has contact with me I am coming down on him?' That response was endorsing Reeces's behaviour, and, incensed, I knew this would have negative repercussions on my relationship with my son. Leon's final word on the subject was, 'You chose to be a single parent, you deal with it!'

Raising the children on my own became so difficult that I contacted Social Services myself and asked them for some parenting advice. They were really good. They arranged for a man to come over once in a while and take Reece out to do 'men things'. It was a way of introducing a good male role model into Reece's life. Social Services even arranged for me to do parenting classes, which were just what I needed. After being controlled for so long, I had a real problem with disciplining my children. Of course, I would teach them right from wrong as best as I could, but whenever I had to be hard with them for their own good, I felt as if I was abusing them. They took full advantage of this, and I found it really hard to cope. With what I had already gone through, I hadn't had enough time to recover and get my head in a good place so that I could conduct my life in a fashion I could be proud of. The children were with me all the time and I rarely got a break, so it was incredibly difficult. Many days I functioned on autopilot in a trance-like state, wondering who I was, feeling completely overwhelmed.

It was tough being a single mother and I had been somewhat gullible believing that when I left Leon that my life would eventually get easier, and I would meet a loving new partner. The children were a handful, and it would take a man made of strong stuff to stand by me as I didn't have the freedom to commit to a relationship. My children and I came as a package.

A Chance to Love Again

Eight years had passed since I had left Leon and I had just ended a relationship with a man who I had been with for five years. He wanted me, but sadly he didn't want all the responsibility I came with. He was immature himself but in comparison to Leon, he treated me very well, and he was alright with the children, although I think Reece had issues accepting him. Devastated, I had lost faith that I could meet anyone who could give me and the children the security we craved and this left me further vulnerable to predatory dark souls.

Adrian came into my life following a recommendation from a friend, as I needed someone to lay some laminate flooring for me. He was very handsome, and similar to Leon in looks: quite tall, with black hair, dark brown, almond-shaped eyes with a twinkle of laughter in them. He seemed a decent man, and as I watched him laying my floor in his T-shirt on his knees, I felt attracted to him.

Sweat dripping off him, he mopped his brow. 'You know, I am not going to take a penny off you for this,' he said, looking at me seriously. As I protested, he waved his arms as if he didn't want to hear, but I insisted he had the money. It was obvious he liked me. I would catch him looking at me and smirking while I was making a cup of tea.

Feeling touched by his kind gesture of offering to do my floor for free, I agreed to go for a drink with him, and that's when I found out more about him. He was a father to three children. He loved them all dearly but had been stopped from seeing them by their mother. He was devastated at not being allowed to see them. He told me how he and his wife didn't get on so he had moved out. There was so much animosity between them it had resulted in her keeping the children away from him. How utterly unfair life can be, I thought, when there are men like Leon who rarely bother to see their children and in comparison, this man, who was clearly heartbroken because he just wanted to see his children and wasn't allowed to.

We began spending more time together and I loved the freedom I was feeling in this new relationship. Ade started to get my house shipshape. All the jobs I couldn't do and couldn't afford to have done, he just got on with. He never even had to be asked to help me. He seemed to enjoy making my house into a nice home. Reece wasn't too keen on Ade, but he would not have been happy with any man around. I was happy for the first time in years. I had that wonderful feeling of being in love again. I was spellbound by this handsome, caring man who had been sent to look after me, or so I believed. I thought that at last my luck was changing. For the first time in years, I felt contented.

One evening, we had gone to the pub for some food, and I had left Reece and Sophie out playing for a few hours. They were now teenagers. We weren't that far away, and I had my phone with me in case there were any problems. We had only been gone for a couple of hours when the phone rang. It was Sophie. She was frantic. She said they Reece had smashed the front living room window.

Ade and I rushed back from the pub. The neighbours were all outside, looking at my house. Feeling ashamed, I got out of the car and walked down the drive, trying to keep myself calm. We went inside the house and the children were still shouting. It was chaotic. Reece was trying to explain what had gone on, but I was very annoyed about the window, and I told him so. Reece retaliated and started to argue with me, and Ade stood up and shouted at him.

The situation escalated and Ade called Reece a little bastard and said that if a child of his had smashed the window, he would have put him in a children's home. That was enough. No way was I standing for that. I told Ade to get out, and he knew from my tone that he had totally overstepped the mark, so he left.

How had things come to this? I put my head in my hands, defeated, as I sat down with two upset children and a smashed window that I couldn't fix, and thought that, as usual, everything in my life was totally out of control. I had no idea how I was ever going to get myself sorted out.

Waking up the next day, I cringed looking at the window and imagined how I would be the talk of the street. I had no intention of seeing Ade again, but he came round the next morning in his van really early, full of apologies about what he had said.

He measured the window and said he would fix it, as he felt it was the least he could do. He came back an hour later with a pane of glass, and, in no time at all, the evidence of the night before had disappeared as he put the final bit of putty around the new window.

It was a relief that someone was there to help me, and, foolishly, I fell back into the relationship with Ade, although I never allowed him to come to the house again.

In general, Reece did not like me having boyfriends and was taking over where his father had left off, always angry and disrespectful to male visitors. He was just a little boy who didn't know any better and I didn't blame him. I just wished he would calm down. It was upsetting for me that the remnants of my past relationship with his dad were continuing to destroy our lives. My relationship with Reece had completely broken down because I could not get through to him and we clashed continuously. It was tiresome and because of it, I still felt Leon's presence in my home.

Finally, Reece decided to go and live with his dad. He had given me an ultimatum that I stop seeing Ade or he would leave. Again, I saw this as controlling behaviour, and whether Reece was right or wrong, I had to make a point that I was not going to let anyone, certainly not a child, dictate to me what I should do. I believed that if I let him rule me, it would be setting a precedence for our lives going forward. So, feeling completely justified in my decision, I told my son that I would not allow him to dictate what I did with my life.

That night, Leon came and took Reece to live with him. Reece wanted to go; he idolised his father and I assumed a few weeks with living with his dad, who would not stand for unruly behaviour, would make him realise how good he had things at home with me, and he would return.

The years with Reece since I left Leon had been turbulent; Reece loved and respected his father. He didn't see Leon very often, but when he did, it was clear he was being manipulated because he would be hostile towards me. Unintentionally, I was causing my boy harm by just trying to live my life. I had come to terms with this and concluded that at least if he was not with me all the time, he could have some peace of mind. Besides, Leon had no problems with discipline, and I felt Reece could benefit from a firmer parent. Both children would get one-to-one attention, which would be good for them.

Ade and I decided to go away for a break. We went to Paphos in Cyprus and I forgot to take my contraceptive pills. All along there had been something about Ade I could not put my finger on.

Something wasn't right, and I don't think I would have continued the relationship after I got back.

Foolishly, I relied on Ade being careful while we were away so that I did not get pregnant, as I intended to continue with the pill when I arrived back in the UK. Just as I was seeing some light at the end of the tunnel with my older children being more independent, that was darkened on discovering I was pregnant again. Being so careless had left me with a dilemma, as I did not want another child.

Why oh why was I my own worst enemy, always making life harder for myself? It was irresponsible and I had to pay the price for that with some tough decisions.

Have you heard the expression that lightning doesn't strike twice? Well in my case it did.

Ade, had come into my life when I still hadn't healed myself mentally after Leon. Therefore, I can understand how I had got embroiled in another toxic relationship. On the surface, Ade seemed quite a relaxed kind of guy, but I sensed there was something bubbling underneath.

Ade lied from the beginning, telling me he had his own business in carpentry. I had seen some of the jobs he had done for his customers, so I was easily convinced. He could look at a bare room, tell me how he was going to design everything, and from scratch build a kitchen that was out of this world, just from how he had envisaged it. He was extremely talented.

Ade was very kind to me at first. He had implied he was a good father and had been a loving husband. We hadn't been together that long. In hindsight, I hardly knew him, and I really didn't relish the prospect of being a single mother again, as I knew things could go wrong. It was hard. Reece and Sophie were now teenagers, and I knew that in a few more years I would have more time for myself. The thought of starting over, having another child, unless I was a hundred percent confident in my new relationship, was daunting.

Ade's sister Tania came to see me at the time. She was a trainee nurse, and a seemingly good mother with a sensible head on her shoulders. I respected her. So when she began singing the praises of her brother louder than a church choir from heaven itself, I naively believed her. She reminisced about what a great father he had been with his own children, how he had made the back garden of his marital home into a children's paradise. He had created a wooden adventure playground, made with his own bare hands. She assured me Ade would look after me, and the children. That discussion with Tanya was enough to persuade me to go ahead with the pregnancy.

A few months into the pregnancy, Ade changed from the laid back, pleasant boyfriend I had known to a moody, aggressive, unpredictable lay-about user. He would disappear for days on end with no explanation of where he had been, and I dared not question him because it would cause an argument. He would go into the blackest of moods.

One of his intimidating habits, when he was stone-walling me for no reason that I could think of, was letting himself into my home with a key I had given him, frowning, and whistling songs loudly. He would make it clear he was ignoring me, yet made his presence known. I wanted to tell him to go, but something inside me was too scared.

It was my house, and he was coming and going as he pleased, unnerving me with his sinister presence. Even today, when I hear people whistling, it makes me think of him in his black mood. My home didn't feel like my little safe haven any more. There was an intruder, and I did not know how to deal with it. Money would also go missing from my house, and if I confronted him about it, Ade would insinuate it was my children, though I knew they would never steal from me.

Then the police turned up looking for him. He was wanted for an assault on a woman. He explained his way out of it, saying that she was exaggerating and had it in for him, because he had ended his relationship with her and she was bitter. His sister backed him up when I voiced my concerns.

Things just went from bad to worse, and it was my worst nightmare come true. I was pregnant, I felt trapped, and he wouldn't leave me alone. Boy, did I wish I had got to know him better before having his baby. He'd had a few moments of shouting and smashing stuff but nothing, after my past, I could see that was crossing a line. But looking back, as the person I am today, I can see it totally was, and I was out of my depth. This is what I mean when I say I wasn't healed properly after Leon.

I wanted to end things, but try as I might, he would not leave me alone. I was on the roundabout again, switching between attempting to end things, then Ade acting loving and stable again. After one

231

awful argument, he had two bouquets of flowers sent to the house, one for me, and one for Sophie, saying how sorry he was for upsetting us. Just like Leon, he wasn't going to leave without a fight.

He would bombard me with flowers and phone calls, begging me to give him another chance for the sake of our unborn child. When I ignored the nice messages, they would turn sinister and he would call me the most insulting names, telling me I was a 'yampy bitch'. I wasn't sure what that meant but that was his nickname for me, and I eventually found out it was his family's name for me too.

The whole situation was so reminiscent of my past experiences, yet he managed to convince me that my hormones were to blame for all of our troubles. When I tried to end it with him, he hung about outside my house, and everywhere I went he seemed to turn up. He even sent his sister Tania to the house with bags of brand-new baby clothes and baby items in preparation for the birth.

It seemed as if he cared; Leon would never have spent his money. My head was in a spin. Had I been too hasty? Was I tarring him with the same brush as Leon, as Ade so often told me I did? Was I depriving my unborn child of the chance of a normal family life with a father?

By the time I went into labour with our daughter, worn down, I had wanted us to sort things out and be a united mother and father. When my waters broke, I wanted Ade to be there, so I called him, and he was delighted to be given another chance. Ade was fantastic during the birth. After our little girl was born, he couldn't have been more attentive and loving. He took me home and looked after me. He wouldn't let me lift a finger.

I had a bath, and he sponged my back, making me feel pampered and cared for. This was a vast difference to the way I had been treated by Leon when I was a new mum, so I grabbed on to these loving gestures and concluded I was in a much better situation than I was back then. I remember looking at our little Chloe lying in her tiny little wooden cot and deciding I didn't want to be on my own any more. I was going to give him one more chance.

Unfortunately, things were only okay for a short while before Ade's mood swings slowly crept back. He was constantly smoking cannabis; he would get out of bed, sit on the garden step and role a joint. For a couple of months, we were on a merry-go-round of splitting up then giving it another go. He stayed with his friend John most nights, so at least I got some respite from him.

Some people can come into your life, take it over and tie you in knots before you have even spotted the warning signs. Why is it that some relationships you get into just cast a spell over you?

My family were fed up with the situation. I understand now why they despaired of me. Every time I got involved with Ade, and we were getting along, I had to keep it secret from them. I wanted them to have some faith in me and believe I had finally got some sense, not realising this was all being taken out my hands. As much as I asked Ade to stay away, he would turn up again, indifferent to my wishes. When I told him I couldn't cope with our relationship the way it was, he would just disregard what I was saying and tell me I was being silly, forcing his way without violence into my life.

He'd talk to me in an insulting baby voice, 'Come on, you know you love me, stop being daft, you know you want me really,' he would say, shutting my fears down. I was so confused but I loved the family feeling when Ade and I were getting along. Worn down, I couldn't seem to properly break it off from him. I desperately didn't want another failed relationship or to be a single mum again, yet I know looking back that would have been the best way for things to be.

It was good when he went to John's because I didn't want my children around the smoking, and I could live in relative peace. As it was when Leon used to work away, I found myself in a relationship desperate for peaceful breaks. Things went on for a few months like that until Chloe was twelve weeks old, and it all came to a head.

It was a lovely hot day, perfect for a trip to the seaside. There wasn't even a hint of a breeze in the air. Sophie had called my mother and arranged to go and stay with her for a couple of days. The minute mum had collected her, and the car had disappeared down the street. I tapped Ade's number into my mobile phone and called him up, thinking that I might as well let Chloe spend some time with her dad. He wasn't living with me, and I only saw him when I didn't have my older children with me.

It felt wrong having to keep the two families in my life separate, but the arrangement worked for everyone, so I just went with the flow. I gave little Chloe a wipe over with the flannel, and placed her in her car seat to go and pick up her daddy. As usual, when I arrived at John's to collect Ade, he was slow to come out the flat, leaving me sitting in the car for ages. He was probably indulging in a smoke, I thought, annoyed. Eventually, Ade came swaggering out of the block of flats with a big grin on his face. He had a distinctive walk whereby he always strode slowly, looking as if he was gliding along. Opening the car door, he hopped in and we set off back to my house.

We were chatting, enjoying the weather, and making the most of it when Ade suggested we should go to Blackpool for a couple of days and stay with his friend Kevin. Kev lived with his girlfriend Rita in a small block of flats just a few streets back from the seafront. Rita had long bleached brittle hair, with grey roots protruding through. She always looked vacant and depressed.

The part about staying with them was a tad off-putting, but going to the seaside seemed a great idea. After such a stressful pregnancy, I welcomed the idea of a break. This would be Chloe's first trip to the beach, I thought happily. The weather was beautiful. We didn't have much money so it would be a nice break away, and, best of all, it was spur of the moment, and such spontaneous ideas were usually the most fun. As soon as we got back to my house, Ade was on the phone to Kev. It turned out that Kev and his girlfriend Rita were already planning on inviting us down there for a few days anyway.

It was all agreed, but I wasn't feeling quite so sure about going to their place. Hearing Kev's voice on the phone reminded me of how uneasy he made me feel. I only tolerated him for Ade. He was overweight and overbearing.

There are a couple of well-known sayings: 'birds of a feather flock together' and, 'you are the company you keep'. I should have paid heed to this. Rita was a nice lady, although she was very timid. She had been with Kev for six years and she did everything for him.

As I raised my doubts about the trip, Ade began throwing all of Chloe's belongings into the boot of the car. The steriliser, the nappies – when you have a new baby there is so much stuff they need. He was keen to get going. I tried to tell him I didn't feel like going if we were to be staying with Kev and Rita, and that I would prefer to stay in a bed and breakfast on our own. Ade said we wouldn't get in a bed and breakfast at such short notice on a nice day like this, and it was too expensive anyway. Why pay when we can have free accommodation, was his argument.

As usual, my concerns were brushed aside with assurances that we wouldn't necessarily have to be in their company, we could stay in their flat, and enjoy the break, just the three of us. My protests were making me feel like a party pooper. Oh well, I thought, what harm can it do? I should let my hair down and be spontaneous more often; we'll probably have a great time. Naively, I thought we could spend some time bonding as a family, and maybe work out a way to sort out the situation with Ade's moods and become a proper happy family unit.

Before I knew it, everything was packed tightly in the boot of the car and I was trying to sort out a few items of clothing for me and Chloe. Ade was shouting up the stairs for me to hurry up. Feeling the excitement in his voice, I also became excited at the prospect of going. We got in the car, me driving, and we were off, the windows open, the radio playing, and our sweet little Chloe sleeping contentedly in the back, oblivious to the fact she was having her first family holiday with Mummy and Daddy.

I must admit there was a nagging feeling of guilt at the back of my head. I so wished Sophie was with us, but I changed my train of thought because I knew she would be happy at her nanny's. I'd made sure I had taken Sophie and Reece on holidays. We had had some great caravan holidays in Somerset. Even when I didn't need to feel guilty, I always found myself feeling anxious about all of my children. As chaotic as my life was, I sincerely wanted the best for them. If this break went alright, I thought maybe next time Sophie could come along too! It might help to put our fragmented family back together.

It took a few hours to get to Kev and Rita's. I drove nice and steadily down the motorway, mindful of our baby being in the back of the car. Finally, we reached Blackpool. There were signs for the seafront, and the calm seaside air blew into the windows of the car as we swept through the narrow streets, people crossing the roads in their shorts and sunglasses, children with ice-creams skipping happily along. We pulled into a well-to-do, quiet back street and parked on the drive of a big old Victorian house that had been converted into flats.

While getting Chloe out of the car, I was planning on giving her a bottle, then taking a nice shower as the journey had left me tired and sweaty. Ade brought the luggage in, and Kev and Rita showed me round the flat. There wasn't much to it – a small living room with a kitchenette, one bedroom, and a tiny shower room; it was quite basic. Rita opened the windows and I could hear the seagulls squawking in the blue sky overhead. This was the life, being by the sea and away from the hustle and bustle of the Midlands.

After we had all changed and showered, we headed to the seafront. Ade and Kev walked on in front; Rita and I lingered behind. She told me how she and Kev had just made up yet again, how he'd promised he'd changed, and things were good between them. She seemed happy. Although it was Rita's flat, Kev took great delight in telling me all about the area, and what was where. He liked to be the centre of attention.

He reminded me of a child, boasting about the seaside town as if he owned the place. Listening to him as he chatted away, I felt there was something about him I could not take to, but I feigned interest, smiling and nodding at the right time as he continued to talk. Regardless of the fact that he was overbearing, I thought it was good of them to offer us the opportunity to stay at their place while we were down here.

We all spent the evening at a seafront pub, drinking and chatting. Rita confided in me that the past two weeks had been the best she'd spent with Kev. He seemed to have learned his lesson, after almost losing her again (that sounded familiar!). She had tried leaving a few times but always went back, much as I had done with Leon. The night went quickly, and finally I went to bed on my own, as Ade stayed up chatting with Kev. So much for the family holiday! I woke the next morning in a strange little room, next to Ade. I hadn't even heard him come to bed.

It seemed that, once again, the day had already been pre-planned with another visit to the pub. I was disappointed, as I was hoping for some family time with Ade. Surely I should have learnt by now that he always seemed to prefer the company of his mates? I didn't say how I felt, fearing it would look like whining. I just hoped that, at some point, Ade and I might go out on our own to the beach with Chloe.

I decided to make the best of it as we weren't here for long. I put on my new white summer dress I'd packed, and I felt pretty and summery. We all strolled along the seafront, Rita and I, with Kev and Ade in front of us again. Maybe he wanted to hang out with Kev because they'd been kind enough to let us stay. We found a little beer garden on the high street that overlooked the beach, and decided to settle there for some lunch.

While Rita went to the bar to get the drinks for her and Kev, I told him she'd confessed to me about how happy he had been making her the last couple of weeks, thinking it was nice for him to know she appreciated him, and in return he might appreciate her. Any caring person would have taken that as a compliment, but I detected a serious nose-dive in Kev's attitude towards Rita when she came back with the drinks. How I wished I hadn't said anything at all.

Rita's self-esteem was extremely low; it was clear from the way she carried herself. She was a lovely, soft, warm person, but I suppose all the years of put-downs by Kev had taken their toll on her.

He started talking to her as if she was dirt, ordering her to fetch him drinks and calling her a 'freak'. He went on and on, dishing out insults to her, until she understandably broke down and began to cry. 'Oh, please, Kev, why are you being so horrible again?' she moaned. This only seemed to fuel his sickening behaviour. He clenched his fists and told her to stop whinging.

A feeling of dread washed over me and I wanted to get up and walk way. I couldn't believe what I was hearing. In the space of a few minutes, the atmosphere had turned extremely unpleasant, to say the least.

Ade didn't seem phased, which was concerning. I was keen to get away from them, so I kept looking at him, motioning my head, trying to signal 'come on, let's get out of here'.

Ade didn't move and I couldn't keep quiet any longer, so I intervened and quietly said to Kev that the only person upsetting the atmosphere was him. Rita and I had been sitting as quietly as mice until he started bullying her.

He told me to mind my own fucking business, and then I was startled when Ade said to me that if Kev hit me for interfering, I shouldn't expect him to stick up for me, because I'd only have myself to blame. To me, there was nothing worse than a bully and I couldn't sit there and see another person be treated in such a vile way. What sort of men were they? What was I involved with here? I was back in the lion's den, it seemed.

Kev even went on to blackmail Rita, saying, 'You better stop crying, or I'll tell these two a thing or two about you.' I was feeling so frustrated that this lazy good-for-nothing was fooling himself that he was above her. It was plain to see that he was so pathetic and insecure about himself that he had to put her down to make himself feel good. He was living off her the way a pimp lives off a prostitute.

I tried to be diplomatic, because I didn't want him to hurt her physically and I had a feeling that this was where it was heading. There was nowhere to go because all our belongings were back at their flat, otherwise I would have got in my car and driven away. To calm the situation down, I tried to humour Kev, telling him he always came across as a nice guy to me, and that his behaviour was uncharacteristic (although it was not – I'd just never witnessed it to this degree).

Then he began reminiscing about his childhood and how his father had never shown him any love, as if that justified him being a bully. We've all had tough times in our lives, but that is no excuse to treat another person so badly. They all carried on drinking, but I wanted to stay in control so I drank only lemonade – that way I could keep my wits about me.

An hour later and worse for wear with drink, Kev and Ade began talking about the fights they had been in, in the past.

Bitterly, I looked over the road to people walking past going about their normal lives, and wished it was me with my children. Instead, I was sat outside a pub, my baby in her pram, listening to the most deviant of conversations. I couldn't quite believe what I was hearing and I just wanted to go home.

Then Kev stood up, announcing cockily to us that he was taking Rita back to the flat to 'have some fun', winking and laughing. He was so matter of fact about it, as if he had said they were going home for tea. She just followed him up the road, like a lamb to the slaughter. I felt sick, but even sicker with Ade that he seemed completely blasé about what was going on.

Ade and I arrived back at the flat about an hour later. In that time, I had told Ade in no uncertain terms we needed to get our stuff and leave.

We arrived at the flat and rang the bell. Kev opened the flat window and shouted down that we'd disturbed them, pulling up the zip on his jeans. He then came down to open the door to us. Almost like a teenage boy being obvious about partaking in a sexual encounter, he began huffing and puffing, saying he was knackered, and went back into the bedroom.

Once in the flat, instead of packing, Ade lay on the sofa and told me to make us some coffees. Although I was desperate to pack and leave, I didn't want to make matters worse, so I bided my time and did as I was told, casually mentioning to Ade that when Kev and Rita came out of the bedroom, he should tell them we were leaving.

As I poured the hot water into our cups, Ade just looked at me unfazed, then he put his head back on a pillow and shut his eyes. I began to wonder how this whole holiday had turned into such a sick nightmare. I was desperate to go home and get away from them all, fearing for the safety of me and my child.

Eventually, Kev came out of the bedroom, fastening his fly, his fat beer belly hanging over his jeans plain to see because his T-shirt was too small. He was plastered in cheap looking tattoos. It was getting more difficult to hide my contempt for him.

I pretended I needed my hairbrush out of the bedroom, but really I wanted to go in and check if Rita was all right. Knocking on the bedroom door, I opened it slowly as she shouted, 'Come in'. She was making the bed. Walking over to her I gave her a hug and told her she had to be strong and get away from him. I was disgusted at what I'd been indirectly involved with. I told her she'd be so much better off on her own.

She said she envied my strength, but she couldn't leave him because he'd threatened her not to leave. How could she envy my strength, I wondered, when I had jumped from the frying pan into the fire and ended up with another deviant? She seemed really frightened. When I went back into the living room, Rita came in and sat by Kev. He kept poking, prodding and pinching her, not leaving her alone. He took great delight in telling her she smelt, and making other derogatory comments.

There was nothing I could do. I needed to get me and Chloe out of there as quickly as possible. So, I stood up, casually hoping it wasn't too obvious that I was making my escape, and announced that I was going to drive back home now. It was almost nine o'clock and it was better to drive now that it was cooler, I implied. It seemed the perfect excuse to make to say our goodbyes. Quite frankly, I was desperate to get away.

I was beginning to wonder about Ade. If he associated with such trash as Kev, and Kev's behaviour didn't seem to concern him, then surely, he was a little sick in the head too? Was he the sort of male role model I wanted around my daughters? The sooner I got home the better. I wanted the sanctity of my own bedroom, and then I could try and get my head round the whole sordid episode and decide what I was going to do from here. Still in shock, I knew it was best not to make a fuss now. My main priority was to get home with Chloe safely.

Night-time was drawing in and I felt relief as I got into my car, bags packed, baby strapped in, ready to go. Kev was hanging out of the flat window above, waving us off, as Ade was insisting I got out of the driver's seat and let him drive. I wouldn't let him; after all, he'd been drinking most of the day. I sensed that Ade was now acting as if he had a point to prove in front of Kev, that he too had to have total control of his woman, and the fact that I wasn't complying was annoying him.

He got really agitated at this point and yelled at me to 'fuck off then', slamming the car door aggressively. With pleasure, I thought, relieved because I didn't want to be anywhere near him. I started the car and drove, but as I got further up the road, my heart began to beat with anxiety. Looking in my mirror, I could see Ade waving his arms in the air angrily and fading into the background.

My head was jumbled with anxiety and thoughts of what ifs. What if I leave him here? He will be so angry with me. What if he comes to my house causing trouble when he makes it back to the Midlands, because I had abandoned him miles away from home? With not much time to assess the situation properly, I hastily decided that it would be best to go back for him, before things got any more out of hand.

I should have carried on driving. Hindsight is a wonderful thing, but in that moment, I was petrified of repercussions. I didn't want to antagonise him any further. So, I turned the car back round reluctantly and started driving back towards Kev's flat. Ade was walking quickly towards the car. He looked furious. Cursing, he strode towards me. I could almost lip-read the swear words that were coming from his mouth.

I started laughing, I don't know if it was because of my nerves, or if I was trying to subconsciously diffuse the anger, making light

240

of it. As he reached the car I was in shock as he punched my window. Then he walked round to the passenger side of the car, fiddling with the door, yanking it and trying to get in. Petrified of being in the car with him, my instincts were screaming at me to jump out.

He jumped in as I jumped out. I continued to pace quickly up the road. I didn't know where to go, but I wanted him to calm down. By now he had jumped in the car, and he began driving alongside me. He was still mad, and shouting at me to get in. My heart was pounding with fear as Chloe was still in the car, and now he was driving it.

Chloe must have sensed the tension and started screaming and crying. I wanted him to get out of the car and leave us, but his temper was spiralling out of control. There was no way I could get in the car, because I knew he would hit me, and he wasn't in a calm enough state to drive, but our precious baby was in the back.

He screeched the car to a halt and jumped out. He leaned across and grabbed the aerial, ripping it off the roof in temper. He was shouting at me to get in the fucking car. He looked like a deranged lunatic. He bounded towards me, so I ran, and he began running after me, chasing me around for what seemed like ages, ordering me to get in the car, saying things like, 'Come here you little cunt before I kill you.' Flashbacks of Leon angrily chasing our dog round the furniture were swimming in my head.

Terrified, I darted up a side street, but he pursued me, leaving the car door open and Chloe still crying in the car. I ran as fast as my legs would carry me, but he was too quick. He caught up with me quickly and yanked my hair, pulling me backwards as I came crashing to the ground, where he began to drag me along, back towards the car. Easing up with the strength of my calves in the chaos, so my bottom was a foot off the floor, I tried to walk in sync with the speed I was being pulled along, in a bid to stop me being scraped along the ground. I knew if he managed to get me into the car, I would be in serious trouble. It was just like the time Leon had found me in Bromsgrove and tried to drag me into his car.

As Ade pulled me along the road, I started to scream, hoping to draw attention to us so that someone would help. In an effort to deter him, I tried to yank his shorts down, as I twisted and turned in a wasted effort to escape his grip.

I was praying that the residents of the street would hear the commotion and come out or call the police, but if they heard anything, no one came to my aid. Ade must have been worried about the attention I might be drawing, as he gave up and let me go, marching angrily back towards the car. All this time, Chloe was still crying and I wanted to get to her.

For a few minutes, I stood by a wall, panting for air under the streetlight, and he got back into my car, leaning towards me out of the car window. We were both out of breath. I knew he had crossed the line with me. We were over now, for sure. I was shaking like a leaf, partly with fear and partly with anger. How dare he lay his hands on me and expose my child to this, causing trouble over nothing?

He seemed calmer now, but he was still telling me to get in the car. I said, 'Who the hell do you think you are, exposing our daughter to this, pulling me by my hair like that? Do you think that I will accept that sort of treatment? I don't want that sort of life again.'

Calmly he got out of the car and approached me. He raised his hands in the air, palms flat, in a gesture of surrender. The adrenalin seemed to have sobered him up. I suspected that the worst was over now. Walking slowly towards me he asked me politely to please get in the car, making a reference to Chloe and how upset she was. 'Come on, Stacey, think of your daughter; listen to her crying. Please just get in the car.' His body language was soft now, his tone was quiet and he seemed very calm. I quickly concluded that Chloe did need me to calm her down, and I couldn't stand in the street all night. I had to get home.

'Look, I just want to get us home, so that Chloe can be put to bed safely, and I can get away from you and never see you again' he said, nodding his head. Ade seemed genuinely calm, and it seemed that we both had the same objective, so I felt reassured that I would be safe to get in the car. Pulling open the door, I got into my seat, adjusting it, and sliding the seatbelt around me.

Then I looked at Ade, expecting him to acknowledge me calmly, but he was looking sternly ahead, face frowning. The calm look he had portrayed seconds ago was now gone. Still staring, he turned the key and started the engine. Chloe quietened down immediately, as I kneeled up reaching into the back seat, stroking her little face. Loosening my seatbelt to do so, I looked at her, glad she was safe as her eyes closed gently. Ade said nothing as I shuffled back into my seat, resting my head back, sighing with relief. I just wanted to get home, be with my children and never see Ade and his scummy mates again.

Seconds later, I felt the force of the car speeding up. Ade had put his foot down on the accelerator. He was driving like a madman, shouting to himself that I had taken the piss. Sitting up, I noticed we were on the approach to a mini roundabout. He almost didn't stop at the 'give way' sign, but at the last minute he braked the car sharply, making us all rock violently in our seats. Panicking because our daughter was in the back, and his driving was reckless, I had no time to think how to get out of this situation. 'For God's sake, Ade, our daughter is in the back. Will you stop the car,' I yelled.

He screeched into a right turn at the roundabout, looked at me with a warning glare and said menacingly to himself, 'Right then!' I knew something bad was about to happen, but I was trapped. Then thwack, my head jolted back, as the full force of a fist smashed into my nose. I felt hot sticky blood splash out of my nose. It was everywhere, lots of it. I couldn't believe what he'd done, and it seemed to take me minutes before my brain caught up with the pain and reacted.

'AAAR,' I screamed, but before I knew it, he did it again, and again, about twenty times in all. He was punching me full force in the face, as he continued to drive the car. He was still steering the car with his left hand and leaning across with his right arm to punch me. All I heard was him panting with the effort to plant another fist into me, then saying, 'Here's one, (panting) and another, (panting) and another', repeatedly, as his right fist connected forcefully with my face.

Petrified, I just sat there and let him take his aggression out on me, because he was still driving the car erratically, and I was worried for our lives, especially the baby. Fearful of struggling with him in case he lost control of the car, I prayed his anger would subside. The horror seemed endless and I had to wait for him to run out of steam. I could feel my face swelling up, my eyes closing, and there was hot, sticky blood all over me. My new white dress was drenched in blood; it had turned completely red.

He finally stopped hitting me but continued to drive recklessly. Frozen in fear, I didn't dare to say anything. I was praying for him to calm down. At one point he panicked and slowed down because the police were driving behind us, but unfortunately, they didn't notice us. They manoeuvred and began to drive by the side of us, but I was too petrified to try and get their attention in case Ade saw me, and it psyched him up.

'Put your fucking head down,' Ade barked, and I did so in an instant, for fear of reprisals. The last thing I wanted to instigate was a police chase with my baby in the back, and Ade seemed reckless enough to let things spiral that way if he had too. My heart sank as they drove off, not even looking in our direction. Had I just lost our chance to get rescued? Silently, I pleaded for a miracle to happen that would get them to notice and we could get away safely.

An industrial estate came into view and Ade pulled on to it, going on and on about what I'd made him do. He pulled up in the middle of some closed factory units. Sat in the dark, he switched the engine off and I could almost read his mind, his face frowning, concentrating with racing thoughts. Though I didn't hear it with my own ears, I was certain he was wishing that we didn't have Chloe with us, and that Sophie didn't know where we were, for I don't doubt for a second that that day could have been the end of my life. That moment, there in the middle of that industrial estate, he could have killed me to save himself facing charges for battery. He must have known that would be my intention once I got back home.

We sat in overwhelming silence for some time, him just staring ahead, deep in thought. What was he going to do next? Finally, he said he was going to take me back to Kev's and get me cleaned up. This was the only time I was pleased to hear that he was taking me to Kev's. It also surprised me, as it meant other people would see what he had done to me, and I would be safe. Surely, I surmised, when Kev and Rita see me, they will most likely phone the police, or get me help. I sat there in a state of shock. I didn't want to say anything that would push him over the edge.

We pulled into the drive of the four-storey block of flats. It was a relief to be back at Kev's. Ade beeped the car horn to get Kev's attention. Thank God, I thought. It was ironic I was now thinking of this as a place of safety in comparison to how I'd felt about it earlier that evening. Pulling the window up and leaning out, Kev shouted, 'What are you doing back?'

Ade opened the car window, and put his arm out, swinging it urgently, motioning to Kev to come down quickly. Kev shut the window as Ade drove me round to the dark car park at the back of the building.

Stepping out, he went round to the passenger side and opened my door. He gripped my wrist so I couldn't escape. I was too frightened to try anyway, and I wasn't going to leave my daughter. As he pulled me onto the gravelled car park out in the open, I hoped someone would see the state I was in and help me get away, but it was dark so there was little chance of that. I stood in the car park with my head hung, looking as if someone had thrown a bucket of blood over me. My face was aching, and I could not see through my right eye it was so swollen.

Kev came rushing down the dark drive to see what was going on. He swaggered over and I expected a change of expression on his smiling face when he approached me. Oddly, he didn't look shocked at the state of me at all. 'What you done that for?' he said to Ade in a joking manner. 'To teach her some fucking respect,' Ade responded, breathless and using one hand to drag me towards the flats, carrying Chloe in her car seat in the other.

My heart sank. How could I have been so naive to think Ade would bring me back here if it meant I would get help? It looked as if things were going to get worse from here if that was possible, but there was hope. Rita was in the flat. Surely when she saw me, she would get help.

The two of them bundled me through to the main entrance of the flats. All the time they were checking to make sure no one was about. Kev was now carrying my baby Chloe in the car seat. A door could be heard shutting upstairs, and I heard the creaks of someone making their way down the stairs. Out of my impaired vision, I could see it was an elderly man.

Ade and I were at the bottom of the staircase, in a tiny bit of the hallway entrance. Ade quickly pushed me into the alcove, leaned over me, and made out we were canoodling to cover me from the view of the unsuspecting man. I didn't want the old man to see me either, because I was frightened the sight of me would give him a heart attack, or they would beat him up too.

Ade leaned over me, overpowering me with his body until I couldn't see anything, only feel the material of his T-shirt against my skin. I could smell his familiar scent, the scent that had once been a comfort to me. He was supposed to be my protector, and here he was protecting himself. Finally, when the old man had left the building, he pulled me up the stairs by my wrist, inside the apartment, and bundled me straight into the tiny shower room.

I was so relieved the violence was over. I caught sight of myself properly in the mirror for the first time; my hair was tangled and matted with blood. It was sticking to my brow like cardboard, so I delicately pulled it off. Then I studied my unfamiliar reflection in the mirror. The right side of my face was badly swollen, my eye was closing and my nose looked fat. The blotchy face that was looking back at me was mine, but it was nothing like me.

Leaning into the shower cubicle with shaking hands, I turned the switch and water came rushing out. Feeling alone and scared, I prayed for help. I thought of my girls, and felt sadness for my Sophie. I had let her down because now she would have to see me in this state. And I had bought another monster into our lives. There was no way I could avoid seeing her, and this bruising was going to take weeks to heal.

Slowly, I stepped into the shower cubicle in my dress, and slid it off. It hit the bottom of the shower tray, which quickly turned red with blood. My head was so tender, it was painful to wash my hair. Every touch stung as I did my best to clean myself up. Stepping out, I dried myself with a towel that was on a rail on the side. As I was so sore, I couldn't wash myself thoroughly, but I'd done it to the best of my ability.

Once dry, I wrapped a towel round my head in a turban style and tucked a towel around under my shoulders to cover my body, then I went into the bedroom. I didn't bother putting the light on I just lay there in the dark, frightened. I wanted to go home. I wanted to get my baby out of this horrible hell hole. There was no way I was going to make a fuss. I just wanted to keep everyone calm for fear of triggering another attack.

The idea crossed my mind to escape later in the evening with Chloe, and I tried to figure out if there was a fire escape or route out of the apartment. My heart sank, as I could see it was too high up to jump out of the windows and I couldn't see any way out of there. My only option now was to concentrate on getting me and Chloe home safely.

I could hear Ade in the living room, ranting and raving about me to Kev, telling him blatant lies about me. I can't remember what they were, but it was as if he was trying to justify what he'd done. I hated him. He was going to pay for this. Yes, I was vulnerable now, but any bully could make their victim feel defenceless through intimidation. It didn't make him a hard man, or clever, just a coward.

There was no way I was going to give him the satisfaction of seeing me upset. So, I got up, got dressed, went into the living room, sat down and began to watch the television. I needed to have Chloe in sight. Rita was lying next to Kev on the sofa, biting her nails anxiously and looking as if she was going to burst into tears at any minute. Kev sat up, clapped his hands, then rubbed them together, ready to make an announcement, but it looked as if he was rubbing them together in glee, aimed at me.

He ordered Rita to go out and get three bottles of wine, almost in an undisclosed celebration. She got up to get her coat but just before she went out, they both warned her not to speak to anyone about anything and to come straight back. 'It should only take you ten minutes,' said Kev, looking at his watch.

'Please Rita,' I prayed silently, 'get the police, help me and Chloe.' I knew she was too frightened to cross Kev though; he had done a good job of terrorising her. To my dismay, she came straight back with the wine as instructed. It upset me that she hadn't got help because I knew that if it had been me, I would have assessed that things had spiralled too far out of control and outside help was now a necessity.

Then again, I completely understood her fear of repercussions.

Kev looked pleased as he opened the wine, giving us all a glass. I think I hated him more than Ade at that point. How could any man witness a woman in that state, who had a new baby in tow, and seem to revel in it? I needed a drink to calm me down, so I took a gulp of it. Then the silly fool offered me some chocolate. Gosh, he was celebrating, wasn't he! I was hardly going to feel like munching on chocolate with my face in so much pain.

Eventually, Kev and Rita went to their room to bed. Ade and I stayed in the small living room. He slept on the sofa bed, and I had been ordered to sleep on the other sofa. I thought that if he went into a deep enough sleep, I could risk phoning the police.

It was impossible to sleep that night. At one point I heard Ade snoring, but I was convinced he was putting it on, to try and lull me into a false sense of security so that I would try and escape, and that would give him the excuse to beat me again. So, I just lay there, unable to sleep, every second a missed opportunity to find the strength to risk sneaking out. After a long night eventually, the sun came up.

At five thirty, Ade woke and put the kettle on. I was curious to see what his mood would be like now that it was a new day. Gently, he came and sat by me, and he seemed back to his quiet self. 'Oh Stacey, what have I done to your face,' he said in his usual mocking baby talk voice, trying to sweep my hair out of my eyes, looking genuinely concerned. I pulled away; I didn't want him even touching me.

He was probably trying to work his charm so I'd have him back, as he knew I'd been through this kind of thing before with Leon, although not quite as extreme. I had to play down what had happened, because I wanted him to think I wasn't too concerned with what he'd done. I didn't want him suspecting that I was intending to go to the police over this once I got home.

'It's nothing,' I lied. We finally got packed up to go home, again. I popped into the bedroom to bid Rita goodbye. They say pride comes before a fall and I felt such a fool I'd been boasting to her that I wouldn't stand to be treated badly by a man again. Now here I was with my face black and blue, hugging her goodbye. I whispered into her ear, 'He's not going to get away with this, you'll see.' I could almost picture myself in the court, months down the line, watching him being sentenced, and me being the instigator of the punishment dealt. I had to show Rita that justice could be achieved. I had to show him the same, and, most importantly, I had to show myself that I was not prepared to let anyone get away with treating me like this again.

The journey back seemed to last forever. It was nauseating. It was still hot, but that didn't matter any more. I stared out of the car window; I didn't even want to look in Ade's direction. Thinking everything over, I looked at the men working on the motorway in their yellow jackets and admired them. They were occupied with their work, good, hardworking men, oblivious to the cars slipping by. *The devil makes work for idle hands,* I thought, with Ade in

248

mind. I wanted to be back around sane, wholesome people again. I felt infected.

We pulled over at the services part of the way back. *Why can't we just get straight home?* I thought, frustrated. The need to get away from him was overpowering. Steering off the motorway, Ade drove to the far end of the services car park, away from all the other cars. Once the car was stationary, he got out, walked round to my side of the car, and opened my door. Squatting on the floor, he leaned into the car, trying to hug me. He was begging me to marry him. What a joke that was! How deluded was he to think I'd marry him after what he had done? I'd finally seen his true colours, and they were dark and murky, like sewer water.

He was promising me all sorts. He'd be a good man. He'd alienate his friends, blaming their influence on him. He'd stop smoking cannabis, he'd get a job, he'd do anything I wanted. Now he was really insulting me. Did he really assume that there was anything he could do to make up for doing this and putting his child's life at risk? He was obviously only trying to sweeten me up so I wouldn't go to the police.

Staying composed, I sat quietly and acted as if I was listening to him and considering what he was saying, but inside I wanted to scream, go crazy and run away from him. The main thing now was to get him to drive that car and get me back to the Midlands.

'Look, can we just get home. I'm hot and dirty, and don't feel too good,' I said. It was the truth. He got back in the car and continued the journey home. Finally, we pulled into my drive. I couldn't run off because he had my door keys on the car key ring, and I had to make sure I got those back. He unloaded the bags out of the car, and I went to the toilet. I could sense that he was watching all my movements. I suppose he was worried in case I went to call the police.

Ade went in the shed outside to get some tools because he'd promised his brother Richard that he was going to do his garden for him that day. As I got the milk from the fridge, I could see him slyly watching me from inside the garden shed. Inside, I was willing him to go. *Just fuck off will you,* I thought. I'd managed well so far to keep myself calm, but I was so near to my freedom now it was getting more difficult to contain my emotions. He came over to me and asked what I was going to do now, adding that it was only a little bruise anyway.

I lied and told him I wouldn't let anyone know I was back, and I'd stay in the house until my face was better. He tried to look sad, and concerned that I had to do that, but I knew he liked my pretend idea of covering up for him. After all, nobody would know then just how low he really was, although I suspect prison was more of a concern to him then what people thought. Linda's words from Bromsgrove refuge came to my head again. 'Just become an actress.' I hated being fake, but needs must when you're dealing with nutters.

He packed my car up with his work gear to take to his brother's house. My lovely little car, which had over the past year became his workhorse, was crammed to the brim with his tools, even a wheelbarrow. This just created more hassle, having to drop them off at John's where Ade lived. Was I ever going to get away from him? It was one thing after another. 'I'll drop you at John's so I can bring my car back here. Anyway, I fancy the drive with you,' I said, not wanting to leave him alone with all my keys and trying to act as if I had no problem with him. Chloe started screaming again. I'm sure she was feeling my inner frustration. This, and the heat, were making me feel more flustered. Ade agreed, and we jumped in my car. Ade started driving in the direction of Richard's place, which was quite a few miles away.

'Look', I said 'I'll have to drop you off at John's for now, because Chloe needs a feed, then I'll bring the rest of your tools down to you later.' He didn't want to do that, he wanted to go to Richards, but I couldn't stand driving any more. I just wanted to drop him off and get away. I thought I was going to explode if I didn't get away from him. I started to cry. My emotions were so hard to contain now, and I was completely exhausted with trying to act calm.

Fortunately, he didn't question me, and allowed me to drop him off at John's. This was amazing. I tried to contain myself. I wanted to laugh with joy, but was it a trick? Did he see through my performance? Did he know that I had no intention of coming back for him, to drop him off at his brother's with his tools? Did he suspect I was really going to go straight to the police?

He got out the car, muttering something about the tools and to not be too long bringing them back. I couldn't quite believe he thought that I was really going to bring them back to him, let alone go anywhere near him again. He leaned over to give me a peck on the cheek, and I leaned in and let him so he would believe I was totally compliant.

He hopped out of the car and as he walked towards the entrance of the flat he shared with John, I started the engine, not taking my eyes off him for a second. I expected him to turn back and get back in the car, but he didn't. He was getting further and further away and then he disappeared inside John's flat. Letting out the biggest sigh of relief I'd ever gasped in my life, I reversed the car and slowly drove away. Once my car had left his street, I put my foot down, and raced home. My whole body racked with sobs, glimpsing at what he'd done to me in the car mirror. I was finally going to get help. It was so good to be free, and I hoped the police could protect me from here on.

Paranoia was eating away at me now that I was finally back home. A combination of the lack of sleep and shock made me fear that Ade was hiding in my house, although logically I knew that was not possible as I had just dropped him off. My ideas of Ade's capabilities were blown totally out of proportion. So, I ran to my neighbours to phone the police as I didn't want to be at home on my own in case he was in there or suddenly came back. The police arrived quickly and took a statement from me. This time I was determined to press charges. In the meantime, the texts and missed calls from Ade started. 'Where's my tools? How long are you going to be?'

A few hours later, mum bought Sophie back. She was horrified at the state I was in. Mum pushed her way through my door, with the best intentions I suppose. 'Nobody is going to hurt my girl any more! I'm going to look after you from now on.' It was honourable of her to decide to take over in one sense, but another part of me was filled with dread. I just wanted to be alone with my children. But, weak from the stress of the last few days, I relented.

Leon had always been careful on most occasions not to damage my face. Ade, on the contrary, let nothing hold him back. There had been no build up, as there had been with Leon, when it used to start with a slap and lead up to punches. This attack had come from nowhere. From nought to a hundred.

251

Back to square one, I had found myself in an abusive relationship again. After all the lengths I had gone to escape from my last one, it was soul destroying. Was there something wrong with me? I seemed to only be attracted to men who turned out to be violent. They were the sweetest, most charming of people, until I had fallen in love with them and then slowly and silently, the rot would creep in.

It was supposed to be a fresh start after leaving Leon, and I felt bitter with life. I had put myself in a bad position again, and so quickly. This time I had a new baby to care and provide for, with another father who was more fixated with me than with the welfare of his child. My body was out of shape, as Ade had constantly reminded me, and I felt good for no one or nothing.

My house had been left like a builder's yard, as Ade had decided to knock the upstairs landing wall out and replace it with wooden spirals. He had not got round to finishing the work, so at the top of the stairs there was no barrier wall between the landing hall floor and the stair well. With no wall for protection against falling, there was the landing floor with a big drop at the side of it, which was very dangerous.

It was going to cost a fortune to replace, and I didn't know how I would find the money. Just before I met Ade, I had a little job and was getting my life sorted. Now I was overdrawn at the bank and had hardly enough money to make ends meet. My life had spiralled so quickly since I had met him, all because I had put my trust in him. How on earth was I ever going to get back on my feet now? It was exhausting. Why couldn't things be simple? Why, again, had I fallen for a man with issues?

I felt completely overwhelmed by my dire situation. Casting my mind back, I thought about how much strength it had taken to leave Leon, to take the children and get out of the marital home. Now I was in my own home, I thought again more positively. It was the home I had fought so hard to get. It was a start. My children were all safe. I could build on this, I could make a good life for myself. After everything I had gone through, I was still standing.

The Aftermath

It turned out that Ade was known to the police, and they were extremely concerned for my welfare. They began looking for him, and as they began their search for him, the news got back to Ade. Then the barrage of texts and calls started. Each day I would receive hundreds of missed calls, with the occasional sneering voicemail calling me a grass, a fat slag, among other things. Abusive insults seem to come with the territory with these kind of men. The texts continued, saying he wanted his money back for the kitchen he had fitted, which I had actually paid for, and that I had started the fight that day because I had insisted on driving the car drunk. I knew I wasn't drunk, but his accusations made me question myself. He was saying anything and everything to get a reaction, to make me give in and respond, because he knew if I responded he could gain momentum and try to lure me back in. Then the tone of the messages would completely change, begging me to take him back, saying he couldn't live without me, how beautiful I was, and how much he loved me. When he felt he was getting nowhere with that, he would resort to the insults.

Eventually, the police caught up with him and arrested him. He got three years in prison but served half the sentence. In that time, he wrote to me daily, telling me he didn't know what had come over him that night, and that he was so sorry – all the usual stuff to pull on the heart strings. I should have blocked the letters but somehow I felt sorry for him that he was in there. Despite the fact it was for his own wrongdoing, I still felt he was in there because of me. I had so much to learn.

He was released after sixteen months and began stalking me. It was a nightmare. He almost convinced me to take him back as it seemed easier than the battle of dealing with his daily pressure. It was constantly wearing me down. Once again, I was out of my depth. Being a woman on my own with children, I felt like a sitting duck in my own home.

One night, the house was in darkness and the children were in bed asleep when I was woken by a noise downstairs. I don't know how, but I knew it was him. I knew I had to prepare myself, be mentally strong and become an actress to pacify him, whatever I needed to do. I needed to handle this. A million thoughts were racing through my head, my heart pumping as the bedroom door opened slowly in the darkness and I heard the click of the bedroom light as it was turned on.

There stood Ade in my bedroom doorway with a victorious smile on his face. My heart was banging so hard I felt it was going to burst through my rib cage. I was grateful that I was on anti-depressants, since it must have been the medication that stopped me from having a heart attack.

How I acted so calmly I will never know, but I knew if I showed him fear and freaked out, it would escalate the situation and I didn't want that, especially with my girls in the next room. So, in a matter-of-fact tone, almost as if I'd casually bumped into him in the street, I said, 'What are you doing here?'

He laughed menacingly, standing at the foot of my bed. 'Well, if you won't speak to me, and you won't take my calls then you give me no choice, do you, Stacey?' he responded sternly, with a superior expression, as if he had the right to be in my house.

With my children in close proximity, I knew I needed to coax him downstairs, out of their earshot. I managed to maintain a calm demeanor and implied that I was willing to hear what he had to say. Gently, I eased myself out of bed in my nightdress and walked past him saying, 'Come on, let's go downstairs and have a drink.' Smiling, he followed behind like a little lap dog, thinking he was getting what he wanted.

We got into the kitchen and I remember finding something alcoholic as I needed to calm my nerves, and knew that's what he expected.

He then started to talk about the incident in Blackpool, completely blaming me, and getting angry that I had reported him to the police. Oh my gosh. I could not believe I had this mad man in my house and not a soul in the world knew he was here with me, and he could do anything he wanted. He could kill me; he might kill me. After all, he had had the nerve to break in, regardless of being on licence and I was terrified.

I knew he was winding himself up, working up to some violent climax and I just could not cope, so I started to hug him, pretending that I believed him and that I was taking on board his views. I found myself apologising, anything to keep the peace.

As I was leaning against the sink unit, he stood in front of me, towering over me. He must have been two inches away from me, looking down into my face; the pupils of his eyes had changed from brown to pure evil black. Flashbacks filled my head of his fists smashing into my face. I knew this man was capable of killing me. Crippled with fear, I envisaged Sophie finding my dead body in the morning, or even worse her walking in innocently to find him beating me and him turning on her.

My head was swimming in panic but then, unexpectedly, he turned round laughing, saying he wanted to take a peek at Chloe. I could not believe my luck as he walked away and headed to the living room, nodding for me to follow him, towards the bottom of the staircase. Here was my chance to escape, as the front door was located at the bottom of the stairs. Walking slowly, I followed closely behind. As he focused on his next step ahead, I pivoted quickly and within two steps I had my hands on the front door, pulling it open. I ran out, leaving the door wide open as I wanted the house exposed for the neighbours to see in.

I ran in bare feet to the neighbours a few doors away. As I looked up the road, I saw him run out into the darkness of the street like a thief in the night, and disappear.

I immediately ran back into the house, bolted the door and called the police. Running up the stairs to check on my girls, I could see they were still thankfully fast asleep and none the wiser. The police came round, and took a statement. As I began telling them what had happened, the sergeant stopped writing and looked at me seriously, 'We will put a camera on your house, get a panic button and keep you safe. Don't worry, we will get him.'

Later, the police managed to speak to one of Ade's friends who lived not too far from where I lived, and he confirmed that Ade had turned up at his house at about three in the morning, knocking on the door and saying he was in trouble. This corroborated my statement that Ade had left my house at approximately two forty five. Ladders that had been stolen from a neighbour's shed a few doors away were also found at the side of my house. They had been laid down on the floor, but it was clear they had been used to help him gain access through my bathroom window.

It was nerve wracking being in my own home, especially at night as I knew he would be lurking about and trying to take his chances. When I was in my living room, if I heard a slight noise my brain would freeze, convinced it was him in the house. It's difficult to keep a toddler quiet when you want to sneak discretely into another room of the house to check no one is in there.

Being in bed at night was the worst. Everything was so dark and quiet, and I'd find myself just lying there, listening hard for any noise, feeling vulnerable.

At times, I thought I could hear him running quickly up the stairs, but soon I'd find I had nodded off, giving into the overwhelming feeling of tiredness. Then I'd sit up sharply, grab my phone, dial two nines for the police, and hold back on pushing the third number nine, waiting for him to enter the room. Then it would suddenly be eerily quiet. Convincing myself he was outside my door, I would sit there trying to breathe quietly, because my breath would be loud and rasping with fear. My heart would thump so loudly as I imagined he was outside the door, lulling me into a false sense of security, waiting for me to settle back down so he could burst in, and the shock would cause me to be unable to move or call the police.

Crippled with fear, I would sit for hours thinking he could hear my breath, thinking he could hear my heartbeat and he was outside listening, sniggering at my heavy breathing. A couple of hours would pass and I would come to the realisation that I must have imagined him being in the house. Overwhelmed with tiredness, I would fall back into a half-conscious sleep.

Eventually, the police caught up with him and he went back to prison. That must have been the lesson he needed, because after that he left me alone for good.

If It's Going to Be, It Starts with Me

Looking at my innocent tiny baby girl Chloe, I felt I had had enough. My children had had enough. It was time to wake up and realise that I was not the one with the problem. Yes, I had issues with putting people's feelings before my own, but life had shown me that this had been to the detriment of me and my children. This little girl did not deserve to go through what my two older children had been through – subjected to seeing their mum upset all the time, if not worse; living in a chaotic environment fuelled with fear and the abnormal behaviour of a strong male figure who got his power by abusing the mother of his children, his woman!

The change in me didn't happen overnight but this was a pivotal time for me. In a bid to help myself heal mentally, I got some self-help books. It was then I discovered the phenomenon known as the Law of Attraction. It changed my life; it was clear to me that I had been a victim all my life through one circumstance or another. In subconsciously labelling myself as an 'undeserving victim', it seemed as if the universe was delivering what I believed. Discovering this new way of perceiving my life was a big turning point for me. For the love of my daughter, and what my children had suffered before, I was going to make it my mission to get life right this time. You can start a new life at any point, no matter where you are in the journey.

It took me years of keeping myself away from these strong characters, and years of new experiences, to replace the old me and get to the normal life I went on to have. The clarity of the Law of Attraction helped me put things in perspective. Why was my life this way, why did I keep going through the same experiences? I realised I had to change.

Things settled down and I decided I knew what I wanted from my life. It wasn't money or a man. I knew the right man would come into my life when I was okay within myself, and I had a long way to go to pave the right path. For now, I needed the basics, a good foundation to build on. Stability, peace and security were must-have ingredients on the path I was now choosing. First, I needed to build my confidence and learn to be my own best friend.

When my mind was in chaos, I couldn't think straight. When the people who disrupted my peace had left my life, I started to see clearly as I had never done before. I had to take a step back and analyse myself, and I could only do that by being on my own. Why had I been accepting treatment that was not right, and why did I keep going back to people who harmed me? Why did I keep messing up, when I really wanted to have a lovely successful life? There was something lacking in me, a void that had developed internally. From a child I had been looking for love, and in my childlike mind I thought I had found it.

I started practising meditation daily. It gave me a deeper understanding of myself, and a chance to step back and see my thoughts and increase my self-awareness.

It was clear I needed time on my own to envelop my children in a healthy environment and to learn to love myself. Once I loved and valued myself, there was no way I would ever accept this treatment again. There was a lot of healing work to be done. I finally understood that until I did this hard work, I was setting myself up for failure in any future relationships. I could not control what I had put up with in the past, but I could absolutely try and control my life moving forward. That was my past, but it did not need to be my future.

My subconscious thought system had always been telling me I was stupid and beneath people. Although I'd always labelled myself as 'thick', I got myself back to college and did an access course to higher education. With my new qualification, when Chloe was one year old, I got myself a good job. It's the best thing I ever did.

Getting into the world of work changed my social circles for the better. I was around people who wanted to make progress, and that made me want to progress. My colleagues at work have been a massive influence on my life. The majority of them, as far as I know (because you never know what goes on behind closed doors!) are respectable mothers, married to decent men who don't hit them. Listening to them over the course of the years, I have learned a lot about love and respect within a relationship.

When I hear them speak of their husbands and how their husbands treat them, I think, *That's how I want to be treated.* They talk with enthusiasm of their children, choosing their colleges, making life decisions within a loving environment, and how they are all involved in this decision as a family. How lovely must it be to take for granted such a normal part of family life! How can you ever have a normal family life if you grow up around violence and live in fear?

The first time Leon put his hands on me in anger, I should have loved myself enough to make it the last time. He told me repeatedly, 'No one will ever love you like I do.' I definitely shouldn't have wanted to be loved like that. If that was love, I would not like to have seen his version of hate.

However, Leon grew up witnessing domestic violence and was a product of that environment, and for that I forgive and pity him. But he could have made the choice not to let the cycle continue. I undoubtedly should have left sooner for the sake of the children, but all is clearer in hindsight and with the wisdom that comes with age, and when you're away from the lies and manipulation and your thoughts are your own, not formed through fear and indoctrination. Only then can you see clearly how utterly depraved domestic violence is. I could never imagine anyone putting their hands on me now.

It has taken me years to see that, and, looking back, I cannot believe it was my life or that I endured that treatment. However, I also know from being healed emotionally now, how easy it is to be battered mentally as well as physically, and to believe you are loved at the same time.

After getting out of the mess I was in and escaping from violent relationships, I knew I could take on most challenges successfully. Everything that snowballed from my childhood confirms that a turbulent childhood can have a devastating impact on your adult life, especially with no loving guidance.

Chloe doesn't see her father, and she is growing up well adjusted, loved and safe. It's so reassuring to know that I am on the right path. I deeply regret, and feel saddened, that my two older children didn't have the stability of a normal childhood like Chloe has had.

I have learned that you should be your own best friend. There is a life after abuse. It's your life and you have choices, and your choices will have such a huge impact on your journey. Remember that the ramifications of your choices will affect your children if you have them. They will infiltrate your home, your friends, your family, your work, your pets, your entire life. Just choose carefully. If you are a victim of physical, mental or emotional abuse, there is help out there, as I proved to myself. Believe me, you can start the change any day. Just reach out and grab it. Be free, be happy.

Fifteen Years Later – Life Goes On

It was December 2018, a far cry from all those years of living in turbulence due to my relationship choices. Almost fifteen years had gone by. 'Buzzing' was the word of the month; I was home and dry. I was getting ready to go out with my girlfriends. Life had never been so good. This was not only because I had lived freely and peacefully since being free of violent controlling partners, but I had just fought and won another of life's battles.

A year earlier, on 4 December 2017 to be precise, I had been to the local hospital to receive unexpected news. Something sinister had crept into my life so subtly I had barely noticed it. Not all life hindrances come in the obvious forms of toxic human beings.

My health had been declining since being bitten by a tick back in 2014 and I went on to develop Lyme disease. I developed the classic erythema rash immediately after the bite, and not knowing anything about the disease, I did not consult the doctor and get antibiotics as I should have done.

I paid dearly for this this sheer ignorance. The disease left me in quite a bit of discomfort with my joints and muscles, not to mention chronic fatigue. Around this time, I also started to clench my teeth at night with a force that would crush metal. I am not sure if that symptom could be attributed to the underlying stress from my past.

I got on with life as best as I could, because there was not one day since I had left Leon or Ade where I had woken up and not felt grateful for the peace and harmony in my life.

Around April 2017, I noticed a little white lump on my tonsil and soft palate. For months, I assumed it was nothing to worry about. Then, on a beautiful summer day the following August, I was driving to work in my little blue Nissan micra, bumping along the road. The radio was on, and I was listening to some music, in a little world of my own. An advertisement came on the radio to promote cancer awareness. It was almost as if the volume had been switched up in the vehicle, yet I hadn't touched the buttons. The advert was

261

running through me so loudly it felt as if it was inside my head, as if I had headphones on my ears.

As quickly as the advert finished, the sound went back to normal. It was very strange, but this prompted me to make an appointment to see the doctor so that they could check out the lump. Still, I was sure I would be okay. At 47, I was relatively young but I erred on the side of caution. The doctor referred me to an ear, nose and throat specialist, who was convinced the inconspicuous little lump was merely a cyst, but to be on the safe side they would perform a biopsy. The appointment came through and I had the biopsy in November.

A month later, I went back to the clinic for the results. It was an icy cold day, and the breeze was making my cheeks cold. As I was approaching the hospital entrance, I could not believe my eyes when Ade drove past me in his BMW. He slowed down and stared at me. Involuntarily, I started shaking and my mouth dried up. I hadn't seen him since he broke into my house many years before, and the last I'd heard of him was when he had pleaded 'not guilty' in the Crown Court to charges of 'breaching a restraining order' against me. The jury found him guilty, of course.

Seeing him now after all these years made me feel vulnerable again, but fortunately he was stuck on a one-way system, where the only vehicles that were allowed to stop were the ambulances, so he carried on his way. For a fleeting moment I did think, *I hope seeing him wasn't a bad omen.*

Still shaking, and my legs a little weak, I made my way up to the third floor of the hospital to the ear, nose and throat department, where my hospital appointment letter had instructed me to go. Finding my way round the hospital was a struggle; it was like a vast and clinical never-ending maze, but walking along the clean tiled floors, I finally reached my destination. I registered with reception and sat waiting patiently until I was called.

Eventually, a nice young nurse led me into the consultant's room. He asked me lots of questions. Had I been in any pain? How long had I had the lump? *Yadda yadda yadda* I was thinking. Just hurry up as I need to get back to work. I'd only popped out of work for this appointment and I had lots of things to be getting on with. I did not want work thinking I was taking advantage by being away from my desk for so long. They had been kind enough to allow me the time to attend the appointment, after all.

Deep in thought, my focus was suddenly back on the doctor, who was sitting in front of me on a tiny stool. 'Cancer.' I looked at him confused as I heard him say it again, 'It's squamous cell carcinoma of the tonsil and the soft palate, though were not sure of how developed it is until we do further tests.' I thought for a minute I had imagined what he had said, but his face portrayed concern, waiting for my response. A nurse sat in the corner of the room stood up and grasped her hands together as she looked over at me.

The tears began to flow as I realised what he was saying, but the tears were not for me, but at the thought of telling my poor children. God those kids loved me, and I loved them. How was I going to tell them? Tentatively, the nurse came over and put her arms around me. She knelt by my side and passed me some tissues. As I sobbed, she gently led me into another room to talk to me further and give me an overview about what I should expect to happen next.

By the time I walked out of the hospital double doors and back out into the fresh air, I had gone into practical mode. The fear had been packed away. I'm not sure if I was in denial but it felt better to be this way. There was no way I was going to go into this without a fight. I hadn't come this far for cancer to finish me off. I had plenty of life left in me to live, and I was still optimistic that I would reach old age, be on my death bed, smiling and knowing I had experienced true love and happiness.

My plan was to structure my cancer journey with an itinerary, take it in bite-size chunks. What was happening to me right now was short term, I concluded. The first task was to start my treatment in January 2018, a six-week course of radiotherapy. I would finish treatment on 18 March and spend the next few months preparing for my end goal of recovery. That was how I intended to deal with it. I knew it was going to be a tough road ahead.

Telling my children was awful. Sophie came back from work and I broke the news to her. Her legs almost gave way as she broke down crying, grabbing onto me affectionately to steady her balance. Putting on my brave face, I assured her everything would be okay. Reece had been a little detached over the years, but he soon turned up after Sophie broke the news to him. He looked like a lost little boy, 'Are you okay, Mum?' he asked, looking hurt.

'I'm going to be absolutely fine.' I assured him. As for Chloe, she was only young and had not long started secondary school, so I thought the least she knew the better.

I didn't know what to expect in terms of how the treatment would make me feel, but it was obvious I had to prepare to feel very sick. I had to stay positive; 2018 was going to be a write-off, and I accepted that, which helped me immensely as I sensed I would get better. I knew the winter would be bleak as I would be having treatment, but I also knew that as the sun started coming out in the spring, the flowers would begin to bloom, and so would my withered body, as it started its journey to recovery and the treatment would be over.

My cousin Charlene was my rock. The daughter of my mother's sister, she had been a light in my childhood. She was the kind of lady who lit up a room. On a Sunday, she would sometimes come round and visit Mum when we were teenagers, and I never wanted her to leave. Her energy was loving and kind, and when she was there Mum always seemed happy. As she left our house, the oppressive energy of our childhood home would settle back in. We had lost touch through being preoccupied with our lives, but I had looked her up and paid her a visit when things had gone wrong between me and Ade.

Her door was always open to everyone, and she made me feel so welcome, accepted and loved. She had four lovely children herself; she was an amazing mother, wife and home maker and from then on, she was my mentor and role model. She helped me so much with Chloe, even looking after her when I had to work the odd Saturday and late night. She had always been there for me after I reached out to her, and she was there for me when I fought my cancer.

On 28 January 2018, I started my treatment. Fortunately, I did not have to endure chemotherapy, as the medics felt the radiotherapy was adequate. I started to feel the effects of the radiotherapy by week two; I was dreadfully tired, and my mouth had started to feel extremely dry. By week three, I was getting sicker. It was at this stage I could no longer eat through my mouth. Well prepared, I was able to start feeding via a peg tube that had been fitted into my stomach earlier that month, which enabled me to get special liquidised yogurts directly into my body.

264

I was taking more paracetamol, but by week four these were no longer adequate for the pain in my mouth, so I was prescribed a morphine patch. I developed oral thrush, which was incredibly painful. I lost my voice, and the term sick as a dog suited me as I felt like an old dog, throwing up or running to the toilet, unable to get there in time. It was not pleasant.

Nights were the worst as my symptoms meant I had to go to the bathroom every fifteen minutes to rinse my mouth out with Caphosol mouthwash to ease the dryness. It was the middle of winter and so cold; I had never been so grateful for the electric blanket my sister Hannah had bought me a couple of months earlier as a Christmas gift. It was lovely to get back into a warm bed, even if it wasn't for long. The disturbed sleep and tiredness reminded me of when I had my newborn babies, except now I was being woken to deal with something harmful, rather than something beautiful and innocent.

Visitors got me down, as well meaning as they were, but I felt I could not turn them away. I feel awful about that now, but I guess being ill made me cranky and unsociable. My loved ones were so kind. My stepmother Helen bought me a beautiful guardian angel necklace as a symbol of her love and support.

Charlene would come to visit me regularly. She would mother me, making sure I was getting calories down me as my weight was plummeting. She would massage me and bring me bits of shopping. She helped me so much and when I felt myself ebbing away, she would keep me on track. She joined the rota with my dear friend Melanie, my father and Sophie in taking me for my daily treatment, as I needed to go to Wolverhampton hospital five days a week.

In April 2018, Sophie and I sat and anxiously waiting to see the consultant, both of us wary to find out if the treatment had got rid of the dreaded thing. We were both overjoyed when I was given the all-clear. I had beaten it, and now I just had to build myself back up again. As I had previously anticipated, the flowers outside started to bloom and the harsh cold weather turned into a kinder, warmer climate.

As I had not left the house in months, my friend Melanie came round one Sunday morning and kindly took me to a local park for a much-needed stroll. It was so lovely walking among the trees, with the sun peering through the branches; it felt good to be alive and appreciating the beauty of nature. Smiling to myself, I was relieved the hardest part was behind me, although I knew there was still a bit to go, as I felt very weak.

Most afternoons, I lay sprawled on the settee, feeling low and exhausted as the sound of the bongs on the TV game show *Tenable* religiously woke me up just before Chloe came home from school. It was depressing. I missed the simple things like shopping, working and going to the gym, but I consoled myself with the thought that this had been my expectation, and things could only get better.

Even cutting the lawn was a mammoth task, considering I used to run for miles before I became ill. It was disheartening that my health was not improving as quickly as I had hoped, but day by day, I began to feel a little bit better. By July 2018, I was back at work, at my old stressful job.

At the time of diagnosis, before I had had my first scan and found out what stage my cancer was at, I had questioned my mortality. When you are having Christmas dinner with your children and asking yourself if this is going to be your last Christmas with them, it makes you realise how lucky you are to be alive. It's so precious to have your health and it made me see how we take for granted spending time with those we love, under normal circumstances.

It had been another wake-up call when the doctors confirmed the cancer was in the early stages, so I had a good prognosis. Maybe I was getting complacent after all the years of peace I had been revelling in. Being sick gave me a lot of time to reflect and realise how far I had come in life. Yes, I had a good job, but it was stressful and that was something I needed to change. Assets are not just financial, I realised; they include your loved ones. It was clear from the support I had just how much my children, family and friends adored me. I was truly blessed to have so many people who cared about me. Once again, I had prayed to God for his help and I truly believe he had helped me.

It made me feel so much more grateful to be well enough to go to work, clean my house and do all the things I had previously moaned about. My taste buds weren't what they were, but this made me realise how I had taken the joy of eating for granted – how lucky we are to be able to eat and indulge in the beautiful tastes that different varieties of food offer.

If this experience had taught me anything, it was that life is too short. Life is your own movie and you shouldn't take anything too seriously. So, I looked online and found a job vacancy working in care. It sounded a lot more interesting than the job I was doing. In July, I had an interview. I was nervous but saw things in a new light. I decided to just enjoy the challenge, and that attitude worked as I was pleased to hear I had secured the job. Everything was going well. My new zest for life was already impacting on the way I was living and that was the first positive change I had made. I left the job I was in, and all the lovely friends I had made over the years, and started my new job.

I was definitely in the right line of work being in care. I got to read all the child protection statements. It was heart-wrenching, but also worthwhile, because I was part of that process of keeping children safe. It made me realise how the law had developed over the years since I had been in the refuges.

Domestic abuse cases were more robust in protecting the welfare of the children. The agencies involved in such cases were aware of the impact that witnessing domestic violence had on children's lives. Should my case of domestic violence have been before the courts in this day and age, there is no doubt I would have had my children removed.

It made me sad witnessing the mothers in front of me, experiencing what I had been through. Not only were they suffering from mental and physical torment, because of domestic violence, and quite often manipulation, but they were also losing their children. It was ironic that they, and the children, had to suffer more because of a situation that was often out of their own hands.

Like me when I was in the thick of it, they could not sort themselves out. Thank goodness for refuges, not only as places of freedom, but as somewhere to take that time and space to get your head straight – an escape from all the manipulation, to give yourself a chance to get your life back on track.

Love at Last

To celebrate my new lease of life I had planned a well-deserved evening out. It was December 2018 and I was getting ready to go out with my girlfriends. We were going day drinking. It was a really cold day, but I was snug at home with the heating on. Dance music played in the background as I ran my bath. An array of clothes was hanging on display on the wardrobe handle so I could select which outfit I was going to wear. I felt like a teenager again, getting ready to go out.

It was only one o'clock in the afternoon, and I had already cracked open a can of beer while getting ready. I loved day drinking. I didn't do it often, but it was the build up to Christmas, and the party season energy was well and truly in the air.

Sophie was living back at home doing her degree and she was going to take care of Chloe for me so I could let my hair down and hit the town. After the year I had had, being stuck in bed ill during the beautiful summer months, I had plenty of making up to do with the good times in life.

My friends and I were meeting at three o'clock in the Wetherspoon's in Birmingham. The plan was to line our stomachs with some nice food, catch up and make our way over the road at about seven to an eighties themed bar. It was free entry before ten, and half-price drinks, so it couldn't be bad.

I'd been to the hairdressers earlier that day and had my hair done. I think if your hair looks nice, you always feel smart. My make-up went on to perfection, and I chose a sparkling silver-grey top with lots of diamante jewels stitched into it, paired with black leather-look trousers and black heels. I put some clips in the side of my blonde hair, scooping it up so my curls fell over them, and finished the look with some silver hoop earrings. Having lost quite a bit of weight with being ill I was pleased with how well I had scrubbed up. After spending the majority of the year with no make-up on, and living in my red dressing gown, right now looking at myself in the mirror I felt a million dollars.

A couple of hours later, driving to my friend Melanie's in my little white Fiesta, I felt a wave of serene pleasure with life wash over me. Sliding a disk into the CD player, I put on a remixed dance song by Taylor Dayne and sang along to it, listening to the words. The beat dropped in and I felt the excitement of love in her voice as she sang about how lucky she was to find a man to love her who didn't try to change any part of her. As I sang along, I remembered the joyous feeling of being in love. Oh, but to be in love with a man who had the qualities described in the words of this song.

Later, my fiends Melanie, Amy and I were climbing in a black cab, all dressed up to the nines, smelling of perfume and slightly, well, on the way in more ways than one. Finally, we reached our destination, hopped out of the cab and went into the pub. We sat in a window seat, chatting and laughing, watching the Christmas shoppers and festive drinkers walking past, all dressed up in elf skirts and Santa hats. Everything felt so perfect. I can't describe how happy I was. That night it was almost like a dream.

Eventually, we headed over to Reflex Bar. What a crazy place that was! As we walked in, 'Freedom' by Wham was blasting out of the speakers. Just a few moments ago, we'd been in the steady vibe of a pub and now we were in the boisterous environment of the club. Ladies were jumping around with pink feather boas, crazy pink afro wigs and oversized illuminous glasses.

The place was brimming with happy party people. As we squeezed through the crowds, everyone was smiling and dancing. I headed towards the dance floor. I may have been on approaching fifty, but I felt better than I had ever did as a teenager. Men smiled and eyed me up and down, moving and making way for me to pass as I shimmered by, shaking my booty to the beat of the party tunes.

The bar was packed with people holding out notes and debit cards, desperately trying to get served with a drink, while my friends and I were dancing. We were having such a lot of fun, with the strobe machines lighting everything up in pink and green, then random blasts of smoke. It was like being in a fun house at an adult fairground. Everyone was smiling, dancing and chatting.

A couple of hours later, I was walking back up towards the dance floor for another boogie, and I saw him, standing by a mirrored pillar near the dance floor – the man of my dreams. At a glimpse, he was around my age. He had black, swept back hair, and was wearing a Crombie-type jacket that made him look like a gangster from one of those old black and white films. It was almost as if the strobe light was on him, highlighting him for me to see. I knew I had to meet him.

Without even thinking, my head swimming with drink, I found my way towards him, skipping over to where he stood. As I hopped up the step to be by his side, I jumped childishly, rotated around and stood by his side. He was tall, about six foot, and stocky. I tapped him on the shoulder and said 'You're nice, are you single?' Straight to the point, I know, but drink is the greatest inhibitor of our usually controlled behaviour, and God, I liked this man.

With a trail of disastrous relationships behind me, and the last one having been several years ago, I found it difficult to relax and meet men. I had been very wary, and, most importantly, God knows why, I rarely fancied anyone. I had found online dating excruciatingly painful and given up on that, and I had realised back in 1999 that going out and actually meeting someone who had the potential of being a life partner was unlikely.

So, for me to see a man, and actually think *Now that's what I am talking about*, then make a beeline for him, was a one-off. This would never happen again, but I had promised myself I was going to live in the moment from now on. I was going to follow my happiness radar and be a little daring. Why not?

I saw his face break into a smile, and then give a little laugh as he turned his head to look at me. He leaned in and whispered something back in my ear – I can't remember what it was, as we were both very tipsy, but I know we were having a mutually pleasant exchange and we were both laughing. I asked if he had children, he said, 'Yes, four'.

This did not deter me, and I had to laugh to myself when I remembered on my old Tinder dating app, that even though I swiped no to everyone, I particularly did not want anyone with more than one child. That was a bit harsh I suppose, when I had three myself. Yet this just made me think of him like me, a parent. Whether he was a responsible one or not I didn't know, but for tonight I just wanted to get this fish in my net. The fish was named Rob.

He had the most beautiful smile and there was no way I was letting him leave here tonight without taking my number, so we moved away from the dance floor. I remember him taking my mobile phone and inputting his number in my phone. We had a bit of a laugh and a joke before he was swept away with his friends to move on to another pub. He left the club, and I stayed a few more hours dancing and enjoying myself, and, if it was possible, I felt even happier then I had done when I walked through the doors earlier that night.

At the end of the evening, my friends and I clambered into our taxi and made our way home. I didn't say much about my encounter with Rob, but I had a little smile on my face. I almost heard the voice of cupid saying in my ear 'My work here is done'!

Elsa

The next morning, I woke with a bad head – not surprising given the amount of alcohol I had consumed the night before. Even though I was hungover, I still thought back to the night before with a smile on my face. Sitting up in bed wearily, I grabbed my phone and looked to see if I had any messages, but there was nothing. Then I checked to see if I had saved the guy's number from the night before, but was dismayed to find that in my drunken state I hadn't.

Even though I felt a bit sad, I had still had a really good night and that would suffice for this new lease of life I had been given.

Thinking about it a little more, the only other times in my life had I felt such an attraction and chemistry with anyone on first meeting was with Leon and Ade. That didn't bode well! They both turned out to be abusive narcissists – it didn't say much for my judgement on men.

However, I was older and more worldly now and had enough experience to spot the red flags. I was going to enjoy all the delights that life had to offer, I wasn't that naive girl any more. I was prepared to give myself the chance of joy and happiness. Whether I heard from him again or not, it didn't matter, as I was in the zone of appreciating life.

Monday morning arrived all too soon and I set off to work. At lunch time, I made my way up to the dreary staff room. There was a big table in the middle, surrounded by sixteen tatty old chairs, a sink, kettle and microwave, and the radio was usually on. Everyone was sitting round the table eating their lunch, absorbed in the world of their mobile phones. How times had changed; I wondered what people did before phones existed.

I unwrapped my sandwiches and hypocritically checked my phone. I had had a WhatsApp message from a number that hadn't been saved to my contacts. An unknown person to me. Could it be…? Anxiously I began to read:

Hi, how are you? Do you remember me from Saturday night?

Oh my God, oh my God! My heart lurched. It was him! Right, now to play it cool and be cautious, because I didn't know for sure it was him.

272

I'm sorry I replied. I had to laugh to myself as that seemed too obvious that I was playing it cool. *Who is it, I don't have your number in my phone?*

Were you drunk? It's Rob.

*I wa*s (embarrassed face emoji) *but I do remember you!!!*

Did you have a good night?

And that's how it all started. Just general chatter about our night, and the party season. He told me he was an engineer and went out once a month drinking with his friends, which was pretty much what I and my friends did too. Life could be strangely serendipitous when it wanted to be.

The messages continued throughout the day and this was the start of our almost daily contact. When I woke in the mornings there would be a message:

Good morning, how's your day going? What have you been up to? Bit by bit we started to get to know each other.

There was no mention of meeting up, or anything smutty, as I was used to getting when previously I had given my number out to men I wasn't that familiar with.

Many times, I had blocked people from contacting me again. I'm not the sort of woman who enjoys receiving pictures of men's penises. What if I had screenshot them and shared them publicly? Were they so sexually obsessed that their common sense had dropped into their pants? Did I ask for a picture of their nether regions? No sir! So, go do one.

This connection with Rob was nice and refreshing, and even better because there was no pressure to meet. It was nice and easy chat, and over time we found we had lots in common. I always looked forward to hearing from him.

He asked me how old my children were, and I told him. His kids were of a similar age. Both of us had a big age gap between our children. I wondered if, like me, his later children were from secondary relationships or all from the same woman.

He had a lovely picture on his WhatsApp profile of the sweetest little girl. She looked about one year old, kneeling up and eating something; she had her brown hair scooped in a little ponytail on the top of her head, and the prettiest little chubby face. She reminded me of Pebbles, the baby girl out of the Flintstones cartoon, she was so cute.

Is that your little beauty on your WhatsApp picture? I asked him.

It was then that I learnt about Elsa. Beautiful little baby girl Elsa was his granddaughter, and she was very sick. The family had nearly lost her, and she had only got out of intensive care recently. Rob told me how tough it had been on his daughter.

Through his texts, I could see what a caring father he was. He was always up at the hospital supporting his older daughter Kirsty with baby Elsa. I explained to him I had just got over cancer myself, but I would much rather it was me than a child who went through it. Our conversations took a new turn after that. They seemed to be deeper.

The texts continued and I encouraged him to be positive, telling him that this time last year, I didn't know if I was going to make another Christmas, but things had turned out well. A year can make the world of difference. Still, I had to be careful about being too positive. No one can predict life. All I could do was be there if he needed to send a message.

On the day of Rob's night out with work, I finally got the text I'd been waiting for. It said, *I'd love to take you out for a drink or two when you're free.*

We arranged to see each other in two weeks' time on the Saturday evening and meet in Birmingham. The texts slowed down a bit to every other day but I knew Rob was just overwhelmed. It suited me too, because I hadn't actually met him properly yet and I didn't want things to be too full on and then discover he really wasn't for me.

The day of our date came, and he texted me on the afternoon saying that he was sitting with Elsa while Kirsty had taken her other children off to see Santa, and did I mind seeing him later than planned, that evening, because he wouldn't be back from the hospital until late.

We were supposed to be meeting at 7.30 p.m. and I didn't relish the prospect of meeting later than that, especially with travelling too, so I politely asked him if we could reschedule. He was fine about it; in fact, I think he was relieved as he said he was really tired. He mentioned he had to be up early in the morning to take his boys to rugby.

Honestly, I didn't mind as I knew he was having a tough time, and I think he really appreciated my relaxed attitude towards it.

274

What he didn't know was that as much as I was disappointed, it was such a cold day I was glad to be able to stay at home in my pyjamas with an early teatime, in front of the television.

He then sent me photographs through of Elsa. I'm not sure if that was because he thought that I might be doubting his reason for cancelling, which I didn't. Actually, I was touched that he trusted me with the pictures, and I felt he was reaching out to me and enjoyed having someone uninvolved to talk to. The poor man was obviously consumed with worry over his family.

Elsa looked so poorly in comparison to the picture of the healthy little child on his WhatsApp profile picture. She was only seventeen months old. It was heartbreaking to see her in her pink pyjamas, lying in a hospital bed with her little knees pulled up to her tummy, almost in the foetal position. She still had her little ponytail on the top of her head, but now her cheeks were flushed with the signs of a temperature. She was sucking her thumb, with a tube coming out of her tummy.

It was Christmas week, and I knew Rob was going out with his work for drinks. I had stayed in with so much Christmas preparation to do. I hoped he was having a good night as he deserved it. Unexpectedly, about seven in the evening, a photograph came through on my WhatsApp. It was a photograph of Rob with a big smile on his face, and his arm round another man, obviously his work mate. I had forgotten what he had looked like, and my memory had served me incorrectly as I thought he had blue eyes, but his eyes were brown.

I studied the picture in a leisurely fashion, as I wasn't sure if my beer goggles had been in operation on the night we met. I had thought he was very good looking, but this picture confirmed my thoughts. He may look a little different from how I remembered him, but he was handsome – he was perfect. He had the most beautiful almond-shaped brown eyes – and I was a sucker for those – and the warmest, kindest smile I had ever seen.

For some time, I sat smiling at his picture. I know that sounds mushy, but I knew this was the start of something special.

Christmas came and went, and on Boxing Day he asked me when he could take me for that drink he had promised me, so we arranged to meet up on the Saturday before New Year's Eve. It wasn't like me to get as far as arranging a date with someone these days, and it was lovely because I felt so excited about it. He texted me on the morning and said he was looking forward to it – and so was I. Life was looking good.

Date Night

Oh, my goodness, it was finally here: the night we would meet. The interesting thing about a first date is that it gives you a sense of direction. It could go either way: I could leave the date thinking never again, or believing there was something worth pursuing. I was as nervous as hell. Since my last relationship had ended, about seven years earlier, I had developed a serious dating phobia. Although that relationship wasn't violent, and an improvement on Leon and Ade, I had still been let down. After that I was hurt, and wary about dating again. My walls were well and truly up and I was closed off to the idea of embarking on a relationship ever again.

I had coped very well on my own, but I felt I had been just existing through life, keeping busy, working, cleaning and gardening. Though I enjoyed my time with my friends, I missed the intimacy of a romantic relationship and now I was ready to give love a chance again. Still slightly reluctant, I felt somewhat reassured that all the self-work I had done on myself had made me wiser and, I hoped, more sensible. I was pretty confident that I could spot the signs of a toxic man before I got too deeply involved, should that happen to me again.

Now all these years later I was getting ready for my first date with Rob. I felt that surviving cancer had changed my whole perspective and I was ready to take a risk. It didn't stop the nerves though, as it had been so long since I had dated. I was having a few vodkas and getting ready for the evening. My son Reece dropped me in Birmingham in his car, which gave me the opportunity to swig another can of beer on the way.

Once in the pub, I scanned the room avidly. It was surprisingly quiet because it was the Saturday before New Year's Eve, and everyone was saving themselves for New Year celebrations by the looks of things. Rob was nowhere to be seen fortunately, so I had time to order another vodka from the bar in a bid to calm my nerves, though I did not seem to be feeling any effects from the drink at all. Drinking beforehand is not something I would recommend for a first date, but had I not done it I don't think I would have mustered the courage to meet him.

Once I had downed my drink, I ran up the stairs to the toilet, then I stood in front of the sink washing my hands. Looking in the mirror I kept saying, 'You've got this, it's just meeting a friend'. My lungs felt tight, and I was struggling to breathe. Eventually, I calmed myself down enough to go back downstairs; he was still nowhere to be seen so I got myself a table out of the way, at the back of the bar, and I sat and waited. I had a perfect view of customers entering the pub.

I watched the double doors at the entrance of the pub swing open as people walked in, but they were just strangers. Having almost given up expecting him to be next, I took a sip of my drink as the doors opened again, and this time I saw him in rush in and head straight to the bar. *This is it*, I thought, *compose yourself.*

He looked round, and I was sat on a table with two chairs at the other end of the room near a window, so I waved at him to get his attention. He smiled, put his hand up to acknowledge me, then paid for his drink and confidently headed over. He pulled a chair out; he was very masculine and sat next to me, and we began to chatter, just idle small talk.

He had just come back from the children's hospital from seeing Elsa, and it was in walking distance from the pub. We talked about different things; I told him bits about my job and my life, and we kept drinking to try and hit the merry high of relaxation.

Eventually, we were both a lot more relaxed. I liked that Rob was a serious person. We had so much in common, both being parents, and that's what we spent the whole night talking about.

He told me had been single for nine months. That was a nice timeframe. I was relieved it wasn't a recent break-up and I wasn't a rebound date.

We moved on to the next bar. It was a freezing cold night, and there was snow on the pavements as we walked along. He offered me his coat, and though I didn't take it, I thought it was a really nice gesture. He was talking, and I looked up at him and admired how tall and stocky he was. With his hand on the small of my back, he made me feel safe by his side. The attraction was undeniable, and I sensed he was feeling it too.

We got to the next bar, and I don't know if it was the fresh air but boy did the drink hit me then. My head was swimming and I remember moving away way from the bar where he stood, walking to the middle of the empty dance floor and dancing. He was smiling at me, so I shimmied back over to him and grabbed his hands and pulled him back to the floor with me. We were both dancing and laughing. Then we went back to the bar to order more drink!

A photographer in the club approached us with a bag over his shoulder, showing us the keyrings and photographs styles available to purchase. This was a night I wanted to remember. Even if I didn't see Rob again, I wasn't going to pass up the opportunity of taking a memory home in my pocket, so Rob stood behind me and we posed, smiling like Cheshire cats, while the photographer pointed the camera at us and literally in a flash the photograph was taken.

Sometime later he came and found us, passing me the finished photograph keyring for approval. Taking it out of his hand I smiled, pleased with the lovely picture of me and Rob. Feeling happy with my purchase, I slipped it into my bag.

We made our way back to the dance floor and danced a little more. Two people with the world on their shoulders had found joy in the company of each other, and the superpower of music had transformed us into teenagers. We started kissing, and stumbled back to the bar with our arms around each other. We spent some time kissing, and it was magical. I didn't care who could see – I was living the dream and I was enjoying it. Then the room began to spin as the alcohol had caught up with me, and any dignity I had disappeared.

The next thing I recall was the doorman gently leading me to a taxi. I was incoherent, trying to explain to him that I was with Rob, but they would not let Rob anywhere near me. Rob watched as I slid onto the back seat and I remember the look of concern on his face as the taxi pulled away. Slinking into the seat, I waved at him, feeling slightly embarrassed. I just wanted my bed.

Hours later, I woke up in bed, still in full make-up and clothes, and recalled the previous evening. What had happened? Checking my phone, I could see a message from Rob: *Hope you got home okay, thank you for a great night.* Oh my God, what had I done? I had not even said goodbye to him properly, and what was the doorman doing putting me in a taxi?

It was 5 a.m. and I texted Rob back. *Thank you for a great night too, sorry I got so drunk. I feel embarrassed, what happened?*

He replied some hours later, explaining that I had disappeared to go to the toilet and when he came to look for me, he found me asleep on one of the chairs with the doorman trying to wake me up. He said he tried to intervene to make sure I was alright, but the doorman was having none of it and insisted on putting me in a taxi.

To be fair to the doorman, I think that was a good thing to do considering I was so wasted. I was surprised when Rob replied, *Not to worry, we've all done it, I had a great night.* With a smile on my face, and a thumping head, I looked at the keyring from last night. We looked so good together. Taking my mobile phone, I took a photograph of it and sent it to Rob. He replied saying it was a really nice picture. There, I had left him with a little keepsake to remember me by. My head was hurting so I nodded off back into a contented sleep.

When I had slept off my hangover, I recalled the events of the night before: Rob's face as I was in the taxi, how worried he looked, and how he had texted me to see if I had got home safely. It was nice that he cared about my welfare and that he wasn't afraid to show it.

New Year, New Life

The new year arrived and it was now 2019. I didn't hear from Rob for a couple of weeks, other than a Happy New Year text message. To be honest, I didn't know if my drunken behaviour had sent him running, so I thought it best to leave it at that. However, some weeks later he messaged me and we started reminiscing about our previous date night. I told him I was surprised to hear from him again.

He said he found me funny, and I replied it wasn't that funny, as I remembered being in the toilet, stooping over the bowl and falling forward, almost headbutting the door. He sent me laughing emojis and I found myself giggling, and happy that I could be myself. He wasn't judging me. That's how I intended my relationships to be from now on – accept me as I am and don't try to change me.

The messages were not coming through every day but I got one every few days. They were mainly about Elsa. He sent me a picture of her in her pretty pink pyjamas; she had started chemotherapy and her hair had been coming out in clumps, so they had shaved her little head. The poor man was very preoccupied with his family, and if I could at least be a friend, I was happy just to be there on the other end of the phone.

In mid-January, I got a message from him: *Hey sexy lady, how are you?* Although there was still no suggestions of a further date, he was making it clear he was attracted to me. I was very relaxed with the situation, as I had previously felt overpowered by messages from men to whom I'd given my number. I found too much enthusiasm on their part off-putting.

I didn't really hear much from him at all. I knew he had a lot on, and I had made it clear I liked him, so I felt it was up to him to pursue things. He was the man, and I had learnt that if a man likes you, you will know about it. There was no way I was risking pushing myself on someone who was either too busy or not bothered, and at this point I could not determine which it was.

Eventually, he messaged me again, asking how I had been keeping. He did make me feel very good about myself, and the messages were giving me a spring in my step. He asked when he could take me out for another drink, and I said I'd go out with him again, but this time I would be taking it easy with the drink. He replied jokingly that he hoped it wouldn't take as much drink for me to relax with him next time. So, we decided our next date would be on 16 February in Birmingham. He had to go and see Elsa at the children's hospital and would come straight up to me again, like last time.

We met again and the date was just brilliant. He came walking over to me at the venue we had arranged to meet in, and as his beautiful brown eyes rested on me I could see a twinkle of excitement in them. He had a great smile and I could sense he was really happy to see me. Even though I was still nervous, I didn't have to hammer the drink down to be able to relax.

He was very nicely dressed, very clean-cut in a shirt and trousers. He obviously took pride in himself and that was good. He opened doors for me, and he insisted on paying for our drinks; he was a gentleman for sure. It was nice to be out with someone who wasn't expecting me to pay for the drinks. He had a good career and his own home, and was a responsible parent – the opposite of Ade and Leon. I felt safe in his company.

We headed into the town, Rob gripping my hand firmly. I could sense he was really proud to be with me. I certainly was not in the prime of my life, but gosh, I felt it. We spent the rest of the evening getting to know more about each other.

As manly has he was, he had a really gentle demeanour. He listened to me without interrupting, and spoke without urgency. He was calm and self-assured. This time we talked more, and the more he talked, the more I liked him. He laughed at my lame jokes and sarcastic asides; he seemed to like my humour, which helped me come out of my shell.

His stories made me laugh about how protective he was over his daughters. It made me think about my own father and how he had been when I first met Leon, and how he too was highly suspicious of Leon's motives. Now Rob and I were the parents who were wary of our children's partners, and they were the adult children who were trying to make a good impression on us. We laughed at the power in our wisdom; we had been there and done that. How the tables turn. I also discovered he had the same birthday as my dad, and I was convinced that was a good omen because I admired Dad.

Rob told me he had shared custody of his teenage sons, Kyle and Ethan, and I figured he was a lot more responsible than any of my exes had been with their children. He must be a really decent man, I surmised, to be working full time, supporting his daughter with her poorly little girl, and so committed to his sons. He was juggling so much and that was a sign of selflessness. A lot of people might not have agreed with my perspective, but after my experience with my own children's fathers, I had the upmost respect for any man who was a good parent.

He told me about all the places he had travelled to and his adventures in Vegas. He asked me about my travelling experiences, and I told him I didn't have many, having been a single mother for the majority of my adult life, so my trips were just beach holidays with the children. He smiled at me knowingly when I said I would love to travel more now I was older, experience different cultures and see what the world had to offer. He said he felt exactly the same.

He asked me in a roundabout way how I felt about things with me and him, and I told him that the only reason it had lasted as long as it had (a couple of months) was because he hadn't bombarded me with messages. I told him I had no real expectations with us and I wanted to just go with the flow. He seemed agreeable to that, and I liked that because it didn't make me feel under pressure. He said he had a feeling that I was a little reserved and he didn't want to push things. We seemed a perfect match.

We went to the Reflex Bar, and the photographer was there again, so I got another keyring. The club was packed this time, but it felt as if it was just me and him in there. We stood by the bar and I put both my arms around his waist, leant my head on his manly chest and snuggled into him. He pulled me to him and kissed me passionately, then he pulled away and looked down at me with a serious look on his face. He was saying something to me and I couldn't hear him because the music was so loud, but the look on his face gave me an idea of what he was saying. I knew he really liked me.

Worse for wear, we eventually left the club at closing time. As we were walking out of the club he said seriously, 'Now can you answer me something, how has a beautiful woman like you been on her own for all these years? How has nobody snapped you up?'

'Now that's easy,' I retorted laughing. 'I have been just waiting for the right one.'

He smiled as he called me a taxi. While we stood outside waiting, we talked about what a great night it had been. It was freezing cold and I was happy snuggled in Rob's warm arms. Next time we meet, I said, you can come to mine and we will make a night of it.

In other words, I was ready to take things a step further and sleep with him. He looked down at me and kissed me tenderly. The taxi came and he said goodnight.

When I got home, he texted me, *Safe journey home, I had a fabulous night, and I can't wait to see you again.* We exchanged a few more messages and he told me he was very attracted to me and felt proud to be out with me. That was such a lovely thing to hear. We laughed about the keyring, and he said he couldn't wait to add more to my collection.

I was very cautious for a long time, unsure if he was trying to lull me into a false sense of security with all the compliments and acts of kindness. For a while, I half expected that it might all be a pretence and eventually he would show his real side, but I have learnt that he respects me too much to be anything less than the perfect man he is for me.

Four years on and we are still together. Everything that has happened to us in our lives before we met made us appreciate each other. Rob and I have had our ups and downs like everyone else but nothing like the ups and downs of my past relationships. Rob had a history all of his own and had known great sadness in his previous life.

We both understand that this is the one journey we get and we are both very much alike in our attitude to life, and that's one of the reasons we work so well. We both know that you can control what goes on inside your head a lot more then you can control what goes on outside. So, when it's good, you need to grab it with both hands and enjoy it, and when it's bad you take it one day at a time until things get better.

Being with Rob puts everything in perspective where my previous relationships are concerned. He is kind, caring and understanding. He treats me with respect, and I have never been so happy. He is my best friend as well as my lover. It beggars belief that I stayed in my relationships in the past as long as I did. But if I had asked them to leave me alone and respect my space, I know they would not have done, hence the strong coercion which ultimately was one of the reasons I stayed put.

Also, I know if the older and wiser me could go back and speak to the younger and naive teenage me about my future just as I was embarking on my life with Leon, with the best will in the world, that younger me would not have listened. I was so desperate for Leon's love, nothing would stopped me continuing down that path. I had so much to learn.

Love is not supposed to diminish you, and break you.

The hardest time of my life was when I left Leon and went to live in the refuges with the children, not to mention the build up to it, and the strength it took to leave. Had I not mustered up that courage, and persevered I know I would not have the happy and fulfilled life I have now.

It was Christmas Eve and I was sitting in my pyjamas watching television, finally getting to relax after a hectic few weeks at work. The door opened and Rob struggled into the room with a big cardboard box and placed it carefully on the middle of the living room floor.

He looked over to me with a mocking smile saying, 'Don't touch!' I jumped up curiously to head over to the box. 'Is this my present?' I said excitedly. Smiling, Rob nodded, but then added that it was heavy and I was best not to pick it up. I sat back down.

What could it be? Maybe a music centre? I had always wanted a better sound system. We had spent many good times, just the two of us, dancing the night away in the house to the lame-sounding speakers blasting out eighties music. How I wish I had met him in the eighties, when we were both young. I couldn't imagine a better life for my children, or me, had I had them with him.

'Can I have a clue?' I said mischievously.

Rob was giving nothing away, 'All will be revealed in the morning.'

Damn it, he was not even going to give me a hint. Eventually, we went to bed, and like an excited child, at 7 a.m., Rob leaned over on top of me, grabbing the warm quilt which was tucked around my shoulders, and shook me awake, laughing.

'Are you excited to see what your present is?' he said, his face beaming with delight. If anyone was excited, I think it was Rob, more so than me.

Rob eased himself out of bed to put the heating on and get me a cup of tea in bed as he did every weekend. Sensing his eagerness for me to open his present, I thought I'd better get myself out of bed and see what all the excitement was about. Waking Chloe, we waited for her to come down and then we did the present exchanges, leaving the big present until last.

Finally, Rob bought the big box over to me, as Chloe looked on wondering, like me, what it contained. Grabbing the box, expecting a struggle to push it forward, the ease with which I moved it surprised me – it was as light as a feather.

'This is really light!' I said to Rob, calling out the obvious lie he had told me last night. Grasping the brown tape that ran down the middle of the box, I tore the strip off it and pulled the flaps open, and before I could even see what was in there, something began rising out of the box. It was a red and gold Christmas balloon in the shape of a love heart, floating gently up to the ceiling.

'Oh my gosh,' I said, taken aback by this wonderful surprise. 'What a beautiful balloon!'

'Mum, look at it!' Chloe shrieked, 'Read it!' I stood up, tugging the balloon down by its red and gold ribbons to eye level to read the words that were on the other side. In gold writing, cleverly painted on the balloon were the words, 'Stacey, will you marry me?' Thinking it was a joke, I looked down at Rob who was now on his knees with a ring box open, a shiny diamond ring on display.

'Well, will you?' He asked, a couple of times, looking worried, excited and concerned, all at the same time. With my hand to my mouth, I almost lost my breath. Oh my gosh, he was proposing to me! It wasn't a joke! A minute went by as my head was stunned with shocked delight, but then looking at Rob dying of anxiety, I put him out of his misery.

'Of course I will, of course.' I dropped to my knees in front of him and pulled him to me, giving him the biggest hug. Leaning away, I looked at him and he looked happier than I did. We hugged again. This was brilliant. I never thought I would want to get married again.

The rest of the morning was full of excitement as my family came to visit and were all happily congratulating us, admiring my ring and Rob's crafty plan. What a difference time can make, when I thought of the awful Christmases I had had over the years, putting on a brave face for the children, and breaking down in tears in private to release the heartache that was weighing on my chest.

Stepping into the garage, I prepared some drinks in for the family, as that's where I stored them when the weather was cooler. Thinking back to those awful days before, happiness surged through me. 'Yes,' I said, squeezing my fist and punching the air, feeling elated. There I was in my fifties and finally I had all the love I had ever wanted.

My children are all thankfully well established in life, and I could not wish for more. Considering what they all went through they have done really well and make me so proud.

Sophie is very level headed. She has a successful career and has bought a house with a lovely young man who idolises her. She, unlike me, would not stand to be treated with anything less than respect. She has been my best friend and right arm throughout my life.

Chloe has left school and is at college, and has a little part time job. Her father got back in touch with her when she was sixteen and they see each other occasionally. From what I hear, he has calmed down and has been diagnosed with autism and bipolar disorder, which makes complete sense to me, looking back.

Reece has a good job and has bought his own house. He has a lovely little family of his own, having made me a grandmother with his lovely little boy. He has been affected by his childhood, though he has done exceptionally well for himself considering the start he had. Guilt for what he went through inside me during my pregnancy and beyond still eats away at me, especially as more recently there has been a lot of evidence in the news of the effects of stress in pregnancy and the harm it can do to your unborn child.

Leon had other relationships and more children. He still sees our children from time to time. I don't have anything to with him. My only wish for him is that he is happy and healed as he did not have the best of starts.

Rob and I have bought a beautiful house together and are very happily married. We had a wonderful honeymoon in Mexico. It was the best day of my life. Though it was a big step giving up my own home and trusting somebody again, and I did struggle initially. Once we moved into our new home, I went into a mild state of shock. Reflecting on how hard it was to get out of those bad relationships all those years ago, in the past. Knowing I had nowhere to run should things go wrong, I fell into a depression. I felt I had put myself in a vulnerable position yet again, because I had not got my own home any more. The memories of the struggle I went through to get that independence haunted me, now that I had given it all up.

Rob has been understanding, patient and supportive, reinforcing my belief and trust in him. I have now settled in, realising that I hadn't totally got over the abuse, even after all these years. The fear of being trapped again still surfaces in me from time to time. I feel reassured now, and have let most of it go. Being happily married to someone I love, who loves me, was all I ever wanted, and this time I am with the right person who wants to see me happy. So, finally, after lots of heartache and pain, love and loss, it's nice to say and I have to pinch myself, but its true... I have my happy ending.

The abused wife. A Poem by the Author

You just don't get it, do you? You wonder why I stay?
You call yourselves my friends, yet you judge me
    every day
The neighbours ignore us, not ones to interfere
My family think all is well, but they have an idea!
He's not just my husband, we have kids together
It's his jealousy that brings him to the end of his
    tether
He suffered as a kid, he's only got me
If I desert him, what kind of wife would I be?
We've been together for what seems like an age
It's the stress of our lives, he can't help his rage
When he raises his hands I scream with fear
My children cruelly listen on, but I don't want them to
    hear
So I curtsey to his anger, bow to his feet
Anything to calm him down, escape to safety on the
    street
Once he's released his thunderous blows
The anger evaporates like melting snow
It's all so quiet after the storm
It's been going on so long now it seems the norm
We've a beautiful house, it's the family pride
I've no money of my own, nowhere to run and hide
My heart swells with love as I watch my kids play
Till my son shoves my daughter, he can't get his own
    way
He scowls at me when I tell him to stop
His father looks back at me saying 'Mum get lost!'
I feel so ashamed, the damage is done
I pray there is still hope for my conditioned son
With trembling hands I pick up the phone
I've made up my mind we're leaving our home

A gentle voice answers saying 'Women's Aid'
A thousand times in my head, this call I've made
With their help, they arrange the move
They provide us with support, shelter, and food
That was some time ago when they put me on the
    right track
And thanks to their help I never went back.

A letter from Stacey

Dear Reader

This story is not recent by any means. It happened a long time ago in my life, but regardless of the era, domestic abuse is very much a current theme today.

If you did enjoy my book, I wondered if you would be so kind as to take the time to leave a review. I read all of my reviews and they mean such a lot to me.

I have written this book using a pen name, and all the characters' names are pseudonyms. This is to protect the identity of the people involved. This book has not been written to upset anyone or to out anybody for their behaviour; it has been written with the intention of helping others who are feeling despondent in a similar situation and are looking for hope.

It has been nice to be able to be so open and put pen to paper and to discover from the readers' reviews that so many people found the story relatable and encouraging.

Warmest wishes,
Stacey

Acknowledgments

I'd like to express my gratitude to all the people who have made the dream of getting my book published come true. I never in my wildest dreams thought that my book would have such success when I set out to write the story.

I would whole heartedly like to thank Women's Aid for all their help in making me and my children safe and giving us the chance to have a better future. Without their financial, and emotional help, support and guidance, and more importantly providing us with a place to stay I dread to think where we would be now. You made a difference to my life, and continue to make a difference to many people's lives.

Thanks to all my readers who left such heartfelt reviews. Especially to the readers who related to the story and found it had helped. It made all the years of toil writing the story worth it. Also, to the readers who believed my story and understood why I endured the abuse and did not judge me for it – that was the point in writing it. I hope it will make more victims reach out for help.

Thanks to my previous editor, Melanie, who made me have faith in the project to get the initial publication out in the public eye.

Thanks to my cousin Charlene, for making me the woman I am today with all her support and guidance. What a mentor she has been!

Thanks to my children for turning out so well and making their lives so good, despite the rocky starts.

Thanks to all my friends and family who gave me the confidence to push through and get the story out there.

Thanks finally to my wonderful husband, my partner and my best friend, for fully supporting me though the writing process and helping me juggle everything, so that I could take time out to get the book finished. Thanks for all the love and kindness you have shown me, and for restoring my faith and making me realise that there are good men out there.

Statement of Truth

Save for where I have changed names, dates, locations and other details for the purposes of protecting the identities of myself and third parties, I believe that the facts stated in this manuscript are true.

Public Interest Statement

I believe that my story will help victims of domestic abuse, and gas lighting recognise that they are in a bad situation and need to leave, especially if children are involved. I truly believe if I had read a book like this when I was going through the experience, I would have recognised the situation I was in and sought help sooner without doubting myself.

Name. Stacey Jameson

Printed in Great Britain
by Amazon

32919839R00172